Health, Human Rights and the United Nations

Inconsistent aims and inherent contradictions?

Théodore H MacDonald PhD, MD, FRSM

*Professor (Emeritus) and Member of Research Institute for Human Rights
and Social Justice, London Metropolitan University
Former Director of Postgraduate Studies in Health, Brunel University
Consultant to the World Health Organization, International Development Agency
and various NGOs in developing countries*

Forewords by

Halfdan Mahler MD

Director General Emeritus, World Health Organization

and

Hani Serag MD

*Global Secretariat Coordinator
People's Health Movement (PHM)*

T0132715

Radcliffe Publishing
Oxford • New York

Radcliffe Publishing Ltd
18 Marcham Road
Abingdon
Oxon OX14 1AA
United Kingdom

www.radcliffe-oxford.com
Electronic catalogue and worldwide online ordering facility.

British Library Cataloguing in Publication Data

A catalogue record for this book is available from the British Library.

ISBN-13: 978 1 84619 241 8

Typeset by Anne Joshua & Associates, Oxford
Printed and bound by TJI Digital, Padstow, Cornwall

Contents

Foreword

As a former Director General of WHO (1973–1988), I can say that it has been my privilege and pleasure to work for justice and equity of access to the global right to health for most of my life. This book reflects pivotal issues in that context, and many of the grievously serious problems besetting our attempts to secure this objective. Indeed, it is with this realization in mind that the People's Health Movement, to which this book is dedicated, came into being. The PHM is a growing coalition of people's organizations, civil society groupings, NGOs, social activists, health professionals, academics and researchers which endorsed the 'People's Charter for Health', a document arising out of the People's Health Assembly of December 2000. On that occasion 1453 participants from 92 countries met to debate strategies for achievement of Health for All. The goal of this organization is to promote global equity as a top priority worldwide.

Théo MacDonald has spent much of his working life in the field of public health, both as an academic and as a medical practitioner in some of the world's poorest countries. His research and writing output has been prodigious, resulting in close to 200 research papers and over 40 books. It is therefore not surprising that his international influence has been great and, among his former students, is a whole army of health promotion and public health specialists practising both in the third world and in the first. All of his books show one characteristic in common: he can attract and hold the attention of lay and professional readers alike.

As he points out, when the UN was established, its aim was to prevent international war by acting as a global mediator of human rights. Indeed, its very first declaration was the Universal Declaration of Human Rights (UDHR) and the establishment of the World Health Organization (WHO) in 1948 as one of its agencies was intended to promote and defend global access to primary healthcare as a basis for all other human rights and personal dignity. To this end, and under my Director Generalship of WHO from 1973 to 1988, as so cogently detailed in this book, the Alma-Ata Declaration was enacted in September 1978, and this document made clear that health attainment was much more an economic (and hence political) issue than a purely clinical one. I retired from WHO in 1988 and, as far as I can judge, since 1990 WHO has become increasingly compromised with respect to its original health-for-all aim through the growing dominance of neoliberal control over global trade and finance. MacDonald underlines the roles played by such UN agencies as the International Monetary Fund (IMF), the World Bank (WB) and the World Trade Organization in this erosion of the WHO's original mandate.

In the closing chapters of the book, Professor MacDonald takes the optimistic line that the inherent contradictions in the UN structure which effectively distort its capacity as a global human rights mediator, are remediable – and he sets out various approaches to this end. But he eloquently argues that such reforms are impossible in the context of neoliberalism. By its very nature, neoliberalism, by producing 'winners' and 'losers', cannot be the *vade mecum* for bringing about a closure of the global inequity gap. We have to elaborate alternative means for laying a groundwork of global survival through sustainable approaches to interaction with the environment and a peaceful and just resolution of conflicting interests.

I thoroughly recommend this book as a passionate, yet reasoned and effectively argued, contribution to this goal.

Halfdan Mahler MD
Director General Emeritus, World Health Organization
September 2007

Foreword

As the Global Secretariat Coordinator of the People's Health Movement (PHM), it gave me great pleasure to be invited to write a foreword to this book. When reading the draft manuscript, I realized how closely it aligned with the People's Charter for Health (PCH), the defining document of the PHM.

The PHM came into being in late 2000 as an initiative of several international organizations and civil society movements, non-government organizations (NGOs) and women's groups that were disciplined to work together towards 'Health for All.' They convened the First People's Health Assembly at Gonoshasthasthaya Kendra in Savar, Bangladesh, in December 2000. At that meeting, 1,453 delegates from 92 countries produced the People's Charter for Health. This document was a response to the fact that, soon after the Alma-Ata document, it became obvious that some of the world's most powerful governments, along with a number of financial interests in the international community, had been effectively blocking many of those policy decisions taken in 1978. As part of the commitment by the WHO to a global objective of 'Health for All' by 2000, it became well understood that the huge inequities in global health could not simply be addressed by a series of clinically run 'rescue campaigns.'

The new PCH defined health as a political, social and economic issue and above all as a fundamental human right. This meant that achieving the highest possible level of health needed to be addressed in terms of its social and economic determinants. In this context, it had to confront a matrix of economic and social factors which themselves caused health deficits in the first place. That is – health, it was realized, is essentially a political issue. In September 1978, the WHO had expressed this coherently and unambiguously in its Alma-Ata Declaration, about which Théodore MacDonald has much to say, and it became WHO policy and hence UN policy. This progress towards diminishing the global health rights gap reached a high point during the time that Dr Halfdan Mahler, from Denmark, was Director-General of the WHO (1973–1988).

He drew up a series of 38 targets which, if reached in the time-frame proposed, would have decisively moved the world very close to the goal of universal health rights by the turn of the millennium. Accordingly, he called the programme 'Health for All 2000' (HFA 2000). However, within only a year of his retirement the entire health rights initiative had begun to falter under the growing impact of neoliberal financial interests. Especially relevant in this regard were the policies of various other UN agencies, such as the World Bank and the International Monetary Fund (IMF), with their systems of punitive Structural Adjustment Policies (SAPs). These compelled Third World countries – as a conditionality for development loans – to cut back on such publicly funded services as health and education, and to privatize them. Even more serious in its disastrous impact on people's health rights was the establishment in 1995 of the World Trade Organization (WTO), with its clearly stated mandate to control global trade through such mechanisms as Trade-Related Intellectual Property Rights (TRIPS) and various free-trade regulations such as the General Agreement on Tariffs and Trade (GATT) and, even worse, the General Agreement on Trade in

Services (GATS). Very briefly, TRIPS renders it possible for genetic materials to be patented, with grossly negative impacts on health and agricultural development in many Third World countries. As MacDonald explains, GATT makes it difficult for such countries to put tariffs on incoming goods, thus compromising their own economies, and GATS extends this to such essential services as health and education. Needless to say, such regulations and procedures are highly profitable to various First World banks and corporations.

The PHM's purpose is to free the WHO (and the UN) from such brakes on their original mandates and to once more make HFA the key objective.

This book, like several others which the author has penned in the last decade or so, provides a closely argued analytical basis for the PHM agenda. Following introductory chapters on how the UN was actually structured and has changed since 1945, the author considers the appalling catalogue of health and human rights abuses currently prevailing in such 'trouble spots' as Darfur, Liberia, Myanmar, the Occupied Palestinian Territories, and even the UK and the USA. He could have picked dozens of sites of such crimes, but his objective has been to illustrate the UN's equivocal and inconsistent approaches to them. Therefore he follows these horror-drenched chapters with one on the political implications of the Alma-Ata Declaration and what must be done to re-establish it as the WHO's overriding goal. He recognizes that this cannot be done without addressing various structural problems within the UN, and this is considered in the final chapter. His view is largely informed by optimism, because most of the reforms required to render the UN effective and authoritative as a transnational mediator of human rights are relatively non-contentious.

However, his writing clearly reflects his concern that we are running out of time if we are to avert catastrophe. Widely experienced at the practical level, having worked as a doctor in much of the Third World, he writes with a compelling sense of urgency, based as much on his capacity for academic analysis as on the life-and-death situations he had to address in the field. His argument is that unless we quickly find alternatives to global neoliberal control over trade and finance, the required structural changes to the UN could never be undertaken. He reminds us that the growing environmental crisis, itself largely a result of neoliberalism, has greatly narrowed our window of opportunity for action, and such action calls for the involvement of us all.

I thoroughly recommend this book not only as a call to arms, but as a source of cogent information and scientifically rigorous analysis for a wide range of professionals, as well as a clear explanation of the issues that we face for the conscientious lay reader.

Hani Serag MD
Global Secretariat Coordinator
People's Health Movement (PHM)
Heliopolis
Cairo
September 2007

Preface

As the horror and degradation of yet another world war were drawing to an end in 1944, what a noble enterprise was the creation of the UN! Its Charter defined and established the bases for mediating global health as the foundation for all other human rights. The definitive document of the Charter, and the one which was intended to guide all UN decisions, was the Universal Declaration of Human Rights (UDHR). With the paramount importance of health rights in mind, the World Health Organization (WHO) emerged in 1948. The first aim of the WHO was to ensure global access to primary healthcare (PHC) for, without health, all other human rights would be but a sad footnote to failure.

However, the UN's remit was not only to human rights, for the Charter also commits it to defend and respect the autonomy of each of its member states. As we shall see, it soon became apparent that this second remit could (and does) interfere with the WHO's activities. However, from its inception the WHO set about its task both directly and indirectly. It is energetic in running mass immunization campaigns and in promoting the spread of public health education. It strives for universal access to PHC by initiating research on specific regional health problems, establishing hospitals and training facilities, etc. However, implicit in the UDHR itself, there is much more to promoting health than the eradication of bacteria and viruses and/or elaborating heroic surgical techniques or high-tech diagnostic methods. Ill health is caused by many factors outside the biomedical realm, and we have been becoming increasingly aware of the cruciality of social and economic factors in causing illness. Poverty is much more of a killer than any disease, because it is the prime factor in allowing disease to become established in a community. Of course, in addressing such social determinants of health, the WHO is as much a political enterprise as a medical one.

As will become evident in this account, the WHO was making enormous strides in this direction, markedly reducing global health inequalities, until around 1990. From then until the end of 2006, its efforts became increasingly sidelined by neoliberal financial policies, promoting the interests of banks and transnational corporations in the developed countries. Hopefully, under the leadership of its new Director-General, Dr Margaret Chan, the WHO will be re-energised in pursuing its political and ideological goals, implicit as these are in the UDHR, as well as its strictly clinical objectives.

However, as this author will argue, the UN itself is beset by many internal problems and by frequent inconsistencies in its decisions and actions. Because of this, it is in many ways failing in its commitment both to the WHO and to the UDHR. Its vacillations and equivocations have, since 1990, begun to undermine the WHO's capacity to mediate the global right to PHC as a priority, because other agencies of the UN, particularly the IMF, the World Bank and the WTO – and such initiatives as the General Agreement on Tariffs and Trade (GATT) and the General Agreement on Trade in Services (GATS) – together with an aggressive promotion of the private ownership of patents in producing pharmaceuticals (TRIPS), have seriously jeopard-ized health in many less developed countries. In other words, the UN's own internal agencies are often working at cross purposes.

To answer the question, therefore, implicit in this book's title, the volume consists of 10 chapters. The first two deal with the origin, development and structure of the UN and some of its agencies, and briefly consider its capacity to mediate the UDHR. Chapters 3 to 7 deal in detail with human rights abuses in Sudan's Darfur province, Burma, Liberia, the Occupied Palestinian Territories and the UK, respectively. Chapters 8 and 9 focus on the development of the WHO and the pressures that are being brought to bear upon it. Chapter 10 returns to a further consideration of the UN. Is it fit for purpose? If not, can we reform it? This would be a complex prospect involving drastic changes in the global political scene and the replacement of neoliberal policies by more equitable ones. Alternatively, can we develop a different transnational body to mediate human rights along with another which, working with it, can arbitrate global trade and fiscal issues?

In the light of impending environmental catastrophe, people all over the world, in all walks of life, are becoming more aware of the pressing need to act globally. The need to base our decisions and actions on parochial national advantage, sequestered in hate and suspicion of other nations playing the same game of Russian roulette, has to give way to a new appreciation of the fact that our global village is indeed very small and perilously frail. We depend upon one another as never before, and unless we ensure the health and human rights of all, we shall surely each perish individually.

Théodore H MacDonald
Littlehampton
UK
September 2007

Acknowledgements

The writing of this book has presented extraordinary difficulties in that many of the author's informants with regard to specific health and human rights abuses had to remain completely confidential. Some NGO humanitarian aid personnel, and even some informants from government agencies, told the author that to divulge their name, or even their locality, could expose them to retribution. This has been especially so with regard to any research on the situation in Sudan and Darfur, Burma (Myanmar), Liberia and the Palestinian Occupied Territories. With regard to my work on the Palestine issue, thanks are due to Manal Masalha, Meisoon Shorafa and Maen Areiket. Maps and information about Darfur and Sudan generally were kindly provided by Rashid Elsheikh.

Without the patience and hard work of Beth Archer, who word-processed my often impenetrably illegible hand-written manuscript, and who in addition accessed some of the material from the Internet, the project would have been severely impeded.

As usual, my editor Gillian Nineham and all of the Radcliffe editorial team, especially Lisa Abbott, Jamie Etherington and Andrea Hargreaves, were not only thorough in maintaining the publisher's high standards, but helpful throughout. Special thanks are due to Gregory Moxon, the publisher's Marketing Manager, for the huge part he played in organizing publicity for the book.

Finally, I thank my wife Chris for her forbearance in helping me to see the task through. Without her eyesight, I would have found much of the necessary computer work insufferably difficult.

Théodore H MacDonald
Littlehampton
UK
September 2007

This book is gratefully dedicated to the work and purposes of the People's Health Movement and all of its agencies and contributors.

Chapter 1

Our partially paralysed United Nations

People with no human rights

Despite the two world wars of the twentieth century, and attempts to organize world affairs in such a way as to guarantee human rights by a multitude of international agreements, including the pivotal UN Universal Declaration of Human Rights, millions of the world's peoples are – even in areas free of war – denied access to primary healthcare. In subsequent chapters we shall examine some of these defects in the 'system.' To do this, we shall have to analyse the apparent inability of the UN to intervene to protect people's rights. However, by way of introduction let us consider first a few real cases, as they illustrate at least five main criticisms of the UN, as summarised below:

1 an apparent reluctance to 'violate' national integrity to protect the human rights of individuals or subpopulations within a nation's borders
2 hesitation on the part of the UN to intervene if doing so would be politically embarrassing or disadvantageous for one of the larger nations
3 inflexibility on the part of UN staff themselves, with such staff even taking advantage of their position to abuse people in their care. Examples abound in several less developed countries
4 use of the UN Security Council to promote the real politics of powerful nations whilst ignoring widespread ongoing gross violations of the human rights of whole populations
5 use of the World Trade Organization (WTO) to put the financial advantages of powerful pharmaceutical transnational corporations (TNCs) ahead of World Health Organization (WHO) dictates with regard to making treatment for HIV/ AIDS universally available where needed.

All of the above compromise, or even eliminate, the basic human rights to primary healthcare (PHC), on which all the other human rights depend.

In this book, the author will consider in detail just five cases, not because they are the only ones, but because each of them illustrates salient points about the UN's ability to protect human rights. This will hopefully enable us to consider methods of improving the transnational mediation of the present glaring global inequities in human rights.

To illustrate some of the points raised above, let us consider the following excerpts and testimonies. The author regrets to say that he has hundreds on file and receives dozens more a week. The selection here is eclectic.

Child soldiers

Consider the UNICEF 2005 Report, *The State of the World's Children*.[1] Most readers are already familiar with the use of children as combatants in the Lord's Resistance Army in Uganda, but the practice is much more widespread than that, involving active conflict in at least 55 countries just between 1990 and 2004. These children are generally kidnapped from remote areas of the country concerned, and often from residential schools or orphanages. A widespread misapprehension is that only boys are exploited in this regard, but the UNICEF report makes it clear that this is by no means the case. The children themselves have to be 'conditioned' – usually by brutality and by the forcible administration of drugs – before they can take to torturing and killing other people. This itself not only violates almost every article of the UN Declaration of Human Rights, and its subsequent Convention on the Rights of the Child (both explained in detail in Chapter 2), but is bound to have an impact on the child's future mental health, even if he or she is eventually rescued. Even more ruthless (if that is possible) is the practice in Burma of using children to walk in front of the real soldiers in order to detonate any mines that may be present.

Studies indicate that girls are primary targets for abduction during armed conflict, with the objective of forcing them to become warriors or sexual and domestic partners. Although precise figures are not available, it is clear that this type of abduction takes place worldwide. Over the past decade, girls have been kidnapped and forced into wartime service in at least 20 countries, including Angola, Burundi, Liberia, Mozambique, Rwanda, Sierra Leone and Uganda in sub-Saharan Africa, Colombia, El Salvador, Guatemala and Peru in Latin America, Cambodia, Myanmar, the Philippines, Sri Lanka and Timor-Leste in Asia, and the former Federal Republic of Yugoslavia and Turkey in Europe.

Abduction is not the only cause of girls' participation in armed conflict. Girls are sometimes given into armed service by their parents as a form of 'tax payment', as happens in Columbia or Cambodia, or for other reasons. After the rape of his 13-year-old daughter, a Kosovo Albanian refugee father gave her away to the Kosovo Liberation Army. 'She can do to the Serbs what they have done to us', he said. 'She will probably be killed, but that would be for the best. She would have no future anyway after what they did to her.'

Some girls may also choose to become part of an armed group. However, their choice is largely a matter of survival. Given the high levels of physical and sexual abuse of girls in most current armed conflicts, taking up arms can be safer than waiting to be raped, injured or killed.

Furthermore, the supply systems of warring groups may be the only source of food, shelter and security available to children in war-affected areas. To describe their enlistment as 'voluntary' is both misleading and erroneous.

Denial of access to effective HIV/AIDS treatments

Antiretroviral drugs (ARVs) can now, in almost all cases, allow victims of HIV/AIDS to live effective lives. However, as this author has pointed out in a previous book,[2] powerful pharmaceutical corporations have successfully used the World Trade Organization (WTO) to prevent countries from producing generic copies of commercially available ARVs, thus condemning hundreds of thousands of the world's poor to distorted, broken and short lives. All too often in such situations, parents die before their young children, leaving such children – despite their tender years – to look after their siblings as best they can.

This obviously constitutes both a most blatant violation of the right of the actual victim to PHC, and the abrogation of children's rights to education. The following two accounts from UNICEF[3] illustrate these points. Both are drawn from Mozambique, but are amply replicated in many other less developed countries (LDCs).

Celina possesses a calm dignity. She holds her head high, her hair is neatly braided, her large eyes look directly at you when she speaks. She rarely smiles, but when she does, her smile is beautiful. It has been two days since the family of six has eaten, but when Celina is given money by an aid worker to go to the market to buy basic food items, her aunt panics. Twelve-year-old Celina is looking after her aunt, Margarida Araujo, and her three-year-old cousin, Paulo. Celina's three other siblings are not at home that afternoon.

The aunt's hollow eyes look scared. Her breathing quickens. Her face grimaces with pain. Her emaciated body is covered by a grubby old sheet, and she is too weak to speak. She can only lie there on an old mat, in front of their family's crumbling mud hut, and look on as Celina disappears through the overgrown weeds. Her aunt is not the only person who is upset. Paulo, who had been sitting on Celina's tiny lap, is screaming hysterically at being left behind.

However, Celina has no choice – food is critical now for the survival of the family. The children are all hungry, and Margarida is dying from AIDS-related illnesses, including tuberculosis, as well as from severe malnutrition. 'I haven't taken my TB tablets for five days, because I'm too hungry', she says in a faint voice. 'The pills have strong side-effects if taken without food', she adds, with tears rolling down her cheeks.

Margarida is only 20 years old, but she has not had much of a youth herself. She dropped out of school when she was 15 to look after her own parents, who she says were ill for a long time before they died. Margarida was married, but she has no children of her own. The children who are living with her are the offspring of her three sisters, all of whom died of AIDS. Three years ago, when Margarida herself became ill, her husband abandoned her. Margarida and the children live in a tiny mud hut, a 15-minute walk from the main road and reachable only by foot along overgrown pathways. Inside, the hut is dank and empty, and when it rains water leaks from the roof. The family's only belongings are some old rusty pots and a few clothes.

Excerpt from Burma (Myanmar)

Refugee International, a non-government organization (NGO), has a vast body of experience in documenting health and other human rights abuses consequent upon people fleeing persecution in their own countries.[4] The following case reflects the dire human rights situation in Burma (Myanmar), especially with regard to its ethnic minorities. The Burmese situation is rendered more impervious to resolution by the UN because of the economic dependence of China and Russia on Burmese oil and gas supplies. As detailed in Chapter 2, Russia and China – both of which have the veto in the UN Security Council – vetoed a US proposal censuring Burma's human rights violations in January 2007.

As an example of the dangers that women face while trying to reach safety in Thailand, I want to share with you the story of Thay Yu, a Karen mother in her forties who was fleeing to Thailand because of oppression by the military in her village. Near the border of Thailand, a group of six Burmese soldiers caught one of the families travelling with her. It was a family of four, consisting of the parents, a nursing baby and a six-year-old girl. Thay Yu hid in a nearby bush, and while soldiers killed the baby with a blow to the back of the neck, others raped the mother while forcing the husband to watch. After killing the mother by stabbing her through her vagina with a bamboo pole, they shot the husband. The six-year-old girl ran away and hid in a tree, where Thay Yu found her and brought her to Thailand after burying the bodies of her parents. This gruesome story is one of many documented accounts. The treatment of ethnic minorities by State Police and Development Council (SPDC) soldiers is inhumane beyond description.

Widespread rape and human rights abuses against ethnic minorities are committed with impunity both by officers and by lower-ranking soldiers. Officers committed the majority of the rapes documented in which the rank of the perpetrator is known. The culture of impunity contributes to the military atmosphere in which rape is permissible. It also leads to the conclusion that the system for protecting civilians is faulty, which in turn suggests that rape is systematic. Due to the well-known impunity with regard to rape, survivors and their families are extremely reluctant to complain about rape. In the rare cases where victims or their families actually do complain to military officials, army personnel often respond with violence. In only two of the 43 cases that Refugees International documented were the perpetrators punished, and these punishments were extremely lenient (e.g. the payment of 1000 Kyat or the equivalent of one US dollar).

As an example of the impunity granted to soldiers, I want to share the story of Naw My Doh, who told us that she saw soldiers take her sister away from their home and transport her to their military camp. She heard her sister calling for her brother and father to help her because 'they are raping me.' They could do nothing to help her. A day after her sister was taken, the soldiers brought her body back for the family to bury. Her wounds clearly indicated that she had been raped, perhaps to death. Despite the fact that the soldiers continued to return to their village after the murder, Naw Mu Doh and her family were too afraid to complain. One month later, her father was killed by the army.

According to Refugees International's conversations with more than 150 people along the Thai/Burmese border over a period of one month, women from ethnic-minority groups along Burma's eastern border experience rape at the hands of Burma's army on a consistent and frequent basis.

Sexual abuse by UN personnel

During the last few months of 2006, such media outlets as the Murdoch Press, ITN and FOX News – and hence much of the UK and other EU media – prominently featured attacks on Kofi Annan, the General Secretary of the UN. This was discussed by the present author in some detail in a previous book.[5] In the present context, it is sufficient to mention that one of the complaints featured against the UN involved a number of incidents, especially in the Democratic Republic of the Congo, in which UN personnel were raping vulnerable women under their protection. The NGO Refugees International has kept records of such abuses – both by UN personnel and by other NGO personnel in close cooperation with UN peacekeepers. In a report issued on 23 January 23 2007,[6] Refugees International stated that:

> Sexual misconduct has long characterized UN peacekeeping missions. During the UN mission in Cambodia (UNTAC) from 1992 to 2003, the number of sex houses and 'Thai-style' massage parlours multiplied and the number of prostitutes rose from 6,000 to 25,000, including an increased number of child prostitutes. Cambodia's HIV rates rose and sexually transmitted infections spread among Cambodian prostitutes. Cambodians complained to the UN mission about UNTAC personnel's disorderly behaviour, drinking and association with prostitutes. The mission's Special Representative to the Secretary-General (SRSG), Yasushi Akashi, infamously replied, 'Boys will be boys', and no disciplinary action was taken.

The following brief excerpt[7] from the testimony of a 14-year-old Liberian girl is germane in this regard.

> When ma asked me to go to the stream to wash plates, a peacekeeper asked me to take off my clothes so that he could take a picture. When I asked him to give me money he told me, no money for children, only biscuit. It is difficult to escape the trap of the NGO people; they use the food as bait to get you to have sex with them.

With respect to the above, however, the question arises as to the administrative link between the UN (as the peace-keeping agency) and its employees in the field. Present restrictions on the UN, as a world body, and the appointment of its field workers in any given country have to be drawn from the local population. Their fitness for the job is decided only locally. The UN administrative apparatus in New York has little or no direct control. In fact, when this author needed to track down a particular peacekeeper in Côte d'Ivoire in 2003, the UN's Personnel Office in New York could not help. I had to make inquiries to NGOs working with the UN in Côte D'Ivoire itself. Also, many such UN peacekeepers only work for 2 or 3 months in that context before taking up employment elsewhere. This, of course, does not absolve the UN, but suggests that any reform of the world body has to involve a tighter control over the selection ad retention of its peacekeepers.

Human trafficking

Another serious area of widespread loss of human rights involves the thousands of individuals who are caught up in the illegal movement of people across frontiers, and without any kind of legal protection, for profit. It has been said that this trade is now even more lucrative than narcotics.[8] It goes without saying that the people who are being trafficked are usually themselves innocent victims of trickery, who have been promised useful employment at their destination and the opportunity to send money home to their families. In reality, they are atrociously exploited in degrading situations of outright prostitution or in conditions of virtual slavery as domestic workers. In the absence of any coordinated effort on the part of the UN itself to protect their human rights, a number of NGOs have sprung up, dedicated to both monitoring the details of this trade and shutting it down. Prominent among these is a Roman Catholic NGO which calls itself Franciscan International. Although an NGO, it is closely associated with the UN and has its offices in the UN buildings in New York.

It claims that at least 2.5 million men, women and children have been trafficked – usually from poor to wealthy countries – for bonded and forced labour activities.[9] This routinely includes prostitution, domestic work, fieldwork or factory work. Such trafficking constitutes a multi-billion dollar business, with approximately two-thirds of those falling into its clutches being used in prostitution or other forms of sexual exploitation. The following two accounts are derived from Franciscan International's 2007 report, cited above.

Maria grew up in extreme poverty in Cameroon in West Africa. When she was offered a job in France that would allow her to support her family, she leapt at the chance to build a better life.

Teresa left her home in the Philippines to work as a maid for a rich woman in Lebanon, where she was assured she could earn enough money both to live on and to help her family back home as well.

Katarina and her young son travelled from their home in the Ukraine to northwest Italy, where they were promised factory work that would ensure a brighter future for both of them.

Their happy endings evaporated. When they arrived in their host countries, their passports were confiscated by local representatives of the recruitment agencies. They were subjected to beatings, confinement, and verbal and sexual abuse. Their earnings were withheld, their work hours were extended, and they were forbidden to communicate with their families back home.

All of the above suggests that, somewhere in its working, the UN is paralysed in its ability to defend human rights. The rest of this chapter establishes a basis for explaining this, and this will be amplified in Chapter 2.

The UN as a paradox

Details about the structure, functions and agencies of the UN will be dealt with in full in the next chapter, but to set the context for our analysis of the problem of defending universal access to primary healthcare (PHC), and other human rights, let us briefly consider what we mean by the word 'nation.'

During the night of Friday 12/Saturday 13 January 2007, the BBC World Service reported a most extraordinary event – namely that at the UN Security Council Russia and China had both vetoed a US Resolution calling for an end to human rights abuses in Burma (Myanmar).[10] The US envoy who put forward the proposal was Alejandro Wolff, and he was referring not only to such well-known cases as the continued restrictions on the pro-democracy leader Aung San Sau Kyi, but also to the less widely known daily assault on the human rights of the minority Karen people. In an interview with the BBC World News after the event, Wolff expressed his disappointment.

However, in this author's view, even worse were the reasons given by the Chinese and Russian representatives for their veto. The Chinese delegate stated that, since the Karen people all lived within Burma's borders, any abuse of their human rights could not pose a threat to peace among the nation state members of the UN. The Russian delegate's views were similar. It would be difficult to find a clearer example of the difference between 'human' and 'national' rights. As will be explained more fully in Chapter 2, and as the reader is presumably aware, the UN's moral authority is primarily based on its initial key document, namely the Universal Declaration of Human Rights. That document, along with various subsequent additions to it, lays out in detail the proposition that a key rôle – and perhaps the most relevant rôle – of the UN is to protect the health and other human rights of *all* people wherever they live. However, another rôle of the UN is to prevent the scourge of international warfare by maintaining peace between nations. Are even these two aims compatible?

What is a nation?

The concept of 'nation' has been with us virtually ever since the first systematic attempts at recording history were made – and probably before then. Thus, in ancient Sanskrit documents, and in the earliest chapters of the Old Testament, references to nations occur. It is clear that these early allusions refer to different ethnic groups. Thus 'nations' were defined not so much by geographical boundaries as by ethnic criteria. By the time the Attic Greeks came on the scene and people like Herodotus were attempting to write about history, the idea of the city state was prominent, so that a geographical element entered into the definition of 'nation.' However, even then different nations tended to be clearly demarcated by the 'race', 'language', etc., of their respective peoples.

In modern times, ease of travel has largely – except in cases such as Tibet or certain remote small island communities – done away with such distinctions. Most large developed nations today are increasingly multicultural, characteristically including among their citizens a variety of languages and cultural values. However, the modern concepts of 'nation' and of 'patriotism' can be very clearly traced to events in European history, most importantly the Treaty of Westphalia, sometimes referred to as the 'Peace of Westphalia.' It gave structure and coherence to the rise of national consciousness, and later to various famous wars between European states and/or against non-European peoples.

The Treaty of Westphalia

The 'Treaty' or 'Peace' of Westphalia, as we were taught in school, ended the Thirty Years War which had raged on and off among the European states since the 1580s. That war had reduced many of the treasuries to dangerously low levels and had reduced vast swathes of the European population to levels of poverty, degradation and disease that had not been experienced since the Renaissance. However, the so-called 'Treaty of Westphalia' was not a single, decisive political act such as, for example, the Treaty of Versailles, but instead referred to a whole range of separate truces and peace deals between pairs of warring states that dragged on from 1618 to around 1647.[11]

Although the devious interplay of diplomacy and realpolitik is of engrossing interest, our concern in this book is that it conferred on the world the modern view of what a nation is. Thus individual nations were defined – to some extent – by the ethnicity of the majority of their citizens – but also by internationally recognized geographical boundaries. This allowed the systematic imposition of workable tariff systems and better organization of trade. It also gave strength and cohesion to the acquisition by European states of colonies in overseas territories. In addition it led to more highly organized prosecution of war between states, culminating in the disastrous events of the two world wars, which so disfigured the twentieth century. Both the League of Nations and, later, the United Nations came into being primarily as attempts to forestall such conflicts in the future.

As we know, the League of Nations ultimately failed in this aim, partly because it did little to address the underlying causes of conflict, such as grotesque variations in wealth and in opportunities available to different clusters of people living in close proximity to one another. Partly in order to avoid this mistake, the UN promulgated the Universal Declaration of Human Rights, with its emphasis on the right of every human being anywhere to be accorded dignity and certain 'basic human rights' simply by virtue of being human. In short, the League had concentrated on trying to prevent war by focusing on protecting the dignity of each nation state, while the modern UN also addressed the vital rights of individual people. Back in 1945, when the UN came into being, the essential paradox implicit in this two-pronged set of aims was not realized.

The UN proceeded to develop agencies to ensure the integrity of its basic declaration, such as the United Nations International Children's Emergency Fund (UNICEF). This agency's title, by the way, has since been shortened to the United Nations Children's Fund, but is still referred to as UNICEF. Another such 'human rights' agency was the United Nations Educational, Social and Cultural Organization (UNESCO), which, among other things, mediates educational development in many of the world's poorest countries. It also provides an international forum that enables educational developments in different countries to be assessed and compared. Important in this respect, for example, are its measurements in different countries of levels of literacy, sexual hygiene, etc. Another very widely recognized acronym referring to such agencies is the WHO (World Health Organization) – probably the best known of them all.

With such an armoury of agencies to give force and authority, if not resources, to the aims of the Universal Declaration of Human Rights, there would surely seem to be few problems. However, as subsequent pages will make clear, this has been far from the case.

Part of the problem is that, over the years since 1945, various other agencies have been put under the UN umbrella, the aims of which often conflict with the Universal Declaration of Human Rights. These include the World Bank (WB), at first referred to as the World Bank for Construction and Development, in keeping with its original intentions to help war-damaged nations to restore their infrastructures. Together with the WB was the International Monetary Fund (IMF). Five decades later the World Trade Organization (WTO) came into existence. Again due more to an accident of history than to design, the IMF and the WB found themselves involved more in funding developments in less developed countries (LDCs) than in helping war-damaged industrial nations to get back on their feet.

The impact of these developments has been immense and, in many cases, quite contradictory to the maintenance or furtherance of human rights among people of the LDCs. These issues will be explained more fully in Chapter 2, but suffice it to say that if the IMF or the WB lent money to a nation, the former had to protect its investment as best it could. One way would be for the IMF to specify how the money should be spent and, more especially, what the debtor nation must do to make sure that the loan would be most effective in mediating development. To do this they impose Structural Adjustment Policies (SAPs) on the borrower nation. These SAPs often intrude directly into the way in which the country is run, because they specify that the government must privatise as many of its public services (such as education and health) as possible, and that it must concentrate as much of its healthcare and education as it can in the areas (e.g. ports) where the development projects most directly affect trade. The SAPs also typically require that the government undertakes widespread domestic infrastructure development (e.g. road-building, etc.). As we shall see, all of this has implications for public health and other human rights.

The emergence of the WTO (in 1995) further exacerbated this widespread undermining of basic human rights, sacrificing them to the need for efficient trade with developed nations in order to pay back the IMF and WB. Insight into how all of this came about will be dealt with in Chapter 2, as will the peculiarly self-contradictory remits and character of some of its agencies. More broadly, it suggests that if we are to take the issue of global equity with regard to health and other human rights seriously, we have to think about how such an ambitious mandate can be mediated effectively. In summary, we must either carry out a major overall reconstruction of the UN, possibly removing some of its agencies to become part of a global finance management body, or perhaps investigate the possibility of establishing another type of world body altogether.

References

1 UNICEF. *The State of the World's Children.* Geneva: UNICEF; 2005. p. 42.
2 MacDonald T. *The Global Human Right to Health: dream or possibility?*
   Oxford: Radcliffe Publishing; 2007. pp. 125–6.
3 UNICEF, op. cit., p. 78.
4 Refugees International. *Testimony: development of democracy in Burma.* Washington, DC: Refugees International: 2006. p. 1; www.refintl.org/content/article/detail/1139/?PHPSESSID =44 (accessed 7 February 2007).
5 MacDonald T, op. cit., pp. 40–42.
6 Refugees International. *Must Boys be Boys? Sexual exploitation in UN missions.* Washington, DC: Refugees International; 2007; p. 2; http://refugeesinternational.org/section/publications/pk_exploit/html (accessed 7 February 2007).
7 Delaney S. *Protecting Children From Sexual Exploitation in Disasters and Emergency Situations.* Bangkok: ECPAT (End Child Prostitution and Trafficking); 2006. p. 26.
8 MacDonald T, op. cit., p. 170.
9 Catholic Online International News. *International Human Trafficking Thrives;* www.catholic.org/international/international_story.php?id=22636 (accessed 5 February 2007).
10 http://news.bbc.co.uk/1/hi/world/asia-pacific/6257921.stm (accessed 25 January 2007).
11 www.historylearningsite.co.uk/peace_of_westphalia.htm (accessed 4 January 2007).

Chapter 2

The UN and human rights

Origins and aims of the UN

As has already been implied, the UN finds itself operating across a wide array of conflicting values, interests and purposes. In order to set the context for this state of affairs, this chapter will specifically delineate how and why the world body came into existence and the bureaucratic mechanisms by which it gradually became enmeshed in contradictory aims. In many respects, the very breadth and, at the same time, inadequately precise definition of its original stated purpose seemed to attract the formation of sub-agencies whose own aims were mutually contradictory. The UN that enunciates such unambiguous declarations as the Declaration of Human Rights and the Declaration of the Rights of the Child is the same UN that incorporates the International Monetary Fund (IMF) as one of its agencies while the IMF's Structural Adjustment Policies (SAPs) often lead to denial of human rights and to violations of the rights of children.

Originally, the UN was established as an international organization to promote international security, cooperation and peace, and this grand venture took place during the closing days of World War Two, when a war-weary world was anxiously looking for ways to prevent future international conflict. Above all, the allied powers sought to create a body that would not fall prey to the sorts of irreconcilable difficulties that had ultimately destroyed the League of Nations. In most respects they were successful. The present UN is far more durable than the old League had ever been, largely because it has spawned a series of agencies, such as UNESCO, UNICEF and the WHO, to mediate its aims globally in such areas as education, care of children and healthcare. However, as we shall see, it is this capacity to create agencies with specific responsibilities that, in many respects, has also weakened the power and consistency of the UN as a universally respected international mediator in preventing wars.

The primary basis for world peace, of course, is an explicit commitment to the concept of the universal human right to dignity. Above all, this requires that all people have a basic right from birth, and before, to health and hence access to primary healthcare. This is basic to and indeed provides the raison d'être of the whole panoply of human rights. It was in this context that, in 1945, 50 nations adopted the United Nations Charter. This document asserts the UN's goals, functions and responsibilities. Human rights are given priority in this Charter from the start. For instance, Article 1 of the Charter states that one of the aims of the UN is to achieve international cooperation in 'promoting and encouraging respect for human rights and for fundamental freedoms for all without distinction as to race, sex, language or religion.'[1]

However, as implied above, the wording of Article 1 is very general. Unambiguous legal definitions were needed before the Charter could be useful in international discussions.

To that end the Commission on Human Rights was established, and it was charged with creating the International Bill of Human Rights. The latter consists of the Universal Declaration of Human Rights (UDHR), the International Covenant on Civil and Political Rights (and its Protocol) and the International Covenant on Economics, Social and Cultural Rights.

The UDHR was the first off the planning table, and its rôle was to define the 'basic human rights' to which we refer in this book and to which all individuals anywhere in the world are entitled. Unfortunately, however, a 'declaration' is not legally binding. For the rights defined by it to have full legal force, they have to be incorporated into 'conventions' (sometimes referred to as treaties or covenants), and it is these which set the international norms and standards. Wherever a government signs (ratifies) such a convention, that nation becomes legally required to uphold these standards.

In this way, the UDHR spawned two covenants critical to our discussion, namely the International Covenant on Civil and Political Rights (ICCPR), along with its Protocol, and the International Covenant on Economics, Social and Cultural Rights (ICESCR). These, and every other such covenant, establish procedures for monitoring and reporting how signatories to the conventions concerned are complying with them. Article 1 in the ICCPR established a Human Rights Committee of 18 independent experts whose rôle was to examine the reports. It is also in the remit of the committee to provide a complaints procedure through which individuals or groups who have a grievance against their government can be heard at an international forum.

Whenever a UN member ratifies such a convention, it not only agrees to abide by the provisions of the convention, but also consents to be monitored. Most of the violations of human rights discussed in this book are exacerbated by trying to agree on procedures for international monitoring. There are no hard and fast rules by which such discussions can be sequenced. Instead, they tend to vary with each issue, not according to any measure of the danger posed by the specific situation, but by the relative political, economic or military power of the nations involved.

Thus, as the reader will be aware, the grievous situation in Darfur involving violation of the health rights (and other human rights) of the people had been going on for some years by 2007, yet did not attract unequivocal UN intervention with regard to Sudan. However, when Iran began to indicate its intention to pursue an independent policy with regard to developing its nuclear programme, the issue was pushed to prominence at the UN Security Council because two of the affected nations were the USA and Israel. That is, real and actual violation of the human rights of the 'economically marginal' people of Darfur has played a subsidiary rôle to the possibility of abuses which Iran might commit.

Even with international agreement, moving a human rights issue into the arena of UN action requires a number of bureaucratic steps. These are discussed more fully in one of the author's previous publications,[2] but the process can be briefly outlined as follows.[3]

1 **Drafting:** The proposed convention is drafted by various interested groups. The UN General Assembly commissions these groups, consisting of representatives of UN member states as well as people representing both existing intergovernmental and non-government organizations (NGOs).
2 **Adoption by the UN:** The proposal is then adopted or rejected by a vote of the UN General Assembly.
3 **Signing by member states:** Whenever a member state signs the proposed conven-

tion, it is indicating that it has started the process required by its government for formal notification. By signing it also agrees to refrain from acts that would be contrary to the objectives of the convention.

4 **Ratification:** When a member state ratifies a convention, it obviously agrees to comply with its provisions and obligations. To this end it assumes the responsibility to ensure that national legislation does not conflict with the convention, while at the same time indicating its reservations about any specific articles of it. As we shall see, this can lead to months and years of delay, during which much needless suffering of innocent people can occur.

5 **Entering into force:** A convention goes into effect when a certain number of member states have ratified it. For example, the ICCPR and ICESCR were originally adopted in 1966, but it was not until a decade later, in 1976, that the specified number of member states (35 at the time) ratified them.

Coherent as this seems to be, the process rarely moves this smoothly. One of the major obstacles frequently arises because of differences in domestic legislation between one nation and another. This again raises the paradox of the UN being expected to protect human rights but without this conflicting with its rôle of 'respecting national sovereignty.' In the USA, for example, the process towards ratification begins when the President endorses the document by signing it. It is then submitted to the Senate, along with any administrative recommendations. The Senate Foreign Relations Committee first considers the convention, conducting hearings to monitor public reaction. The Foreign Relations Committee may then recommend the convention to the Senate, possibly with reservations or qualifications. Such reservations are often based on the need to enact new legislation in order to conform to a convention. However, the federal system of the US government gives individual states, not the national government, the right to make law in many areas, such as criminal and family law. Next the full Senate considers the convention. Finally, if the Senate approves the convention, the President formally notifies the UN that the USA has ratified and thus become a state party to the convention.

The Convention on the Rights of the Child provides an example of the evolution of a UN convention. In 1959, a working group drafted the Declaration on the Rights of the Child, which consisted of 10 principles setting out basic rights to which all children should be entitled.

From declaration to convention

The only criterion by which the worth or strength of any UN Declaration can be judged is the extent to which its various clauses can be brought to the fore as UN Conventions. Let us consider the UN Declaration on the Rights of the Child as an example.

Pivotal as a major concern in this book is the impact on the health rights of children. The basic principles were easily agreed upon by member states, and agreement on the declaration was not difficult to secure. It was in codifying these principles into a convention that problems arose. A summary of the whole convoluted process is highly instructive, and provides a basis upon which improvements in securing global rights might well be initiated.

The formal drafting process lasted nine years, during which representatives of governments, intergovernmental agencies (such as UNICEF and UNESCO) and NGOs (such as Save the Children and the International National Red Cross) worked together to create consensus on the language used in the convention.

The resulting Convention on the Rights of the Child (Children's Convention) contains 54 articles that can be divided into three general categories as follows:

1 protection – covering specific issues, such as abuse, neglect and exploitation
2 provision – addressing a child's particular needs, such as education and health care
3 participation – acknowledging a child's growing capacity to make decisions and play a part in society.

The Children's Convention was adopted by the General Assembly in 1989 and was immediately signed and ratified by more nations in a shorter period of time than any other UN convention. As a result, the Children's Convention entered into force shortly thereafter, in 1990. Furthermore, the total number of member states which have ratified the Children's Convention has surpassed that of all other conventions. As of December 1998, only two member states – Somalia and the USA – have not ratified it. It goes without saying that if the most powerful and wealthy nation on earth cannot ratify something as basic as the Convention on the Rights of the Child, we are facing an uphill struggle to truly make 'primary healthcare' a basic human right.

In the 58 years from 1948 to 2006, the UDHR has produced 20 human rights conventions. Many of these have come into force, while the others are still in the process of ratification. One in particular that has not yet even been drafted is a convention on the rights of indigenous people. Indeed, as will be cited later in this text, the *British Medical Journal* has considered this crucial point in recent issues, not only with respect to indigenous people living in First World nations such as Australia and the USA, but also with respect to indigenous people in India, the African nations, South America and elsewhere.

From declaration to action: the World Health Organization

Probably one of the best known of the UN agencies is the World Health Organization (WHO). It was established on 7 April 1948 as the UN's specialist agency for health. In its constitution,[4] it states that the objective of the WHO is attainment by all peoples of the highest possible level of health. The constitution then goes on to define health as a 'state of complete physical, mental and social well-being and not merely the absence of disease or infirmity.' This definition obviously casts its remit very broadly indeed, for if we are not speaking only of the 'absence of disease', we are referring to much more than clinical or biomedical criteria. Indeed, we are referring to health promotion.[5] This in turn must involve – at the very least – primary healthcare (PHC). PHC is defined in slightly different ways by different health agencies. For instance, within biomedical circles, PHC is just the first rung of a three-rung hierarchy consisting of primary healthcare (PHC), secondary healthcare (SHC) and tertiary healthcare (THC). PHC refers to access to a general medical practitioner and possibly a nurse or health visitor, SHC refers to clinical facilities and more diagnostic tests (e.g. X-ray), and THC refers to the most esoteric levels of medical technology, specialist surgery, etc. However, this is not what the WHO meant by PHC, nor was it what the UN

Charter had in mind when it referred to PHC as a 'human right.'[6] Not only does PHC have a wider remit than the 'operational' definition given above (because it includes access to dentistry and pharmaceuticals), but it embraces all of the social contexts that enhance health.

The working definition of PHC in this context was elaborated by the WHO in 1978 in its now famous Alma-Ata Declaration.[7] In general, it was held to be a strategy that not only responds equitably, appropriately and effectively to clinical healthcare needs, but also deals comprehensively with social, economic and political causes and consequences of poor health. At a meeting of the International People's Health University (IPHU) in Cuenca, Ecuador, in July 2005, PHC was defined by David Sanders[8] as including the following.

1 It must be applicable universally and converge on the basis of need only.
2 It must be comprehensive in that it emphasizes disease prevention and health promotion.
3 It must embrace both the individual and community involvement, and inculcate responsibility in maintaining health.
4 It must be intersectorial, involving cooperation between all relevant agencies – education, law enforcement, medical agencies, etc.
5 It must include access on the basis of need alone to all available medical or diagnostic technology that resources allow.

However, the extent to which this policy could be applied equitably soon became compromised by the UN's own activities through its other agencies, especially those mediating finance. Things started to unravel with regard to equitable application of these policies in the late 1980s. In fact, the WHO hit its high point in this enterprise when Dr Halfdan Mahler of Denmark was Director-General. He assumed that post in 1973 and his tenure ended in 1988. He had been tireless in promoting the WHO's PHC policy, and he organized committees which drew up strategies for creating 'Health For All' (HFA) by the turn of the millennium (by the year 2000). Moreover, his HFA (2000) policies formed the basis of the famous 'Healthy Cities' programmes. The first of these – 'Healthy Ottawa 2000' – gave rise to what is known in health promotion circles as the 'Ottawa Charter 1986.'[9] This turned out to be a major influential vehicle for popularising the radical and seminal ideas of Mark Lalonde[10] with regard to health promotion as a political and social enterprise as much as a biomedical one.

The WHO has continued to play a key rôle in promoting the need to make a PHC realisable as a 'human right', and indeed in this it has been perfectly consistent with the UN Charter. However, since 1988 it has been running into difficulties. As the author pointed out in 2005,[11] the original guiding WHO principles of PHC as a basic human right have been increasingly sidelined as financial globalization, under such mechanisms as the International Monetary Fund, Structural Adjustment Policies and World Trade Organization imposition of policies under the General Agreement on Trade and Services. Instead of health being regarded as a basic human right (as in the UN Charter), it has been becoming more and more of a 'desideratum if it can be afforded.'

Indeed, in this author's view, from 1989 through to late 2006 the whole idea of PHC became increasingly contingent on an integrated system of global finance, rather than being regarded as a basic human right per se. However, on 10 November 2006 another Director-General of the WHO was appointed, who may well take up the PHC flag and continue to carry it forward from where Halfdan Mahler left off in 1988. This new Director-General is Dr Margaret Chan. In her inaugural address when she assumed the post, she was reported as saying that her priorities would be 'the health rights of the very poorest and dispossessed women everywhere.'[12] So far, as of late 2007, her tenure as Director-General of the WHO appears to augur well for her stated intentions, although some criticisms have been raised (*see* Chapter 8).

However, even if Dr Chan could restore the primacy of PHC for all as the undergirding policy of the WHO, the latter is not the only UN agency that has an impact on the global human right to health. In particular, the UN is 'foster parent' to at least three other agencies whose actions often obstruct access of people in the Third World to human rights. A brief account of how this has come about follows.

The IMF, WB and WTO

These three acronyms – household words to international health workers – refer respectively to the International Monetary Fund, the World Bank for Reconstruction and Development and the World Trade Organization. An insight into their history is necessary if one is to understand their impact on global health rights today.

The IMF and the WB came into existence before the UN itself did. In 1944, representatives of some of the leading allied powers in World War Two met to consider questions related to how global trade and finance could best be mediated once victory had been achieved. The most pivotal of these meetings were held in the Bretton Woods Conference Centre, situated in rural New Hampshire, USA. The key players at these meetings were Britain and the USA. The IMF and the WB were formalized at these meetings, but in fact both agencies were originally planned as far back as 1930, well before the war had even started, by the US Senate Committee for Foreign Relations (CFR).[13]

The reason for this was that the rapid growth, vigour and innovativeness of business and industry in the USA were engendering increasing levels of demand for world trading markets. This was bringing US commercial interests into conflict with those of the then British Empire, because the latter had already established a matrix of trading and tariff arrangements all over the world to enhance its own economic well-being. Back then the CFR agreed that some kind of international banking system would need to be established by which the USA would exercise decisive control over global commerce. Therefore, by the time of the Bretton Woods Conference, the US delegation, led by their president Franklin Delano Roosevelt, had a clear idea of what they wanted.

At that time the USA was by far the most powerful and undamaged nation in the world, and was of course under Roosevelt's leadership. He was a most remarkable man, passionate in his commitment to his country and its people. Even to this day he is remembered by many people – not only Americans – with almost reverential affection. While many individuals and nations had been brought to the edge (and over it) of economic ruin during the Great Depression, he had introduced the New Deal and such enterprises as the Tennessee Valley Authority. Thus his legislation brought financial salvation and security to millions of his own people. When he was 39 years of age, he was severely crippled with polio but, although he was wheelchair-bound, this did not prevent him from becoming President in 1933 and from being re-elected three more times subsequently in 1936, 1940 and 1944. He died of a brain haemorrhage in 1945.

His administration had consistently reflected his devotion to the ideal of the rights of ordinary people and his almost visceral detestation of royalty or anything that smacked of privilege gained by unearned wealth or social class. For this reason he felt an intense animus toward the British Empire, which at the time constituted a serious check on US international trade and influence, by virtue of its complex matrix of tariff and trading arrangements with the British Empire. Thus on coming to office for the first time in 1933, he aggressively promoted US trading interests. Needless to say, many of the world's colonial people lauded the first of these aims, while regretting more recently his success in achieving the latter one!

It was in this context that Roosevelt, along with the famous English economist, John Maynard Keynes (1883–1996), played such a pivotal rôle in setting up the two major economic bodies which today control the levers of global trade. These two bodies are the WB (officially called the International Bank for Reconstruction and Development) and the IMF. They, at Keynes' insistence, were also about to set up a World Trade Organization (WTO) to ensure equity in international trade, but Roosevelt finally vetoed this idea because it would have imposed restraints on US economic power. The WTO was eventually set up in 1995, but in such a way as to embrace US control over global trade, rather than the reverse.

A pivotal decision, agreed at the Bretton Woods Conference, was that the US dollar would be the global medium of exchange. This was initially opposed by Keynes but, especially without his version of a WTO to arbitrate trading dispute, he was over-ruled. The consequences of this fateful decision have been immense and, as explained later, may yet undermine US global hegemony in finance.

Rôles of the IMF and the WB

Because both of these bodies were agreed to and established formally at the same session at Bretton Woods, they are often referred to as twin sisters. However, their functions are different and their relationship with one another has a significant impact on development programmes in many countries, even in the wealthy industrialized nations. The IMF agrees on broad lines of policy in matters such as establishing and maintaining currency convertibility, and trying to avoid competitive exchange depreciation. In that sense, and unlike the WB, its main rôle was as a fiscal policy think-tank and not merely a financial institution. Initially its basic financial policy was to adhere strictly to the gold standard in adjudicating loans to member countries. However, the USA came off the gold standard in the early 1960s. Thus the IMF was restrained from high-risk lending. Indeed, it only lends to treasuries and central banks of member countries and generally over only five years. Originally, then, the IMF saw its function as helping member states in the short term if they should run into temporary balance-of-payments problems.[14]

It must be borne in mind that the official rationale for the establishment of the WB and the IMF at the Bretton Woods Conference was that it was designed to help the major developed countries that had been damaged by the ravages of war to get back on their feet. The long antecedent history of the WB (alluded to above) and its importance to US trading interests did not feature in the official statement! In this regard, too, even at Bretton Woods, no one could have foreseen that the WB and the IMF would – within 30 years – find themselves focused almost exclusively on poor less developed countries (LDCs) rather than on major industrialized nations. How this came about will be explained later.

Before discussing how the IMF could mediate short-term loans to temporarily cash-strapped nations, let us consider the IMF's twin sister, the WB. The latter has virtually the same membership as the IMF, but is endowed with much greater financial flexibility. For instance, it can make long-term loans over periods of up to 20 years, and can now even lend to private projects in LDCs. As we shall see, it can – and frequently does – finance such private projects as setting up water purification facilities, in turn only allowing users to access safe drinking water by paying for it. In such ways it is seen as directly influencing the running of poorer countries. The WB makes very wide use of private banks in both the developed and less developed world as principle and intermediary lenders. Furthermore, it can even sell outstanding debts on the financial markets. Indeed, it is this capacity of First World banks to 'sell outstanding debt' that keeps them safe, while mortgaging the LDCs even further.

We can now explain how the WB and the IMF became involved in lending money to very poor LDCs whose economies had never been strong and had not been ruined suddenly through war. The scenario unfolded as follows. Between 1944 and 1972–73, the WB and the IMF loaned very little money to impoverished LDCs, especially those with no domestic oil reserves. However, the Organization of Petroleum-Exporting Countries (OPEC) began to put the squeeze on the oil-hungry heavily industrialized nations in Europe and North America by raising the price of oil. This brought huge profits in US dollars to the OPEC countries, which then invested them in developed-country banks. These banks would then have to pay heavy interest rates on the deposits. They, linked with the WB and the IMF, had to find some way of reinvesting the deposits to extract a higher interest rate than they would have to give to the original depositors. In effect LDCs, especially those which had no access to domestic supplies of oil, saved the banks in the developed world. The World Bank and the IMF shifted their interest to the LDCs, offering to make them development loans without too great a regard as to whether or not the loans could ever be paid back without jeopardising the recipient country.

In order for the LDCs to repay, they needed to industrialize rapidly. This required the importation of oil from OPEC countries at high cost, which drove the LDCs to default on loan repayments and to ask for extensions on existing loans at even higher interest rates. Of course, now the banks were awash with US dollars that had to be reinvested quickly, and were only too glad to help out in this way. Over time, this has led one LDC after another into an unbelievably perilous financial situation. For example, some African countries are actually spending more on compound interest rates (not the principal!) than they can spend on health and education in their own countries. And it is here that the question of how the WB and the IMF can ensure that debt repayment comes in.

As soon as a loan is made by the IMF, the debtor nation has to agree to certain Structural Adjustment Policies (SAPs). These are conditions imposed by the banks on the country in order to ensure that its economy can maintain the repayments. Thus a common SAP requirement is that the debtor nation drastically cuts down on expenditure for government services. In any government, two major government services are health and education. Thus the debtor nation is compelled to privatize such services as far as possible. This means that there follows a great reduction in these services in the debtor country. Teachers and healthcare workers who were once employed in the public sector are dismissed and driven to seek employment in newly established private enterprises, which of course have to make a profit (which a public service is not required to do). All of this results in a deterioration in working conditions in health and education at the same time as excluding a large proportion of the population from these services.

Remember also that borrower nations, by the original Bretton Woods agreements, must transact their business – including making repayments to the IMF – in US dollars. This puts them under greater pressure to mortgage the long-term welfare of their own country and people in order to secure US dollars as expeditiously as possible on the global market.

This is routinely coupled with what is referred to as 'verticalization', which means the tendency to concentrate medical and educational services in the main urban/ industrial areas, near ports, in order to further sustain the growing need of the debtor country to export goods for foreign sale in US dollars. All WB and IMF loans have to be paid off in US dollars. A country that is free to spend its resources running health and education as public services will try to 'horizontalize' those services, the obvious aim being to reach all of its citizens. Thus, increasingly after 1973, the IMF and the WB became accused of widening the gap in health rights between the developed and less developed countries.

A new version of the WTO

As we have seen, Keynes' idea for a World Trade Organization, raised at Bretton Woods in 1944, was rejected by the US delegates as being potentially damaging to US interests. Keynes' original proposal included the idea that the WB should print its own currency as the global trading medium, with all nations paying into it according to their trading strength. In the short term this would have entailed US bankers footing a higher bill than those of other participating nations, but it would also have cushioned international trade in the long term from such shocks as sudden devaluation of national currencies. The US dollar has already suffered several such setbacks in the last few decades and – as will be suggested later– this opens the way to a calamitous collapse of the entire basis for US financial hegemony.

Indeed, the USA-felt need for some mechanism to maintain its hold on global financial control meant that ultimately a WTO would have to be called into existence. It was finally established about 50 years after Keynes first suggested it, but still under the rubric that the US dollar should remain the only legal currency for international exchange. The new WTO is buttressed by various bilateral and multi-lateral agreements, such as the General Agreement on Tariffs and Trade (GATT) and the General Agreement on Trade in Services (GATS), and by such regulations (binding on all member states to the WTO) as Trade-Related Intellectual Property Rights (TRIPS).

Basically, the latter are mechanisms by which the WTO can mediate free trade globally between nations, often with disastrous health consequences for poorer nations. For instance, GATT allows – say – a large power, such as the USA, to trade freely and without restrictions or protective tariffs either way, with, say, Chad. In theory, each of these countries has one seat at the WTO and they therefore meet on equal terms. However, as explained in the preceding chapter, this 'equality' is an illusion, and in effect the more financial power a nation can call upon, the better leverage it has in WTO mediations. This is because wealthier nations can afford armies of highly qualified financial advisers who (under WTO regulations) can attend its meetings with the one WTO delegate allowed from that country.

A number of GATT-style agreements have recently become famous, such as the North America Free Trade Association (NAFTA). This represents an agreement between Canada, the USA and Mexico by which no one of these nations will erect protective tariffs to impede free trade with another. Although it is obvious that such an agreement would have a negative impact on the health rights of citizens in the economically poorer nation, it also works the other way. Thus, on the Mexican side of the US/Mexican border, a legion of manufacturing plants (maquilladoras) have been set up. They obviously provide local employment for desperately poor Mexican workers who would otherwise have nothing, but of course these maquilladoras do not come under US health and safety legislation, but only under such protection as Mexican laws allow. Likewise, pay is not determined by US union negotiation with the owners. Thus the Mexican workforce consists of people who work longer hours for lower pay and under less health protection than would US workers. This represents at least a temporary gain for some Mexicans, but it leads to higher levels of unemployment among US highly unionized workers. The automobile industry in the USA provides a dramatic example, as thousands have been laid off from automobile plants in Michigan and manufacturing has been moved to maquilladoras in Mexico.

Even more sinister in many respects is GATS, because 'services' include a wide array of critical activities – education, health, etc. – that can completely undermine a poorer country's efforts to provide for its own social needs with its own resources.

Both GATT and GATS have attracted a great deal of adverse comment over the last few years with regard to their negative impact on health, but any account of the WTO's arsenal in enforcing free trade would be incomplete if it failed to mention TRIPS (Trade-Related Intellectual Property Rights). TRIPS is really a radical re-interpretation of patent law. It means that if a region is known to have traditionally been particularly successful in producing a particular crop, and if agronomists over time succeed in isolating the particular gene complex and, better still, in reproducing it, they can patent it. Even if the original local producer wants to continue exporting their unique product, they can be charged a fee to do so under TRIPS regulations. This applies to pharmaceuticals isolated after years of research by large multinational companies. A telling example that has recently appeared in the news is the production of antiretroviral drugs (ARVs) for the control of HIV/AIDS. Such pharmaceuticals are hugely expensive and cannot be routinely purchased by the vast majority of victims of HIV/AIDS in the LDCs. However, both India and Brazil have recently earned a reputation for being able to mass-produce generic copies of these expensive ARVs at as little as 4–5% of the cost. Yet TRIPS regulations under the WTO may well prevent the widespread sale of these generic copies to countries in Africa or elsewhere.

One of the major criticisms of the WTO is that, despite its democratic pretensions, its successive meetings have failed to address the LDCs' objections to the adverse impact on health and other human rights of its rulings with respect to trade, and the application of TRIPS to medicine, agriculture, etc. To set the scene for further analysis of these pivotal issues, let us summarize the state of play.

A quick history of WTO resolutions

As already stated, the purpose of the WTO is to bring about global free trade, and to this end the International Technical Barriers to Trade (TBT) Agreement was negotiated at the Uruguay round of GATT and then culminated in the Marrakech Agreement, out of which the creation of WTO was actually negotiated (in 1994). It formally came into existence on 1 January 1995. At the very first of its ministerial conferences (in Singapore in 1996), disagreements arose over the issues discussed previously between the delegates from developed and less developed countries. They were not satisfactorily resolved, and were reserved for resolution at the Second Ministerial Conference (in Geneva in 1998). The debate was acrimonious, and it was decided to defer the issue until after a new Director-General had been elected. On 1 September 1999, Mike Moore (from the USA) assumed the post, but not without protracted argument. Another contender was Supachai Panithpakdi (from India), and a compromise was reached, with the two sharing the post for 3 years each, and Mike Moore holding the post first. Again, attempts to settle the concerns of the LDC delegates were deferred until the Third Ministerial Conference in Seattle in December 1999. It was during those deliberations that the now famous riots occurred, as popular antagonism to the WTO began to mount. The Seattle conference was followed in November 2001 by the Fourth Ministerial Conference in Doha, Qatar. At this conference the Doha Declaration was drawn up. This is a pivotal document, and it contains clauses purportedly designed to protect less developed nations from detrimental impacts on health and trade arising from WTO rulings relating to TRIPS, etc. These clauses did not themselves have the force of law, and were sufficiently general in their formulation as to make enforcement ambiguous. For a more complete discussion of the Doha Declaration, the reader is referred to a previous book by this author.[15]

Since the Doha Declaration, the WTO has been at the forefront of concern among people working for global equity in human rights, and its subsequent ministerial conferences have been anticipated with a mixture of cynicism that nothing will change, and the hope that protective clauses will become binding. The Fifth Ministerial Conference took place in Taiwan in January 2002. However, the Doha Declaration barely got a look-in there, as the debate focused on the issue of customs and trading rights vis-à-vis China and Taiwan. China had finally become a member of the WTO a year before, in January 2001. The conference was on this occasion under the chairmanship of Supachai Panithpakdi, so there was an expectation that perhaps the concerns of the LDCs would be given greater priority. Instead it was resolved that they would be discussed at the Sixth Ministerial Conference, scheduled to take place in Cancún, Mexico, in September 2003!

At that meeting, an alliance of 22 delegates representing LDCs led by India, China and Brazil resisted developed-world trading interests. In particular, they called for an end to agricultural subsidies within the EU and the USA. However, these talks also broke down, although there was agreement to solidify the Doha Declaration clauses at the next meeting. These delays of course continued to exacerbate the problems in the LDCs and, as we shall see, the health right inequities between the developed and less developed nations widened. Progress seemed to be made at the Seventh Ministerial Conference in Geneva in August 2004. In summary, the agreement was that the EU and the USA, along with other developed countries, would lower tariff barriers to manufactured goods from the developed world.

The significance of these concerns may seem to the casual reader to be remote from health rights issues. However, this is far from being so. Consider the case of Burkina Faso, one of the world's poorest nations and a former French colony in Africa that achieved independence in 1960. Its soil and climate are such that it produces prodigious crops of cotton cheaply and easily, and cotton is its principal export. However, in the USA, cotton farmers in Mississippi receive agricultural subsidies that allow them to use expensive fertilizers to produce cotton. The USA does not produce cotton as easily as Burkina Faso does but, because of the subsidies, it is able to sell what it does produce on the international market at an even lower price than Burkina Faso. As Burkina Faso's cotton farmers face economic ruin, a precipitous derogation of domestic health and other human rights there is an obvious consequence.

Therefore, with regard to the Geneva Ministerial Conference, what has been the result? The prevailing view is that it has been another 'thumbs down' for LDCs and their people. The well-known NGO, Oxfam, has condemned the Geneva meeting and the Eighth Ministerial Convention at Hong Kong in December 2005 as failing completely to make meaningful decisions with regard to the Doha Declaration. Indeed, on 27 April 2006, Oxfam called upon New Zealand (where it was meeting at the time) to do its part with regard to reigning in agricultural subsidies to help to revive the Doha Development Goals.[16] Oxfam went on to say that the chances of a trade deal that helped to reduce poverty being completed in 2006 were looking increasingly slim.

Oxfam's report, *A Recipe for Disaster*,[17] states that although a new deal is badly needed, current offers are not good enough and poor countries would have been better off missing the 2006 deadline and holding out for better offers. This is despite the fact that, once the US administration loses its authority to negotiate trade deals without the involvement of Congress, a new deal could take years to agree. That view has been upheld by subsequent events.

The UN's authority to protect human rights

In this chapter the reader has been brought face-to-face with a context in which the global human right to health, enshrined in the UN Declaration of Human Rights, is routinely ignored in the name of free trade and – more broadly – of the neoliberal orthodoxies that currently control global finance and trade. Can the UN act to address these grave and persistent inequities? The answer is that it cannot because, although the WHO is an agency of the UN, so are the IMF, the WB and the WTO. True, the UN itself did create UNESCO, UNICEF and many others specifically to enhance its Declaration of Human Rights. However, as we have seen, the WB and the IMF were created by politicians, with a particular agenda, at the Bretton Woods Conference. When the UN came into being, disproportionately financed by the USA, whose territory had barely been scratched by the ravages of World War Two, and on US soil, the WB and the IMF were placed under UN control. When the WTO was finally established in 1995, very much under US financial control, it was taken over almost as an arm of the IMF, and thus also found itself often regarded as a 'UN agency.'

This, together with the anomalous confusion between 'national rights' and 'human rights' alluded to in Chapter 1, does much to account for what this author has referred to as the 'schizophrenic view' of the current UN in its response to human rights more broadly. Structural changes to the UN are required before it can transcend these difficulties and regain global authority.

One of the problems of enabling the UN to transcend its present limitations lies in the way in which it is structured administratively. These aspects of its difficulties will be dealt with in greater detail in Chapter 10, but for now it suffices to point out that the UN from the beginning has consisted of two main divisions – the General Assembly (on which every member state has a seat) and the Security Council (on which 15 member states have seats). The problem is that 5 seats have been reserved for the five Permanent Members – the USA, the UK, France, Russia and China. The other 10 seats on the Security Council are allocated by a ballot of the General Assembly every two years, but in such a way that, broadly speaking, every geographical region of the world is represented. However, the Permanent Members – the Big Five – are the only ones with the power of the veto, and they have not changed since the end of World War Two.

In summary, then, there are four major 'contradictions' and/or 'inconsistencies' inherent in the UN's origins and structure.

1   Its controlling powers (the 'Big Five'), which have veto power, have not changed since the end of World War Two. They represent the victorious powers and tend to reflect a neoliberal bias. Indeed, throughout much of its existence the UN has often acted as little more than an extension of US foreign policy.
2   It cannot simultaneously promote and defend basic human rights while also being obliged to promote and defend the rights of individual member states. This will become evident when we consider the case of Burma (*see* Chapter 4).
3   Some of its agencies are committed to mutually contradictory programmes.
4   The concept of the 'nation state' has undergone radical changes since 1945, due to great advances in global travel and communication.

Any improvement in the UN, or any replacement for it, must take these problems into account if it is to have the global authority that it needs.

In the next chapter we shall consider the Darfur crisis in more exhaustive detail, and illustrate how and where the UN's ambiguous position is reflected in the furtherance of amelioration. For, as was pointed out as far back as 2001, by Christof Heyns and Frans Viljoen,[18] the actual success of any international human rights system should be evaluated in accordance with its impact on human rights practices at the domestic level. At the beginning of the new millennium, it is clear that the concept of human rights is widely accepted. The conceptual battle is over, and the focus has shifted to the implementation of human rights. Universal ratification of the main UN human rights treaties might be appearing on the horizon, but ratification in itself is largely a formal (and in some cases empty) gesture. The challenge now is to ensure that the promises contained in the treaties and affirmed through ratification are realized in the lives of ordinary people around the world. It is with this in mind that we begin with an analysis of an actual case in the next chapter.

References

1 United Nations. *Charter of the United Nations*; www.un.org/aboutun/charter/-2k (accessed 2 March 2007).

2 MacDonald T. *The Global Human Right to Health: dream or possibility?* Oxford: Radcliffe Publishing; 2007. pp. 9–18.

3 United Nations. *From Concept to Convention: how human rights law evolves. Part 1;* www.1.umn. edu/humanrts/edumat/hredustries/hereandnow (accessed 6 January 2007).

4 World Health Organization. *About WHO;* www.who.int/about.p.1 (accessed 2 March 2007).

5 MacDonald T. *Rethinking Health Promotion: a global approach.* London: Routledge; 1998.

6 Global Policy Forum – Peace Action International Office. *Convention on the Rights of the Child.* Article 6 (Para 2) and Article 24 (Par 1); www.globalpolicy.org/security/sanction/lawstds.httu (accessed 6 January 2007).

7 World Health Organization. *The Global Meeting on Future Strategic Directions for Primary Health Care: a framework for future strategic directions.* Global Report – Alma Ata Declaration; www.who.int/primary-health-care (accessed 6 March 2007).

8 Sanders D. *Primary health care and health system development: strategies for regeneration.* Paper presented at the International People's Health University, Cuenca, Ecuador, 2005.

9 Seedhouse D. *Health Promotion: philosophy, prejudice and practice.* New York: John Wiley & Sons; 1997. p. 36.

10 Lalonde M. *A New Perspective on the Health of Canadians.* Ottawa: Information Canada; 1974.

11 MacDonald T. *Health, Trade and Human Rights.* Oxford: Radcliffe Publishing; 2005. p. 3.

12 US Information Service. *Report on Dr Margaret Chan assuming office as Director-General of WHO;* www.usinfo.state.gov/xarchives/display.html (accessed 8 January 2007).

13 Shoup LH, Minter W. Shaping a new world order. In: *Imperial Brain Trust: the Council on Foreign Relations and United States Foreign Policy.* New York: Monthly Review Press; 1997. p. 117.

14 Rachman J, Black E, editors. *Multinational Corporations.* Chicago: Trade and the Dollar Publishers; 1974. p. 46.

15 MacDonald T. *Health, Trade and Human Rights.* Oxford: Radcliffe Publishing; 2005. p. 15.

16 Oxfam. *Rich Country Greed Diminishes Prospect of WTO Deadline;* www.scoop.co.nz.stories/P0000604/500211.htm (accessed 6 May 2006).

17 www.oxfam.org.nz (accessed 6 May 2006).

18 Heyns C, Viljoen F. The impact of United Nations treaties at the domestic level. *Hum Rights Q.* 2001; **23:** 483–97.

Chapter 3

The Darfur crisis

Geographical context

The Darfur crisis in Sudan, especially with regard to apparent reluctance by the UN to intervene either through trade sanctions or otherwise, is much more complex than much of the media coverage would have us believe. In this chapter the author will try to analyse the events in such a way as to ultimately (*see* Chapter 10) provide a basis for considering what has to be done to render transnational mediation of global equity with regard to the health rights specified in the Universal Declaration of Human Rights more of a reality than it is at present.

We start with the crisis in Darfur, but this cannot be approached without a clear understanding, first, of the geography of the area involved, because much of the analysis will involve references not only to Darfur itself, but also to the geographical positions of various tribal groupings within its borders. For this reason, constant reference will need to be made to Figures 3.1 and 3.2.

Figure 3.1: Sudan and its surrounding countries, and position of Sudan's Darfur Province.[1]

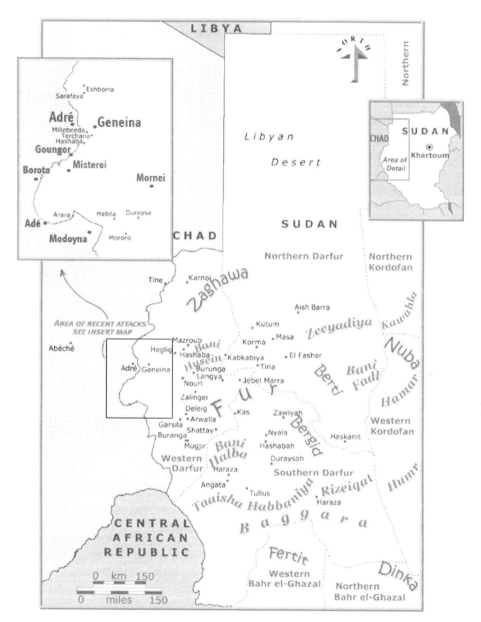

Figure 3.2: Map showing details of Darfur's tribal regions.[2]

First, however, let us look carefully at the purely geographical context. Sudan is the largest country in Africa (in terms of area) and lies in the north-west of the continent. It is bounded on the north-east corner by the Red Sea, but is otherwise surrounded by a number of African countries. Going in a clockwise direction, these are Chad, Libya, Egypt, Ethiopia, Kenya, Uganda, Congo, the Democratic Republic and the Central African Republic. The province of Darfur extends down almost the complete western side of Sudan, bounded to the north by Egypt, to the north-west by Libya and to the west by Chad. This means that it is difficult for any protracted unrest in Sudan to be kept hermetically sealed from the rest of African politics.

The north of Sudan is largely desert or scrubland, and the south is mostly savannah suitable mainly for livestock farming. Almost three-quarters of the workforce are engaged in agriculture, mainly at the subsistence level. Sudan's chief agricultural exports are cotton, groundnuts, sesame seed and animal skins. Sudan remains one of the world's poorest countries, subjected to both drought and floods, and it has incurred immense levels of foreign debt. However, its rivers have great potential for irrigation, and the Jonglei Canal conserves water, draining much of the Sudd (*see* Figure 3.1), and this provides extensive areas of good farmland. In addition, Sudan's mineral resources include extensive oil and gas reserves. The latter obviously imposes a degree of hesitancy by powerful nations in the UN Security Council about interfering in Sudanese affairs.

From 1898 until 1956, Sudan was ruled jointly by Britain and Egypt. In 1956 Sudan became independent. In 1969 a military coup brought General Nimeiry to power and a long-lasting civil war (1955–1972) between the predominantly Arab north and black south was brought to an end. However, in 1983, Nimeiry imposed strict Muslim law, and this restarted the civil war. This eventually led to a democratically elected civilian government which was displaced by another military coup in 1989. Since then there has rarely been peace within Sudan, as the next section explains.

Historical context

Starting in 2003, the situation with regard to Sudan and Darfur seemed to suddenly burst into public consciousness, as though Sudan had suddenly embarked on a campaign of rape, plunder and murder among the defenceless and peaceful people of Darfur. A sinister group called the Janjaweed, we gathered, were armed and supported by the Sudan government to facilitate their gratuitous assault on the human rights of internally displaced people (IDP) in Darfur. Widespread violation of human rights is certainly going on in Darfur, the Janjaweed do exist and the Sudanese government is clearly obstructing human rights in Darfur, but the situation is much more complex than the media accounts suggest. In order to effectively understand the rôle of the UN as the putative defender of human rights in this dreadful débacle, it is necessary to have a more complete insight into the real context of the situation. A glance at the geographical relationship of Sudan and Darfur with surrounding African countries[1] (*see* Figure 3.1) will help to clarify the matter.

It was probably a speech by Colin Powell, US Secretary of State, on 9 September 2004 to the Senate Foreign Relations Committee – avidly taken up by the media – that created the widespread impression that the conflict between the government of Sudan (GOS) and the people of its western province Darfur was a recent development. In that speech, Powell raised the issue of whether what the Janjaweed and its supporters in the GOS were doing to civilians in Darfur constituted 'genocide' or not. If it did, then the UN would definitely have been able to intervene – initially by imposing trade sanctions, but also by sending in military forces if the sanctions failed, although as will be mentioned in Chapter 10, the military option is rarely the best.

However, there are several minority ethnic and religious groupings in Sudan, and for many years these have been in open conflict with one another. These conflicts have usually distilled into binaries, such as Christian against Muslin, black African vs. Arab, rebel vs. government, etc. Thus when considering the huge influx of refugees from Darfur into Egypt, say, it is important to realize that their flight was due largely to the Darfur vs. GOS conflict going back as far as 1980. Precise information about the numbers of asylum seekers and/or refugees is almost impossible to assess, but such conflicts were as brutal as anything with which we have been made familiar since 2003. Extreme violence in Sudan pre-dates the outbreak of the Second Civil War way back in 1983. However, the Islamicization reform campaign and subsequent state of emergency declared by President Nimeiry on 26 April 1983 are normally thought of as reintroducing the North–South violence that had raged for nearly 20 years, and had tentatively ended with the 1972 Addis Ababa Accords.

However, the current complicated crisis has strong links to environmental and natural resource issues, a fact that must be reflected in humanitarian response and rehabilitation efforts. The consequent violations of human rights relating to health are therefore routine and numerous. For example, competition over land and water between sedentary farmers and nomadic tribes has long been a part of Darfur's history. However, environmental degradation, desertification in northern Sudan and the impact of prolonged droughts exacerbated the situation, causing nomadic groups to move further south in search of suitable land and water. This intensified friction with farmers in Darfur's more fertile agricultural belt, and contributed to the current crisis. Related factors that are compounded by environmental issues include poverty and underdevelopment.[3]

Effects on the environment are also expected where the movement of large numbers of people occurs. For example, refugee populations can contribute to soil erosion and deforestation. Greater impact is also expected where background natural resources and other conditions are poor. In the case of refugees, the United Nations High Commissioner for Refugees (UNHCR) recognizes that environmental considerations must be integrated into operations and planning to ensure both environmental quality and the well-being of human populations.[4]

Political context

Of course, the above references to environmental degradation are crucial because the maintenance of primary healthcare (PHC), if not of health itself, is a fundamental prerequisite of all human rights, and disruption of the environment undermines this. However, the political context is also critical to the human rights agenda. Furthermore, it is in analysing the political context that we can detect serious sources of 'blockage' of reaction to human rights violations. In the account that follows, we encounter a plethora of committees communicating with one another without reference to specific remedial actions to safeguard human rights.

After a 21-year civil war, the Government of Sudan and the Sudan People's Liberation Movement/Army (SPLM/A) signed the Comprehensive Peace Agreement (CPA) in Nairobi on 9 January 2005. The CPA provides operational modalities for a 6-year interim period, at the end of which the people of Southern Sudan are to determine through a referendum whether they wish to remain part of a united Sudan under the system of government established in the CPA, or to secede.

Following the signing of the CPA, General Omar Hassan Al-Bashir, who had been

President of Sudan since the military coup in 1989, was sworn in as President of the Government of National Unity (GNU) on 9 July 2005. Dr John Garang de Mabior, the Chairman of the SPLM/A was sworn in as First Vice-President of the GNU and President of the Government of Southern Sudan (GoSS). Ali Osman Mohamed Taha, the previous First Vice-President and chief negotiator at the Naivasha peace negotiations, was sworn in as Second Vice-President of the GNU. An Interim National Constitution was signed by President Bashir on 9 July 2005, and a state of emergency was lifted in all states except Darfur, Kassala and Red Sea. On 30 July 2005 the first Vice-President, Dr John Garang, died in a helicopter crash and was succeeded by Salva Kirr Mayardi as both the First Vice-President of the nation and President of the GoSS.

The human rights provisions in the CPA and the Interim National Constitution therefore marked a watershed in Sudan's commitment to end a history of widespread human rights violations. The Constitution states that 'all rights and freedoms enshrined in international human rights treaties, covenants and instruments ratified by the Republic of the Sudan shall be an integral part' of its Bill of Rights. Key to respecting this constitutional commitment is the Government's respect for the CPA and the variety of mechanisms it put in place to combat the pervasive marginalization of certain populations in Sudan. Many of these mechanisms are aimed at distributing political power, Government institutions and the dividends of Sudan's natural resources throughout Sudan in a fair and equitable manner.[5]

The implementation of the CPA has generally been slow, but there was some progress. Late October and early November 2005 saw the formation and staffing of the Assessment and Evaluation Commission (AEC), the National Petroleum Commission (NPC), the Ceasefire Political Commission (CPC), the Fiscal and Financial Allocation and Monitoring Commission (FFAMC), the Technical Ad Hoc Border Committee and the National Judicial Service Commission (NJSC). On 8 January, the SPLA and the South Sudan Defence Forces (SSDF) signed the 'Juba Declaration', which outlined the process for integrating former SSDF forces into the SPLA. On 17 January 2006, the National Assembly endorsed the Joint Integrated Units (JIU) Act, which provided for establishment of JIUs, their mandate, areas of deployment, uniform and common doctrine. In February 2006, the CPC convened its first meeting, and two Demobilization, Disarmament and Reintegration (DDR) institutions (the National Council for DDR and the Northern Sudan DDR Commission) were established by Presidential decrees. A ceremony to launch the National Mine Action Authority (NMAA) was held on 7 March 2006.[6]

In contrast to this progress, as of 30 March 2006 many of the established institutions and committees did not regularly meet or establish substantive changes on the ground. Actual reconstruction had yet to start in the South, and overall progress in the three transitional areas (Abyei, Southern Kordofan and Blue Nile States) was limited. The National Petroleum Commission had not met regularly and there were no agreements on the rules of procedures or the mandate and composition of the commission's Secretariat. The National Human Rights Commission, the Civil Service Commission and the National Land Commission had yet to be established. The National Constitutional Review Commission was re-established through Presidential decree on 7 January 2006, but its new membership had yet to be named, and by 30 March 2006 it had still not convened. The establishment of the National Security Council and the National Security Service, which would be critical to the reform of Sudan's security apparatus, had not taken place. The Abyei area submitted its final report to the Presidency on 14 July 2005, but its decision had yet to be implemented. Various committees in Southern Sudan had also not been established, and this too slowed down the CPA implementation process.[7]

The UN High Commissioner for Refugees[8] estimates that the 21-year civil war in Southern Sudan sent more than half a million people into refugee camps in seven neighbouring countries, and displaced between 4 and 6 million people within Sudan, including 2.5 million in the capital, Khartoum. In 2005 there were over 500,000 spontaneous returns in Southern Sudan. This included North-to-South and South-to-South return movements. The UN 2006 Work Plan projected the return of 680,000 IDP and refugees for 2006. These movements required a committed effort to implement the CPA so to reduce the considerable strain that the movements were having on the already resource-deficient communities in the south and the three transitional areas. The movements also raised serious concerns about security for the returnees both in transit and upon their arrival home.

In Western Sudan, the conflict in Darfur has left thousands dead and around 2 million people displaced. On 29 March 2005, the Security Council took special note of the conflict in Darfur and passed resolution 1591 (2005), which established a Panel of Experts charged with, among other things, conducting fact-finding activities to identify individuals who were impeding the peace process, threatening the stability in Darfur and the region, or committing violations of international humanitarian or human rights law or other atrocities. Based on its findings, the Panel was to recommend to a sanctions committee the names of individuals who should have financial and other sanctions imposed on them. On 9 January 2006, the panel submitted its findings to the committee with a list of names that included high-ranking officials. In April, the Security Council passed resolution 1672 (2006), which placed sanctions on four individuals – one Government official, one militia leader and two rebel members.[9]

Two days after the Security Council passed resolution 1591 (2005), it passed resolution 1593 (2005), which referred the situation in Darfur to the Prosecutor of the International Criminal Court (ICC), The Government has repeatedly objected to this, claiming that Sudan is capable of bringing justice to Darfur and that it would refuse to allow its nationals to be tried in an international court. Since the conflict escalated in late 2003, the dynamics of the violence have become increasingly complex and volatile, with splits within the rebel groups and tensions existing between Chad and Sudan. As of December 2005, an estimated 3.6 million people in Darfur were in need of humanitarian assistance due to the combined effects of violence, displacement and restrictions on movement, as well as economic breakdown and loss of livelihood. Half of the 3.6 million individuals in need are internally displaced persons.

Despite ceasefire agreements,[10] peace talks in Abuja, Nigeria and an African Union military presence in the region,[11] there continued to be human rights violations and protracted violence between Government forces, militias and rebels, as well as between rebel factions. Numerous civilians were killed, arbitrarily arrested, raped, sexually assaulted, displaced, and tortured and subjected to other ill-treatment in custody.[12]

The issue of accountability

Reports from field workers in Médicins Sans Frontières and other NGOs working in camps for internally displaced civilians are all frighteningly consistent in addressing the issue of accountability with regard to violations of health rights in Darfur. The central Government of Sudan (GOS) in Khartoum has consistently denied direct involvement in these outrages, and it is with them that the UN must negotiate in trying to assess the levels of humanitarian aid required. The issue is further muddied by the large number of rebel subgroups fighting among themselves and with GOS security forces.

However, the UN Security Council has throughout much of 2006 and 2007 been much more seriously concerned about the possibility of Iran developing an independent nuclear capacity than it has been about the situation in Darfur. From July to November 2006 the question of whether or not the large-scale molestation and murder of civilians in Darfur – because of the above-mentioned inter-group conflicts – constituted 'genocide' created debate but little action. Until that was decided, the UN was ostensibly powerless to intervene. What the UN *did* do was to set up the UN Mission in Darfur (UNMIS), and it derived its humanitarian 'authority' from two pivotal sources.[13]

1   The Government of Sudan (GOS) and the UN signed a joint communiqué in July 2004 that committed the GOS to allow the free entry of human rights monitors into Darfur.
2   The UN Security Council itself, by Resolution 1590, officially established the UNMIS and charged it with ensuring 'an adequate human rights presence, capacity and expertise to carry out civilian protection.'

However, by the beginning of 2007, it was abundantly clear that almost 2 years after the signing of the Comprehensive Peace Agreement (CPA), the Sudanese government was falling seriously short on its commitment, as summarized below.

- The incidence of human rights violations, including rape and murder of civilians, has increased greatly.
- There has been a failure to identify most perpetrators of these crimes or to hold anyone responsible for them. This is despite the fact that even high-ranking Sudanese officials have been named in connection with such crimes.
- Incarceration and ill-treatment of people who have tried to bring details of violations of human rights to the attention of the authorities have increased. This has effectively silenced such complaints in many areas. People are afraid to speak out, even in the presence of ICRC (Red Cross) officials under guarantees of confidentiality.
- Direct obstruction of the work of UNMIS human rights officers has been intensified.
- There has been no attempt on the part of the GOS to establish a National Human Rights Commission, as promised under the CPA.

As a result, now, at least 4 years after the systematic violation of human rights against Darfur civilians had attracted the attention of the media worldwide, UNMIS has made the following recommendations.

- The government should continue the initiatives it has taken to respect human rights. This should lead to the strengthening of a human rights infrastructure that is capable of ending Sudan's history of gross human rights violations. At the centre of this project should be a strong, independent National Human Rights Commission that provides oversights of, and impartial advice to, the Government. The Commission's findings should be made public and be widely disseminated.
- In Darfur, the Government and rebels should immediately respect the governing ceasefire agreement, recognizing its impact on reducing further displacement and reducing violations of international humanitarian law and international human rights law. The Government should also disarm the militia and protect the physical security of all Darfurians by putting in place a credible, capable and professional police force and judiciary.
- Those responsible for human rights abuses and violations of international humanitarian law should be held accountable. This should occur regardless of where the crimes took place, when they took place, and who committed them.

It should be obvious to the reader that not only the GOS, but also the UN itself has a lot of ground to cover if any of these observations are to have any effect. At the very minimum, they must involve establishment of a greatly strengthened judicial system in Sudan, especially in Darfur. Moreover, this must be seen to meet international standards of impartiality and independence and be staffed by sufficient numbers of judges, prosecutors, etc. However, the question inevitably arises as to the authority of the UN itself, for it is not intervening. The GOS has reneged on the CPA agreements and has even insisted on not allowing any increase in the number of UN peacekeeping forces in Darfur. Not only that, but it has also insisted that the peacekeeping forces already there – all from the African Union – are the only ones it will recognize.

The African Union forces that are present are far too few to be effective (about one person for every 400 square kilometres of terrain), and have often indicated that they are hopelessly overstretched. In fact in November 2006 they threatened to withdraw altogether and only remain there on very precarious terms. As the reader will see, this is not the first time that the UN has found itself in a similar position. Within the last decade alone, it has happened in the Rwanda-Burundi situation in Africa and the Bosnian situation in Europe. As things stand now, UNMIS officials do not even have access to military establishments in Darfur, or to detention centres, and only have highly monitored access to camps provided for IDP.

As it has done on a number of occasions, the UN could get around all of these obstacles simply by imposing trade sanctions. These worked remarkably well on apartheid South Africa. Such issues need to be addressed in some detail if we are to remedy the situation. The determination of the GOS to prevent UN involvement is reflected by the fact that its security forces in Darfur grossly outnumber its numbers of humanitarian personnel, which it was obliged to provide under the terms of the CPA.

Worsening access to primary healthcare in Darfur

As we have seen, it is PHC – the most basic of all human rights – that is the first to suffer in situations of conflict. Darfur has been no exception in this respect. The author has drawn relevant data directly from the good offices of the UN Resident Humanitarian Coordinator for the Sudan.[14]

By 30 June 2004, it was estimated that only 52% of the civilian population throughout Sudan had access to basic food, while 54% were in receipt of non-food items (NFI), such as tents. Only 38% of IDP had satisfactory sanitation facilities. An Expanded Programme for Immunization (EPI) to protect against measles was protecting around 88% of the children of IDP between the ages of 9 months and 15 years. However, all of these indices have deteriorated from these figures in the last 2 years. An overview of the PHC situation is shown in Figure 3.3.

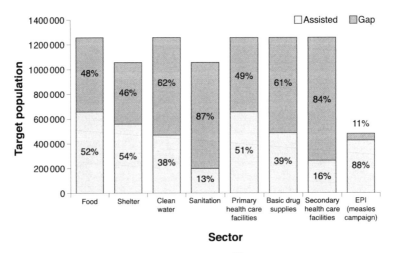

Figure 3.3: Estimated sectoral needs and gaps in Darfur.[15]

Access to essential PHC remains low. As is shown in Figure 3.2, the gap in access to PHC facilities is estimated to be 49%, compared with 84% for access to secondary healthcare. Many health facilities are providing only the most rudimentary and possibly even sporadic care. Given the current low capacity, facilities in many areas remain of poor quality and are in need of increased monitoring in such a manner that minimum humanitarian standards are systematically met. The matrices therefore actually reflect the theoretical number of people assisted by those PHC facilities, regardless of the actual quality of or access to the services provided. Consequently, actual coverage may be somewhat lower than is indicated in the matrices. Although the gap in the provision of basic drug supplies is estimated to be 61%, this figure takes into account mainly drugs supplied by the WHO and UNICEF. Some facilities are supported by NGOs that supply their own drugs, and thus the gap in provision of basic drug supplies may be smaller. Information gaps still exist, and further monitoring and assessment are required to verify the present and projected needs with regard to PHC facilities and basic drug supplies.

Figure 3.4 provides a similar overview of the gaps, but this time as a percentage of the accessible population. The gaps (food, 45%; shelter, 43%; water, 61%; sanitation, 86%; PHC facilities, 47%; basic drugs and medication, 58%; secondary healthcare facilities, 83%) should be cause for alarm.

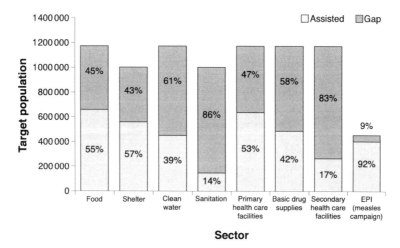

Figure 3.4: Estimated sectoral needs and gaps in areas accessible to the UN.[16]

Tables 3.1 to 3.3[17] demonstrate even more explicitly and in more detail the desperate nature of the health rights crisis.

How conditions have deteriorated since 2004

While conditions for civilians in Darfur continue to worsen, as shown in Tables 3.1 to 3.3 above, the GOS continues to play diplomatic games with the UN even to the extent that it takes pride in attacks by the Janjaweed on civilians in IDP camps, in which GOS forces have not actively aided them. In addition, there has even been a proliferation of anti-government rebel groups and fighting between them, creating a whole new raft of abuses of civilians and – in some areas – the total suppression of PHC initiatives. One of the most active of these rebel groups is the Sudan Liberation Army (SLA), whose focus has been on attacking civilians fleeing across the border into Chad (*see* Figure 3.1).

This in turn has even led to incursions into Chad itself and the pillaging of refugee camps in Chad. The GOS response to this has been to become involved as well in violating Chad's border. In fact, since 2006 the combined impact of these events has very greatly increased the health problems of civilian refugees from Darfur and civilians in Chad who are cut off from their own health services. To appreciate more fully this involvement of another country, and the diplomatic dangers that this poses for UN action, it is necessary for the reader to step back a little to see how the African Union itself first became involved, as it also has diplomatic responsibilities to Chad and more especially to the International Red Cross representatives in that country. It also illustrates how lack of decisive intervention by the UN back in 2003 has led to a much more complex series of international problems.

The sequence of events was as follows. Following appalling acts of violence against women and children in Darfur in 2003 – widely reported by such media as TNN and Fox News, but without comment on the social context – the GOS, along with the SLA and the SLM (Movement) and the Justice and Equality Movement (JEM), signed a ceasefire agreement in N'djamena in Chad on 8 April 2004. Chad was chosen as the

Table 3.1: Humanitarian needs and gaps in Greater Darfur Region: effect of conflict on people, food, shelter and clean water. Data collated on 1 June 2004.[17]

State	People				Food			Shelter			Clean water		
	Total number	IDPs	Affected residents	% accessible by UN	Persons currently assisted	Gap (number of people)	Gap (%)	Persons currently assisted	Gap (number of people)	Gap (%)	Persons currently assisted	Gap (number of people)	Gap (%)
North Darfur	397,707	324,215	73,492	–	260,270	137,437	35	170,384	153,831	41	152,876	244,731	62
South Darfur	259,224	225,543	33,681	–	73,227	185,997	72	94,948	130,595	58	87,160	172,064	66
West Darfur	603,490	500,748	102,742	–	316,701	286,789	48	299,737	201,011	40	238,269	365,221	61
Total	1,260,421	1,050,506	209,915	–	650,198	610,223	48	565,069	485,437	46	478,405	782,016	62

Persons assisted: shelter/NFIs and sanitation = number of IDP.

Table 3.2: Humanitarian needs and gaps in Greater Darfur Region: effect of conflict on sanitation, primary healthcare facilities, basic drug supplies and secondary healthcare. Data collated on 1 June 2004.[17]

State	Total number	Sanitation			Primary healthcare facilities			Basic drug supplies			Secondary healthcare		
		Persons currently assisted	Gap (number of people)	Gap (%)	Persons currently assisted	Gap (number of people)	Gap (%)	Persons currently assisted	Gap (number of people)	Gap (%)	Persons currently assisted	Gap (number of people)	Gap (%)
North Darfur	397,707	90,800	233,415	72	232,247	165,360	42	110,244	287,463	72	98,258	299,449	75
South Darfur	259,224	14,260	211,283	94	111,631	147,593	57	55,508	203,716	79	–	259,224	100
West Darfur	603,490	30,920	469,828	94	300,926	302,564	50	327,546	275,944	46	100,216	503,274	83
Total	1,260,421	135,890	914,526	87	644,904	615,517	49	493,298	767,123	61	198,474	1,061,947	84

Persons assisted: shelter/NFIs and sanitation = number of IDP.

Table 3.3: Humanitarian needs and gaps in areas of Darfur accessible to the UN: effect of conflict on EPI (emergency measles campaign), nutrition, agriculture and education. Data collated on 1 June 2004.[17]

State	Total number	EPI (emergency measles campaign)			Nutrition			Agriculture			Education		
		Persons currently assisted	Gap (number of people)	Gap (%)	Persons currently assisted	Gap (number of people)	Gap (%)	Persons currently assisted	Gap (number of people)	Gap (%)	Persons currently assisted	Gap (number of people)	Gap (%)
North Darfur	397,707	136,859	26,201	16	944	12,578	93	85,650	312,057	78	18,299	69,197	79
South Darfur	259,224	99,172	11,038	10	1,777	6,924	80	39,302	171,514	81	16,087	34,533	68
West Darfur	603,490	193,616	18,251	9	5,815	14,704	72	25,622	577,868	96	6,552	126,216	95
Total	1,260,421	429,647	55,490	11	8,536	34,206	80	150,574	1,061,439	88	40,938	229,945	85

Persons assisted: shelter/NFIs and sanitation = number of IDP; EPI/measles = children aged 9 months to 15 years; nutrition = malnourished children under 5 years of age; agriculture = conflict-affected population with access to land; education = children aged 6–13 years.

venue precisely because at that time it was not implicated in the conflict. It was then that the African Union (AU) became involved. In August 2004, the AU headed peace negotiations in Abuja, Nigeria, between the Sudanese Government, the SLA(M) and the JEM. These negotiations are still ongoing. The ceasefire agreement that was signed in N'djamena, Chad on 8 April 2004 established an international Ceasefire Commission (CFC) to monitor the accord. The CFC was the precursor to the African Union Mission in Sudan (AMIS), which as of 10 March 2006 had a total strength of 7,031 personnel (4,915 protection force members, 726 military observers and 1,390 civilian police personnel) out of 7,731 provided for in the decision of the AU Peace and Security Council on 28 April 2005.

By February 2007 the situation had worsened even further, with humanitarian agencies and associated NGOs actually having to abandon various IDP camps in Western Darfur when their field personnel were harassed and some were killed.[18] The proliferation of incidents involving civilians – an increasingly common phenomenon in modern warfare – in fact violates a pivotal clause of the Universal Declaration of Human Rights, which identifies what it calls the 'Principle of Distinction.'

Alongside the intensification of the conflict, isolated incidents in which people, and especially IDP, were killed, physically abused, sexually assaulted or harassed by the militia continued daily. In addition, Sudan's security apparatus continued to arbitrarily arrest people and abuse detainees for assumed rebel affiliation.

The humanitarian crisis, which was made worse by the renewed fighting, deteriorated further, with humanitarian access seriously limited due to insecurity and real or de facto blockades on civilian populations. In some locations the Government and militia appeared to try to isolate the SLA by making roads impassable and implementing fuel embargoes. This was done without concern for the civilian population, and is a violation of the Government's obligations under the International Covenant on Economic, Social and Cultural Rights not to prevent people from enjoying, among other rights, an adequate standard of living and the right to health. In other locations, the SLA ambushed and attacked humanitarian agencies and hindered their access to those in need. On 28 April 2006, UNMIS issued a press release which noted that:

> Over the past few weeks, aid workers operating for non-governmental organizations (NGOs) and UN agencies have come under continuous attacks and harassment by armed groups in the areas of Shangli Tobayi, Tawilla and Kutum in North Darfur. Several reports indicate that many of these attacks have been waged by SLA factions.
>
> (Darfur Consortium: www.darfurconsortium.org)

The principle of distinction, which is a cornerstone of international humanitarian law, is being flouted in Darfur by nearly all parties to the conflict. Fighters are not distinguishing between civilian and military targets. In many cases, fighters are targeting people on the basis of their ethnicity rather than their participation in hostilities. Rebels in particular must do a better job of distinguishing themselves from the civilian population when hostilities are taking place.

In the Gereida area of South Darfur, militias and Government forces attacked well over 20 villages between January and April 2006. On 24 April, hundreds of Arab militia, jointly with Government forces, attacked Joghana town (30 kilometres southeast of Gereida in the Buram locality). The attackers used land cruisers, two Government attack helicopters, and one Antonov, painted white. On 21 April 2006,

Dito village (north-west of Gereida) was attacked by Government forces that were reportedly supported by armed militia. Starting on 16 April 2006, Government forces began clearing the road from Nyala to Buram, with the alleged intention of attacking SLA positions in the area.

On 18 March 2006, mainly armed militia – most of them in military uniforms – attacked villages north of Gereida, including Abdus, Misroh Sanamanaga and Abujabra Dakma villages. In the attacks approximately 12 people were killed and 9 people were injured. On 10 March 2006, armed militia riding horses attacked the villages of Sugur, Mitea, Haraza, Chudul, Gundiko, Karfala, Jazira, Bagmara, Umjamania, Umkirkir, Helat Naga, Nutty, Baloom and Twomat. A total of 29 people were killed and 11 people were injured. In some of these fights, tribes joined in at a late stage in order to benefit from the looting and land grabs.

This and other fighting has brought approximately 60,000 newly displaced people to Gereida town since November 2005. The fighting exacerbated the humanitarian crisis, which was further worsened by a fuel embargo that was imposed in March and April. The embargo impeded the ability of NGOs to carry out their work, as they needed to use fuel for their operations. In addition, as water pumps could not function without fuel, the embargo threatened the water supply and thus threatened the livelihoods, health and hygiene of IDP and the host community.

In the Shearia area of South Darfur, the Government and militias targeted the Zaghawa community as a whole. The Zaghawa are of the same ethnicity as the dominant faction of the rebel opposition in the Shearia area, and are perceived by the Government and militias as SLA supporters and spies. Violations against the Zaghawa included beatings, systematic looting, arbitrary arrests, closure of schools, and denial of access to water resources. This has resulted in thousands of Zaghawa being forcibly displaced from Shearia town, nearly emptying the town of disputing tribes. In late 2005, IDP started to return to their houses. However, there was a significant deterioration in the human rights situation in Shearia town and the surrounding villages between January and March 2006. New cases of SLA retaliation attacks against tribes perceived to be Government-allied tribes have also been reported.

In addition to the targeting of the Zaghawa community in Shearia, on 13 April 2006 approximately 500 members of the Arab militia, described as being from the Misseriya tribe, attacked Kurunji village (in the Shearia area of South Darfur). Kurunji is inhabited by approximately 7,000 people, primarily from the Birgit tribe. The attack was well coordinated. The attackers dragged men and women from their homes, beat them, looted their houses and stole livestock. At least 15 villagers were killed and 19 were wounded. There appeared to have been no SLA presence in the village, although some villagers did take up arms to resist the attack. AMIS personnel saw militia gathering 5 kilometres north of Kurunji, and the day before the attack (12 April) the militia were only 2 kilometres from the village.

On 14 February 2006, Government forces and allied militia carried out a joint attack with air support on Rahad El Reel (10 kilometres east of Shearia town in South Darfur). The SLA and IDP reported that a mixed force of Government soldiers (with air support) and 300 militia members attacked the town. While there was an SLA presence in the area and the SLA shot down one Government attack helicopter, during the fighting seven civilians were allegedly killed and five injured in a manner that appeared to contravene the laws of war. Houses were burned and militia and Government soldiers looted property.

In a similar manner to the Gereida area, humanitarian access in Shearia was restricted. Among other locations, people travelling on roads in and out of Labado in late March and April were attacked by militia or arrested and detained by National Security. This created a de facto blockade that prevented necessary humanitarian assistance from reaching people in need, and also prevented people from accessing goods and services available outside Labado. The situation was made worse by the fact that there was no healthcare facility except for an NGO clinic that operated once a week. It was reported that people, including young children, died in Labado due to lack of any kind of medical facilities – not even rudimentary first aid was available. Lack of mechanical transport, because the only available sources of either petrol or diesel had been garnered by the various militia groups, meant that injured civilians had to be transported by donkey cart. As a result, people died while en route to Muharija to obtain medical care.

One could provide any amount of detailed information about the general and escalating worsening of the health situation in Darfur. However, enough has been said above to indicate the extent to which the situation has moved far beyond the borders of Sudan. It is this gradual involvement of other nations in Africa which reflects the problems with the present capacity of the UN as a global protector of the human right to health and healthcare. However, before analysing the various UN-sponsored and other diplomatic events to enforce the Universal Declaration of Human Rights, it is appropriate to examine the violation of the health of the most vulnerable members of the civilian population, namely women and children. As this author has already shown in a previous publication,[19] concerns about protecting the health rights of mothers and children has been so important as to have attracted further UN Declarations over and above the clauses of the Universal Declaration of Human Rights itself. A large proportion of these concerns revolve around gender-based violence. In Darfur, the situation as of mid-2007 is drastic, and demands an international response that is unimpeded by the traditional acquiescence to national integrity protocols.

Gender-based violence in Darfur

Across Darfur, women and girls continue to be sexually assaulted and raped. Most often this happens when they go outside the confines of their IDP camps to collect firewood or hay, to fetch water, or to farm. In many cases the perpetrators are armed men in military uniform or civilian clothing, travelling in groups on horseback or camel. The perpetrators often ridicule the women and tell them that they should not be collecting grass because the grass is for grazing their livestock. They also tell the women not to return to the area. These acts not only affect the individual victims, but also effectively terrorize and imprison IDP by making them afraid to leave their homes, thereby preventing them from accessing income-generating items and items that are necessary for their livelihood. Acts of sexual abuse are also taking place during larger attacks on villages by militia or joint militia and Government operations. Much of the following is drawn from the UN Report 2007.[20]

From late February 2006 to March 2007, UNMIS Human Rights documented 15 separate incidents of sexual abuse involving at least 250 IDP in an area outside a single West Darfur IDP camp (Ardamata), by small groups of armed men from nomadic tribes. In Kalma camp in South Darfur, UNMIS Human Rights learned of three women and two girls who were raped in March. UNMIS Human Rights confirmed that in late January and February in Manawashi in South Darfur, at least 12 women who were IDP were raped. The women had come to Manawashi after fleeing violence inflicted by militia with police support in Marshing (South Darfur) in mid-January. Human Rights Officers also spoke with nine women who were the victims of gender-based violence during the mid-January violence in Marshing. In early January 2006, when armed militias attacked four villages in West Darfur, UMNIS Human Rights documented 75 victims of rape, at least five of whom were children. Most of the victims were subjected to beatings and gang-rape.

The Government has taken some positive rudimentary steps towards addressing the problem of sexual violence in Darfur. The absolute denial by the authorities of the existence of rape in Darfur has receded. In November 2005, during the national campaign against violence against women (25 November to 10 December 2005), the Government held a press conference in Khartoum in which it admitted that rape was a problem in Darfur and stated that it was committed to addressing it. It presented a National Action Plan to end violence against women in Darfur, with time-bound targets and activities. State committees to combat violence against women were created in South, North and West Darfur. In December 2005, the Government created a new unit to combat violence against women and children under the Minister of Justice, to institutionalize and coordinate the Government's response to the problem. However, no UN-based international mediation was involved.

Government representatives have also conducted joint assessment missions with UNMIS Human Rights, which demonstrates a degree of willingness to engage in the issue. One of these missions was to Morni (West Darfur) in December 2005, prompted by allegations that members of the Central Police Reserve were involved in committing serious violations, including rape. Other visits took place in Nyala (South Darfur) in March 2006 to assess the work of the South Darfur Committee to Combat Violence against Women, and to make proposals for strengthening its effectiveness in dealing with sexual and gender-based violence. In March, UNMIS Human Rights was informed that additional Government funds were being sought to support the South Darfur Committee, and the Government has promised to involve civil society.

Prior to these steps, in October 2005 the Minister of Justice issued a decree, known as the Rules of Application for Criminal Circular 2. These rules confirmed that victims of rape could obtain medical treatment without first having to notify the police, as had formerly been the practice. The rules also stated that healthcare providers would not face negative repercussions or harassment if they provided treatment for victims. The Government has committed itself to disseminate the new rules to police and healthcare providers, and has taken action in cases of non-compliance. On 13 March 2006, UNMIS Human Rights was informed that the Ministry of the Interior had sent letters to police stations in Darfur informing them of Criminal Circular 2 and requesting the distribution of Form 8 to the authorized clinics. However, at the time of writing (2007), people who report rape and other violations by the military are routinely penalized.

Despite all of these steps, the above-mentioned cases of violence against women and girls demonstrate that far more needs to be done by the Government to combat sexual violence. Factors that have contributed to a lack of improvement include a poorly resourced law enforcement system that is not sufficiently supported by the Ministry of the Interior, failure on the part of the police to investigate complaints properly, and social stigmatization and fear of reprisals which prevent victims from reporting the incidents to the police. In a positive contrast to this, incidents of sexual and gender-based violence in the area outside of Ardamata IDP camp in West Darfur decreased dramatically in March. Many of those concerned attribute this to the combined positive effects of increased Government and AMIS Civpol (African Mission In Sudan; Civil Police) patrols and the opening of a new police post in the area on 12 March. However, the UN Declaration of Human Rights, in theory, calls for international intervention in such circumstances.[21] It should be explained that the African Union is the only body that is allowed to have any peacekeepers in Darfur, and there are far too few of them to be effective. It is they who set up the AMIS to try to help the local police to maintain human rights.

The mechanisms and initiatives put in place to address sexual and gender-based violence could have a positive impact through their mandate to monitor and help to facilitate proper police response and medical attention for victims. However, they could be more active and could be receiving more support from State authorities. The National Action Plan continually missed its target dates for various goals. Although some workshops have been held in Darfur to raise awareness of local authorities on the issue of sexual violence and Form 8 compliance, more needs to be done on this front, especially in areas outside towns. In eastern West Darfur, women are still obliged to report to the police and obtain a Form 8 before they can receive medical treatment. In other locations in West Darfur, police and Ministry of Health healthcare providers are unfamiliar with the Rules of Application for Criminal Circular 2, the Rules have not been circulated to many rural areas, some officials continue to insist that victims visit police before seeking medical treatment, and some healthcare providers continue to express fear of possible repercussions.

In late January 2006, UNMIS Human Rights documented two cases (one in West Darfur and one in South Darfur) where medical staff failed to abide by the Rules of Application for Criminal Circular 2 by refusing to provide medical services for abused women who did not present them with the Form 8 from the police. In one of these cases a medical examination was eventually performed, but the final medical report demonstrated the ignorance of the examiner, who stated that 'she has been beaten seriously on her back, there are marks showing the beatings, but there was no indication of rape, her hymen was torn a long time before.'

In South Darfur, where the State Committee is more active than in the other states, UNMIS Human Rights accompanied members of the Committee on 21 March 2006 to Mershing and Manawashi police stations to investigate the implementation of policies to combat sexual violence. The team observed that there were no proper procedures for registering sexual and gender-based violence cases at police stations, there was no presence of female police in the police stations, and in Mershing no sexual and gender-based violence cases had been reported or registered. However, the Officer in Charge admitted that such incidents were occurring. In Manawashi, the police admitted that a few cases had been reported and registered, but they did not know how many. In both areas the IDP community has little confidence in the police, the police stations lack any welcoming space in which survivors can report incidents in a confidential manner, and the police stations have no vehicle or radio allocated for logistical support.

In Kass (South Darfur), a judge informed Human Rights Officers that seven cases of sexual violence, including rape, had been tried in the last year, with six convictions. The conviction of rape offenders is crucial to ending sexual violence in Darfur, regardless of who is the victim or perpetrator. However, in Kass none of the cases dealt with crimes against IDP. Yet YNMIS Human Rights documented 12 cases of IDP from Kass who were raped between 15 February and 15 March 2006. This reflects the pattern of police inaction towards crimes against IDP, as well as reluctance on the part of IDP to report incidents.

In the light of all the above, it is important to realize that ordinary civilian-organized NGOs have not been silent. All too often, however, such people are regarded by the GOS and its various agencies as troublemakers. We shall therefore consider their present status in Darfur as providing further bases for usefully criticising the apparent inertia of the UN.

Human rights advocacy in Darfur

In March 2007, UNICEF[22] reported in the following terms. The conflict in Darfur is described by the UN as one of the world's worst humanitarian crises, affecting up to 4 million people. Fighting between rebel groups, security forces and the Janjaweed militia continues largely unrestrained. Entire villages have been wiped out, and 400,000 people have been killed. Persistent conflict and continued widespread displacement characterize the crisis, which started in February 2003.

Around 2 million people are internally displaced, half of whom are children. In the last 6 months alone, 250,000 people have been newly displaced. As more communities become affected, access to them becomes more difficult due to insecurity, with the delivery of assistance to the most vulnerable being compromised. Humanitarian workers have been targets of violence in all parts of Darfur, and many aid agencies have had to end their operations in the region.

In Khartoum, Darfur and Eastern Sudan, people are being harassed, arrested, detained and physically abused for voicing their human rights concerns. Victims include members of NGOs, journalists, politicians, people who file complaints with the police or other Government officials, and people who discuss human rights issues with the international community. NGOs and forums that discuss human rights issues, as well as rule of law, conflict resolution and peace-building, have had their meetings shut down.

As a result of the Government's response to individuals who voice their human rights concerns, people are less willing to discuss human rights issues or to file complaints. In Zalingei, IDP cancelled a demonstration, planned for 24 March 2007 in protest at the Government's failure to protect IDP, due to fear of reprisals. Members of UNMIS Human Rights are increasingly concerned about the welfare of the victims and witnesses with whom they speak.

Sudan's security apparatus is largely responsible for the human rights violations against people who voice their human rights concerns. This indicates that the Government has yet to truly appreciate the value of human rights, and instead considers advocating that the exercise of such rights is a threat to its national security. Often, and without foundation, the Government confronts human rights proponents with accusations that they are enemies of the State. This attitude is antithetical to the commitments that the Government made in the CPA and to democracy.

On 9 March 2006, the West Darfur HAC (Humanitarian Aid Commission) Commissioner issued a letter to a prominent national NGO that engages in, among other activities, protection and human rights work. It was ordered to suspend its activities in West Darfur. This letter, which was copied to National Security and Military Intelligence, followed a series of threats to and harassment of the NGO's staff members by security officials in West Darfur. The NGO's El Geneina office was reopened on 4 April 2006 after receiving a letter from the State's Ministry of Social Affairs and Information on 28 March, stating that it could resume its activities in El Geneina. However, when on 4 April the El Geneina director of the NGO requested a letter from HAC confirming that it could resume its activities, the acting HAC Commissioner for West Darfur State replied that he would not provide such a letter until the NGO had presented its new annual registration certificate. The NGO's annual certificate expired in March 2006, and according to the organization's director in Khartoum, it is in the process of re-registering in accordance with the procedures of the new Organization of Voluntary and Humanitarian Work Act of 2006, which came into force on 16 March 2006. However, the request by HAC appears to be inconsistent with the Act, which gives NGOs 90 days from the time when the Act comes into force to re-register.

On 23 January 2006, a Government delegation from El Geneina visited Kerenek (West Darfur) to investigate an attack on four adjacent villages that took place in January. Three sheikhs spoke to the delegation about assaults and torture of civilians, theft of livestock, and the rape of 36 women. They also told the delegation that soon after the attacks the police refused to open a file on the incidents. Three sheikhs were arrested the next day by police who alleged that they had made false allegations. One of the sheikhs said that after he was arrested he was beaten with a stick for 15 minutes by a police officer outside the police station. On 25 February 2006, the three sheikhs were released by a guarantor.

On 5 December 2005, police and National Security officers arrested a sheikh from an IDP camp in South Darfur and detained him for 14 days. He was accused of 'speaking to foreigners.' He was beaten on the head during police questioning, and had death threats made against him. He was told 'We will make an example of you to all the sheikhs.'

The restrictions imposed on people and organizations who voice human rights concerns are not limited to Darfur. On 21 February 2006, Parliament approved the national Organization of Voluntary and Humanitarian Work Act of 2006. The Act came into force on 16 March 2006. It prescribes values and goals for the work of civil society operations, and it appears to allow the Government to rely on and to organize civil society operations to address humanitarian crises and other issues without their consent. The Act allows the Government to reject and revoke an NGO's registration without adequate judicial review, and it grants broad powers to the Registrar and the Commissioner of the Humanitarian Aid Commission that leave potential for abuse. The Act also establishes burdensome procedural requirements that could impede the work of civil society actors. (Amendments provided for judicial review by the Committee of Humanitarian Affairs did not survive the final vote.)

On 22 January 2006, National Security officers raided an NGO forum meeting in Khartoum around the time of the African Union Summit, detaining for a few hours all of the participants, including European diplomats, members of the foreign press, a member of the National Assembly of Sudan and a Human Rights Officer. The raid happened just before 6 pm, as the meeting was drawing to a close and a final communiqué was to be adopted criticizing the Government's human rights abuses. All of the detainees were eventually released.

In Khartoum on 30 December 2005, National Security officers arrested a journalist for writing an article that was critical of the President. The interrogating officer stated that the words were humiliating to the President and undermined the Presidency. The journalist was formally arrested on the charge of inciting hatred against the State under article 30 of the National Security Act. He was released on bail on 2 January. Upon release, he was informed that he was going to be charged with joint criminal responsibility with the editor-in-chief, and for contravening the values and rules of the journalist. The article 30 charge was withdrawn. It was a welcome event when formal censorship ended with the lifting of the state of emergency in 2005, but this case demonstrates that other applicable laws can be used to achieve the same goal.

In Kassala, in Eastern Sudan, National Security officers arrested five members of the Kassala Beja Congress between 3 and 4 April. It appears that the group that was arrested in April was arrested in relation to a peaceful sit-in the Beja Congress organized on 27 March in front of UNMIS in Kassala to protest against the continued detention of their three colleagues and the general harassment they faced from security officials in Kassala. The authorities were apparently unhappy at the attempts of the Beja Congress to involve UNMIS, and believed such involvement was an infringement of sovereignty. The individuals concerned were released on 6 April.

Throughout the Sudan, Government officials have, on occasion, also obstructed the work of UNMIS Human Rights. This has included authorities intimidating or physically abusing individuals in order to deter them from speaking to Human Rights Officers; the uninvited and often surreptitious presence of State authorities at meetings between IDP and Human Rights Officers, denying UNMIS Human Rights access to various detention facilities in Darfur and Khartoum and to certain IDP camps in Darfur and Kassala, the Humanitarian Aid Commission (HAC) requiring Human Rights Officers to inform them of their presence upon arriving in Darfur IDP camps (implying that HAC or National Security will monitor their activities), and prohibiting UNMIS Human Rights officers from travelling to certain areas in Abyei.

The harassment, arrests, detentions and physical abuse of people who voice their human rights concerns are in stark contrast to the initiatives that Sudan took to allow civil society to operate freely. The Government relaxed media restrictions in Khartoum immediately after the adoption of the Interim National Constitution in July 2005. It did not interfere with many of the community-based activities surrounding the international campaign of 16 Days of Activism against Gender Violence that started on 25 November 2005. The Government has, on various occasions, allowed national organizations and the international community to carry out civil society human rights training and capacity-building activities in Khartoum, Southern Sudan, Eastern Sudan, the transitional areas and Darfur, including the training of independent journalists, and human rights training for human rights activists, lawyers and community leaders.

However, the Government's intolerance towards people who voice their human rights concerns is also a significant threat to the larger CPA implementation process. Actions by the Government that place restrictions on freedom of expression and even of association between ordinary citizens and their politicians hamper the Government's commitments in the CPA to promote political participation in anticipation of the local, state and national elections, as well as the referendum on Southern Sudan in 2011.

Implications for intervention by the UN

All of the above serves to highlight specific deficiencies in the UN's response to its human rights responsibilities as defined in the Universal Declaration of Human Rights. Although these (and different ones derived from consideration of other specific cases in subsequent chapters of this book) will be considered in Chapter 10, it is important that the issue of the integrity of the nation state be more flexibly defined so as to enable intervention in a nation's domestic affairs in defence of human rights.

With respect to Darfur in particular, this point becomes much more relevant if we consider the social and political impact on ordinary civil life once a nation has tried – for whatever reasons – to marginalize one of its ethnic sub-populations. Indeed, an almost inevitable consequence of such a course of action is a change in the ordinary rôle of the police in preventing crime and prosecuting criminals, instead organizing those same police as agents of repression against the population as a whole. This in turn increases the tendency of ordinarily 'loyal' opposition to become both radical in its expectations and violent in promoting them. As this author once heard Martin Luther King comment when addressing a demonstration in Alabama in 1961, 'The problem with outright revolution is that, if it succeeds, the new regime has to find some way of living in harmony with those elements of the population its radical demands have alienated.'

We shall therefore close this long chapter with a consideration of how Darfur's police became a 'security force' against its people rather than agents of protection of civil society.

From police to security in Darfur

All reports by humanitarian agencies involved in Darfur since 2005 have documented how National Security and Military Intelligence officers have engaged in acts of torture. They have arbitrarily inflicted inhumane punishments and degraded detained people over prolonged periods of time. UNMIS Human Rights personnel have been obstructed in their attempts to access these detention centres. Such personnel argue that, unless they can thus gain access, they are unable to determine whether or not the GOS is honouring its agreements under the peace accords to which it signed up. UNMIS Human Rights personnel have been rebuffed not only by the GOS in this regard, but also by the SLS. Does this constitute a valid reason for the UN not to intervene? What is obviously required is not only free access to detainees, but also guarantees that they can be interviewed individually without guards being present and in complete confidence. The UN could insist on this as a minimal requirement if trade sanctions are to be avoided.

In fact, this author would argue, it was precisely the fear that the UN might be moved to impose sanctions that led the GOS to agree, as far back as August 2005, to give UNMIS Human Rights personnel free access to all detention facilities in Sudan. However, since then the GOS has seriously reneged on this agreement. For example, in Geneina (*see* Figure 3.2), prison wardens informed UNMIS that they were under instructions not to allow humanitarian officers access to detainees. UNMIS asked GOS to put their agreement in writing. However, at the time of writing (2007) they have yet to do so.[23]

In fact, reports indicate that it was in 2005, when it had become evident that the UN was not going to intervene effectively, either by imposing trade sanctions or by any other means, that National Security officials in Darfur suddenly changed from being fairly open to UNMIS requests, and became much more resistant. In some other Darfur detention centres, UNMIS visits were still allowed – although with a security guard present throughout – but only if permission was requested in writing at least 7 days ahead of time. Reports[24] suggested that prison officials used that week to conceal equipment used to torture inmates, and some detainees were removed to reduce overcrowding. Even those who were released were told that their freedom was conditional on them not communicating with human rights personnel!

In North Darfur, National Security officers have insisted that Human Rights officers must provide a letter from El Fasher, North Darfur, National Security office granting access on a specific date. At the same time, National Security officials have maintained that their detention cells in North Darfur have not held detainees since the signing of the N'Djamena Peace Accords in 2004. They have insisted that all detainees held under emergency and national security laws are kept at the Shalla detention centre, the largest prison facility in North Darfur. On 21 October 2005 the director of the El Fasher National Security Office showed Human Rights officers around one empty detention facility adjacent to their El Fasher office to prove his point. Nevertheless, UNMIS Human Rights continues to receive reports, the most recent one dated 3 March 2006, of people being arrested and detained at various locations in El Fasher that are run and controlled by National Security.[25]

The above-cited UNMIS report goes on to state that UNMIS officials attempting to access facilities in Zalingei (*see* Figure 3.2) had been refused admission. Indeed, since December 2005, the head of National Security in Zalingei has changed three times and, without a written agreement from the Government permitting UNMIS Human Rights detention access, this has created a significant obstacle. With each new head, UNMIS Human Rights had to explain its mandate and start negotiations all over again. However, access has been granted in principle. On 14 December 2005, National Security said that it would grant access to detainees. When Human Rights officers followed up on this access, they were informed that the detainees had been moved to a Military Intelligence facility. On proceeding to the facility on 14 and 15 December 2005, Human Rights officers were informed that the detainees had been transferred back to National Security. On returning to National Security, the head was absent and other National Security staff refused access. On 2 February, UNMIS Human Rights was denied access to National Security detention facilities in Nertiti. The head of National Security in Nertiti informed them that access would only be granted upon presentation of a written agreement.

Even in Khartoum, UNMIS Human Rights has not been allowed access to National Security detention facilities. At Kober and Dabak prisons the directors informed Human Rights officers that National Security detainees did not fall under their jurisdiction and they had no authority to grant access.

Present rôle of military intelligence

In any civil society, once the ordinary function of the police as protective of civilian rights is superseded by security concerns, it is not long before the perceived needs of military intelligence assume priority in national life. Darfur, and Sudan as a whole, are no different in this regard. Civilians who are held under military intelligence are already bereft of most of their rights to humanitarian intervention. They often even claim that – in the name of military intelligence – they are not covered by government agreements with such transnational agencies as the UN or even the International Red Cross.

In Nyala (South Darfur), where Human Rights officers have twice requested access since December, the Director of Military Intelligence has consistently refused this, claiming to lack any knowledge of the UNMIS Human Rights mandate to monitor detention facilities. The Director has further stated that military detention facilities in Nyala only hold members of the SAF who are not subject to UN monitoring. In North Darfur, where UNMIS Human Rights has not sought access since 21 November, Military Intelligence has maintained that it does not have prison facilities, but rather it has what it describes as 'temporary holding cells' where detainees are kept for very short periods while investigations are pending. Notwithstanding these assertions, the team continues to receive numerous reports of people being arrested and detained under inhumane conditions in various facilities within the El Fasher locality that are believed to be run and controlled by Military Intelligence.

Prospects for amelioration of the Darfur situation

The question must naturally arise as to what must happen before any significant improvement in the human rights situation can occur. Even before an organization like the UN, or any of its agencies, can intervene, there have to be national agencies which are prepared to cooperate with a variety of domestic agencies. They include the National Intelligence and Security Service, Military Intelligence, Border Intelligence, the Sudanese Armed Forces, the Popular Defence Forces and the Central Reserve Police. Members of the security apparatus in Sudan have arrested numerous people. In a number of cases these arrests were arbitrary, the use of force was excessive, and the people who were detained were denied fair trial guarantees, held for unlawfully prolonged periods of time, and subjected to physical and psychological abuse. The security apparatus has also been responsible for restricting individuals' rights to freedom of association and expression. These abuses were documented in Darfur, Khartoum and Eastern Sudan.[26]

As the above-mentioned UNMIS report points out, the international community is greatly impeded in acting unless some internal reforms occur. There is an urgent need for legal and institutional reform of the security apparatus in the Sudan. Legislation governing these agencies gives officers broad powers of arrest and detention with little in the way of effective judicial oversight mechanisms to hold perpetrators of human rights abuses accountable. If the respect for human rights, rule of law and democracy promised by the CPA is to become a reality in the Sudan, the Government needs to drastically rethink the powers and purposes of its security forces. On 26 April 2006, the Special Court in Bahri, North Khartoum, delivered a verdict that acquitted 10 men whose confessions were obtained under torture at the hands of National Security officers. The men were accused of plotting a military coup in September 2004. This is a commendable verdict that is in line with international human rights standards, which prohibit a court from relying on evidence gained through torture. This case should be applied throughout all of Sudan.

This example, as well as reforms that the Interim National Constitution envisages for the National Security Service, advises them to focus on 'advice, information gathering and analysis', rather than arrests and detentions. It also requires its officers to be representative of the people of the Sudan, and to behave in a professional manner. The number of Southern Sudanese working for the National Security Service is increasing. These reforms must also be read in conjunction with the general spirit of the Constitution, which places a premium on respect for human rights. A new National Security Act is being prepared, and was scheduled to be submitted for Parliament's approval by the end of 2006. At the time of writing (2007), it has still not been submitted.

Unfortunately, the Act that was in place prior to the adoption of the new Constitution almost 11 months ago remains in place.[27] This Act effectively removes detainees from the legal system for long periods of time. In contravention of Sudan's human rights obligations, it authorizes detention by the Director of National Security for up to 6 months without judicial review, and it does not provide the right of access to counsel. The Act also does not provide adequate oversight mechanisms for National Security Service activities. It promotes immunity by providing officers with immunity against ordinary civil or criminal proceedings for any act connected with 'official' duties. Cases can only be brought with the approval of the Director-General of the National Security Service, and the Act provides for officers to be tried by special Security Courts, which lack independence and transparency. The human rights shortcomings of National Security legislation are made worse when provisions in the Act that aim to protect an individual's rights are not implemented. UNMIS Human Rights documented cases (see above) where the rights provided for detained individuals (such as protection from inhumane treatment and notification of charges) were not respected.

However, pressure can be brought to bear on the GOS in Khartoum to make clear that they are committed to reform national security in such a way as to allow internationally validated human rights agencies to interact with it. Such pressures could include little more than the kind of trade sanctions that were so effective in bringing about changes to the human rights situation in apartheid South Africa.

It is crucial for the Sudan to adopt a holistic approach to security reform. The abusive powers of the National Security Service must not be relocated into another agency. For example, immunity provisions should be struck from the Police Act and the People's Armed Forces Act. Emergency laws, which broaden the already excessive powers of the State Protection Act, provide the President of the Republic, the governor, or anyone delegated by the governor, apparent carte blanche powers to enter any premises or to search places and individuals, and organized movement of individuals, and to arrest individuals suspected of involvement in a crime in connection with the declaration of emergency. It also provides 'any other powers which the President of the Republic may deem necessary.'

The International Covenant on Civil and Political Rights (ICCPR) allows States to derogate from certain rights in times of emergency. However, the emergency laws are overreaching in application, ill-defined, and arbitrary to the point of being inconsistent with Sudan's obligations under international human rights law. In accordance with the ICCPR, any National Emergency Act of 1997 can be invoked in times that could fall short of this requirement – for example, in times of 'disruption of work or public utilities' or 'criminal acts of mutiny or riot.' Moreover, the ICCPR requires that derogations do not extend beyond what is 'strictly required by the exigencies of the situation.' This means that a derogation cannot extinguish an entire right and it must be proportionate to the stated purpose of the limitation.[28]

Non-derogable rights under the ICCPR include, among others, the right to life, the prohibition of torture or cruel, inhuman or degrading treatment or punishment, the prohibition of slavery, and the right to be recognized everywhere as a person before the law. Under the Interim National Constitution, the State cannot derogate from, among others, the right to life, prohibition of slavery and torture, the right to litigation and the right to a fair trial.

All of the above allows ample scope for a more focused UN intervention in Sudan's internal affairs than most of us have been conditioned to believe possible. The last chapter will consider this proposition in the general context of reform of the UN (or the creation of an alternative transnational authority to replace it). The Darfur crisis, as the reader will now appreciate, raises complex problems with regard to the UN's present ability to sustain its stewardship of the Universal Declaration of Human Rights. Some of these problems are peculiar to Sudan itself, while others have wider applicability. These differences will become more apparent as we move on in Chapter 4 to consider the current human rights situation in Burma (Myanmar).

But before doing so, let us touch on the Sudan President's fall from grace. The Sudanese president, Omar Hassan Bashir, was convinced that this year (2007) he would assume the mantle of President of the African Union. This appointment had been deferred twice before because of the Darfur crisis, but he and his supporters were confident that the apparent reluctance of the UN to get him to accept a larger UN peace-keeping force, consisting of troops from outside the AU, had strengthened his status among the AU nations. However, things have not turned out that way.

On 29 January 2007, Alpha Omar Konaré, the AU boss, stated in Addis Ababa, Ethiopia, that the AU peacekeepers would be withheld from Sudan. At the Addis Abada meeting, Tawanda Hondora commented: 'Electing Sudan as Chair of the AU while Sudan defies the UN would undermine the credibility of the AU and of Africans' attitude to human rights.'[29] He went on to state that Amnesty International had said that the objectives of the AU, as set out in its Constitutive Act, include the promotion and protection of human rights, peace, security and stability on the African continent.

'The AU already deferred a decision to grant the chairmanship to Sudan in 2005 and 2006 due to Sudanese government violations in Darfur – we hope that African governments will stop human rights abuses in Darfur', said Mr Hondora.

Human rights activists have been blaming the Sudanese government for its consistent failure to protect the people of Darfur from gross human rights violations, including mass killings, rape and forced displacement. Sudanese forces continue to act in violation of international standards of human rights and international humanitarian law in Darfur, including recently launching air attacks that killed scores of civilians.

Sudan is also said to be continuing to support the Janjaweed militias, which are responsible for continuing grave human rights violations in Darfur and eastern Chad.

Since the current conflict in Darfur began in 2003, around 85,000 people have been killed, while 200,000 have died of hunger or disease and more than 2 million have been displaced, mainly due to attacks by Sudanese forces and by Janjaweed forces armed by the Sudanese government.

While Sudan's bid for the AU presidency was therefore again turned down, Ghana – with its positive human rights record and stable government – turned out to be a good alternative. Ghana, which houses a peacekeeping institute founded by ex-UN Chief Kofi Annan, has long experience of playing a positive rôle in ending the many conflicts in neighbouring countries such as Côte d'Ivoire, Togo and Liberia.

In Ghana and within the Ghanaian government, the news that Mr Kufuor was taking over the AU presidency was received with great pride. Citizens and the press saw the appointment as a testament to the great democratic and economic successes of Ghana during the last decade, which had made this West African nation a model country.

Ghana, when elected, will take over the AU presidency from Congo Brazzaville, where President Dénis Sassou-Nguesso has represented the continental body during the last year. We have yet to see whether this improves matters.

References

1 http://commons.wikimedia.org/wiki/Image:Darfur_map.png (accessed 25 February 2007).
2 Human Rights Watch; www.hrw.org/campaigns/darfur/map.htm (accessed 6 December 2006).
3 Van Hear N, McDowell C. *Catching Fire: containing forced migration*. New York: Lexington Books; 2005. pp. 201–5.
4 United Nations Refugee Agency; www.unhcr.ch (accessed 6 December 2006).
5 United Nations High Commission for Human Rights (UNHCR). *Third Periodic Report of the UNHCR on the Human Rights Situation in Sudan in 2006*. Geneva: UNHCR; 2006. pp. 7–9.
6 United Nations Mission in Sudan (UNMIS). *The CPA Monitor Monthly Report*. New York: UNMIS; 2006. p. 26.
7 United Nations High Commission for Human Rights, op. cit., p. 8.
8 Ibid., p. 21.
9 Feinstein International Famine Centre, Tufts University. Darfur: livelihoods under siege; http://nutrition.tufts.edu/pdf/research/famine/darfur_livelihood_under_siege.pdf (accessed 11 December 2006).
10 United Nations High Commission for Human Rights, op. cit., pp. 21–3.
11 Ibid., p. 23.
12 Ibid., p. 24.
13 Ibid., pp. 11–13.
14 United Nations. *Darfur Humanitarian Profile No. 4. Addendum;* www.unsudanig.org (accessed 9 March 2007).
15 United Nations High Commission for Human Rights, op. cit., p. 20.
16 Ibid., p. 21.
17 Ibid., pp. 22–3.
18 United Nations. *Office of the UN Deputy Special Representative of the UN Secretary-General for Sudan;* www.un.org/news/ossg/srg/africa.htm (accessed 9 March 2007).
19 MacDonald T. *The Global Human Right to Health*. Oxford: Radcliffe Publishing; 2007. pp. 111–17.
20 United Nations Mission in Sudan (UNMIS). *CPA Monitor Monthly Report on the Implementation of the Comprehensive Peace Accords (CPA)*. New York: UNMIS; 2007. p. 27.
21 United Nations. *Addendum to Darfur Humanitarian Profile. No. 6*. 1 July 2007.

22 UNICEF. Crisis in Darfur, Sudan (in *Current Emergencies*); www.unicef.org.uk/emergency/emergency_detail.asp (accessed 3 March 2007).

23 United Nations. *Addendum to Darfur Humanitarian Profile*, op. cit., pp. 19–21.

24 United Nations Mission in Sudan (UNMIS), op. cit., p. 28.

25 Ibid., pp. 28–9.

26 Ibid., p. 30.

27 United Nations. *Second Periodic Report of the UN High Commissioner for Human Rights: Human Rights Situation in Sudan – January 2006*. pp. 12–13.

28 Ibid., p. 15.

29 Afrol News. Ghana gets AU Presidency as Sudan snubbed. 1 February 2007; www.afrol.com/article/204074 (accessed 21 February 2007).

Chapter 4

The well-hidden regime of Myanmar

Context of the current situation in Burma

Unlike Sudan, Burma (Myanmar) was closely monitored by the UN after its military elite overthrew the political party elected by the people in fair and free elections in 1990. Indeed, the UN had observers in the country during the run-up to these elections because of fears that the existing military government might use illegal tactics to influence the votes. In order for the reader to understand where and how the UN, certain of its agencies, such as the International Labour Organization (ILO), and various NGOs have attempted to monitor and prevent abuses of health and other human rights in Myanmar today, it is necessary to briefly outline a little of that country's history.

The country was internationally known as 'Burma' until the present military regime overthrew a democratically elected party (the New League for Democracy – NDL) in 2000. After that the new regime changed its name to 'Myanmar.' Use of this name is not universal, and in such international relationships (trade, politics, etc.) with which the government does business both names, Burma and Myanmar, are used.

The army first seized power from a conventional democratic government in 1962. Many people at the time regarded this as both a temporary state of affairs and as possibly a good thing in itself, as the previous democratic regime had not inspired confidence, and was widely regarded as being somewhat corrupt. However, it soon became obvious that 'rule of the generals' was in no way a temporary transition to democracy, as had been promised at the time of the coup, nor was it any less corrupt than the previous regime. From 1962 until 1990 its levels of corruption grew so that, by the time democratic elections were permitted in 1990, the military regime featured corruption at every level as one of its more salient features.

Several parties contended for office in the 1990 elections, but one led by a young Burmese woman, who had spent much of her life abroad and had attended a number of leading universities in the USA and the UK, seemed to attract huge interest among the electorate. Her name is Daw Mung Suu Kyi, and she led a loose coalition of liberal democrats called the New League for Democracy (NLD). In the 1990 election, the NLD won about 80% of the vote, and the elections – observed by foreign UN agents – were declared 'free and fair.'[1] Suu Kyi's family background had psychologically prepared her for the iconic rôle she occupied in 1990 – and which in the eyes of human rights activists she still occupies today. Her father was the Burmese General Aung San, a popular hero who helped to establish national independence in 1948. Aung San was assassinated in July 1947, and 2-year-old Suu Kyi left Burma and lived and studied in India and the UK.

In 1988 she returned to Burma at a time of political upheaval and ended up leading the National League for Democracy in opposition to the ruling military regime. Inspired by the non-violent practices of Mohandas Gandhi and Martin Luther King

Junior, she became a national hero and an international celebrity. She was placed under house arrest in 1989, but the NLD still convincingly won popular elections in 1990. The military junta refused to give up power, and held her under house arrest until 1995. She won the Nobel Peace Prize in 1991. She was detained again from September 2000 until May 2002, during which time the NLD was having secret negotiations with the junta in an effort to break the political deadlock. In May 2003 Suu Kyi was again detained, and was taken into 'protective custody' as confrontations between the NLD and government supporters increased. Despite diplomatic pressure and international pleas for her release, she continues to be held in Myanmar. In May 2007 the ruling military junta announced an extension of her house arrest for an indefinite period.[2]

The ruling regime, glorying under the acronym SLORC (State Law and Order Restoration Council), declared the election result invalid and resumed military control. Again many of the SLORC leadership insisted that suspension of democratic rule was 'only temporary.' However, Suu Kyi was put under house arrest and attempts on her part to meet with her party colleagues were prevented. SLORC changed its name, to give it a more democratic-sounding flavour, to the SPDC (State Peace and Development Council). In Myanmar, exponents of democracy are generally afraid to speak out and their access to the print media is strictly controlled. Despite this, a group called the Democratic Voice of Burma manages to appear online three or four times a year. In 2000, the SPDC widely broadcast the view in Myanmar (they control all of the media) that people might as well forget about the NLD because it was no longer a 'valid political force.'[3]

However, if that is true, the SPDC should feel confident that they have conditioned the electorate well enough and can, in any case, determine which groups can stand, and that they need not fear the prospect of calling a new election. This would not be an act of magnanimity, but of crucial importance to Myanmar's international image. However, at the time of writing (2007) they have made no more attempts to do so. In a sense the Myanmar tyranny is in an even stronger position than that in Sudan, with regard to the UN. This is because China, Vietnam and Russia will always support it at UN deliberations – and both Russia and China have the veto in the Security Council. All of these countries benefit from Myanmar's natural resources – not only its oil, but also its widespread destruction of its forest of teakwood in complete violation of international environment accords to which it is a signatory. China is an eager customer for such wood. Another strong appeal of Myanmar as a trading partner is that, due to its huge exploitation of slave labour (as will be discussed later) it can produce commodities at much lower prices than many of its competitors.

The most disheartening evidence that the UN cannot or will not defend human rights was made explicit on 12 January 2007, when the US representative at the Security Council put forward a motion calling for condemnation of Burma's serous and continuing violation of human rights – especially those of such ethnic minorities as the Karens – and calling for UN action to be taken. It was vetoed by both Russia and China. Indeed, the Chinese delegate's comment was most revelatory. He pointed out that whatever the Burmese government was doing to peoples entirely within its own borders was not in any way violating the interests of other nations, nor was it creating international conflict. Therefore, since the UN's purpose was to maintain inter-national peace, the UN could not condemn the Burmese government!

UN involvement with Myanmar

The above comments would seem to render the Myanmar regime safe from any prospect of UN-approved human rights intervention. However, Myanmar plays an active rôle in the Association of South-East Asian Nations (ASEAN), particularly in military matters, and ASEAN shares many of the organizational links with the UN in the area of human rights.

As far back as 1998, the UN Secretary-General had made a proposal to the current Chairman of the ASEAN Standing Committee that an ASEAN Troika be set up to help to resolve the political deadlock in Burma. The aim of that initiative was to ultimately bring about dialogue between the ruling junta and the opposition movement, the NLD, headed by leader Daw San Suu Kyi. The concept of an ASEAN Troika was agreed upon by the 10 member countries in July 2000 at their ministerial meeting in Bangkok.

The US President had warned the junta that 'those who rule Burma should know – all of us are watching carefully what happens.' The junta's Foreign Minister's rather predictable response was that Rangoon would not bow to any outside pressure. It is inevitable that the proposed ASEAN Troika would not receive the requisite support to ensure its adoption, due to the various political alliances across this complex region. This was yet another grave disappointment in the face of many such attempts to achieve constructive engagement, the economic sanctions adopted by big powers and quiet diplomacy – all of which have failed to bring about restoration of democracy within Burma.

It is clear that any initiative against Burma that is proposed at the Security Council level will be aborted by China's veto. The international community seems to have been hamstrung by such regional politics being played out in the UN forum with regard to Myanmar. The challenge of addressing these barriers must be taken up by the international community – not only for the sake of Myanmar but also for the larger cause of establishing an international mechanism to enforce measures against violations of human rights by a state against its own people. Developments afoot should be analysed and, where possible, supported. Myanmar is an eminently suitable case study. The arguments for international humanitarian intervention are both compelling and vast.

The junta's systematic violations of human rights, their flagrant disregard of the 1990 democratic election results and their failure to adopt a Constitution all constitute democratic and unambiguous breaches of the UN Charter. The time had come for a major initiative, formed by a 'coalition of the willing' – a peaceful responsible approach that costs nothing in terms of lives or capital. Such an approach should not require the consent of the military junta. The matter was seemingly simple – civilians under military rule who are subjected to brutal and inhuman suppression are entitled to immediate protection.

For the past 9 years the UN has adopted resolutions condemning the violations of human rights in Burma and seeking some kind of political settlement. On 8 November 2000 it passed the strongest resolution so far, and condemned the regime's persecution of democratic opposition. This seemed to be yet another step closer to intervention, providing another cogent ground for the establishment of an ad hoc body to intervene on the principle of widely accepted international law. However, no intervention was proposed or forthcoming.

The immediate need is to have a UN presence inside Burma, to monitor abuses and prevent an outbreak of civil war. The junta's ongoing suppression and attempts to undermine and abolish the NLD and general pro-democracy movements are leading the country towards an uprising of volcanic proportions.

Even by 2004, it was reported[4] that the government was still flagrantly violating all international humanitarian principles and, as we shall see in the next section, health rights remain a hollow joke. In fact, arbitrary military brutality has increased. The government has reinforced its firm military rule with a pervasive security apparatus. The Office of Chief Military Intelligence (OCMI) exercised control through surveillance of the military, government employees and private citizens, and through harassment of political activists, intimidation, arrest, detention, physical abuse, and restrictions on citizens' contacts with foreigners. The Government justified its security measures as being necessary to maintain order and national unity. Members of the security forces committed numerous serious human rights abuses.

Although it is resource-rich, the country is extremely poor. In 2006 the estimated annual per capita income was approximately \$300, and most of the population of more than 50 million was located in rural areas and lived at subsistence levels. Four decades of military rule, economic mismanagement and endemic corruption have resulted in widespread poverty, poor healthcare, declining education levels, poor infrastructure and continually deteriorating economic conditions. During 2006, the collapse of the private banking sector and the economic consequences of additional international sanctions further weakened the economy.

Health and human rights in Burma since 2005

There has been comparatively little media comment about the increasing violation of the health rights of the Burmese people, especially some of its ethnic minorities, during the last two or three years, with the exception of the occasional poignant reference to the heroic figure of Aung Suu Kyi herself. We must conclude that this is because Russia and China – both of which benefit from the Myanmar regime – have the veto in the UN. This weakness in the system of transnational protection of human rights will be addressed in Chapter 10. However, as recently as 2006, Health Unlimited[5] has been able to point out the continuing decline in access to primary healthcare in most areas of Burma. By 2006, the Government's extremely poor human rights record had worsened, and it continued to commit numerous serious abuses. Citizens still did not have the right to change their government. Security forces continued to commit extrajudicial killings and rape, forcibly relocate people, use forced labour and conscript child soldiers, and they re-established forced conscription of the civilian population into militia units. During that year, government-affiliated agents killed as many as 70 pro-democracy activists. Disappearances continued, and members of the security forces tortured, beat and otherwise abused prisoners and detainees. Citizens were subjected to arbitrary arrest without appeal.

Arrests and detention for expression of dissenting political views occurred on numerous occasions. During the year, the Government arrested over 270 democracy supporters, primarily members of the country's largest pro-democracy party, the National League for Democracy (NLD). The Government detained many of them in secret locations without notifying their families or providing access to due legal process or counsel. During the year, the Government stated that it had released approximately 120 political prisoners, but the majority of them had already finished their sentences, and many were common criminals and not political prisoners. By the year's end, an estimated 1,300 political prisoners remained in prison.

Prison conditions remained harsh and life-threatening, although in some prisons the conditions improved after the International Committee of the Red Cross (ICRC) was allowed access. The Government did not take steps to prosecute or punish human rights abusers. On 30 May 2006, Government-affiliated forces attacked an NLD convoy led by party leader Aung San Suu Kyi, leaving several hundred NLD members and pro-democracy supporters missing, under arrest, wounded, raped or dead. Following the attack, Government authorities detained Aung San Suu Kyi, other NLD party officials, and eyewitnesses to the attack. By the year's end, the Government had not investigated or admitted any rôle in the attack. The Government subsequently banned all NLD political activities, closed down approximately 100 recently reopened NLD offices, detained the entire 9-member NLD Central Executive Committee, and closely monitored the activities of other political parties throughout the country.

The Government continued to severely restrict freedom of speech, press, assembly, association and movement. During the year, individuals suspected of or charged with pro-democratic political activity were killed or subjected to severe harassment, physical attack, arbitrary arrest, detention without trial, incommunicado detention, house arrest, and the closing of political and economic offices.

The Government did not permit domestic human rights organizations to function independently, and remained hostile to outside scrutiny of its human rights record. However, it allowed the UN Special Rapporteur on Human Rights (UNSRHR) in Burma to conduct two limited missions to the country, although the Government did not allow the UNSRHR to visit all of the sites requested or to stay for as long as was requested. It also allowed the International Labour Organization (ILO) to operate a liaison office in Rangoon. However, after the May 2003 attack on Aung San Suu Kyi, the ILO deferred finalizing a draft agreement with the Government on forced labour. The problems of violence and societal discrimination against women remained, as did those of discrimination against religious and ethnic minorities. The Government continued to restrict workers' rights, ban unions, and use forced labour for public works and for the support of military garrisons. Forced child labour remained a serious problem, despite recent ordinances outlawing the practice. The forced use of citizens as porters by SPDC troops – with the attendant mistreatment, illness and sometimes death of these individuals – remained a common practice, as did Government forced recruitment of child soldiers. Trafficking in people – particularly women and girls, primarily for the purpose of prostitution – remained widespread, despite some NGO efforts to address the problem.

The above reference to the attacks on 30 May 2003 needs some elaboration. It must not be imagined that the ethnic minorities that were being suppressed – and which saw in the NLD some sympathy for their plight – were themselves entirely blameless. The Karens in particular had developed a capacity for armed resistance and engaged in widespread violation of human rights, but to nowhere near the same extent as that practised by the Myanmar government.[6] However, even this can be attributed to a long-evolving and defensive response to repression. The Burma document cited above describes in detail the 2003 events, which can be summarized as follows.

On 30 May 2003, government-affiliated forces attacked an NLD convoy led by party leader Aung San Suu Kyi near the village of Depeyin in the north-west region of the country, using bamboo staves and metal pipes to kill or injure pro-democracy supporters. The attackers killed at least six pro-democracy supporters, including NLD members San Myint, Tin Maung Oo, Thien Toe Aye and Khin Maung Kyaw. The two others killed were Min Zaw Oo (a student) and U Panna Thiri (a Buddhist monk from Monywa). Diplomatic representatives received credible reports of two more victims who later died of their injuries, including Tun Aung Kyaw, a political activist from Mandalay who died in early September. Local villagers and survivors of the attack reported to diplomatic representatives that the attackers might have killed as many as 70 pro-democracy supporters who were accompanying the NLD convoy. By the year's end, the fate of the many other wounded individuals, including 10 NLD members and 47 pro-democracy supporters from the convoy, remained unknown.

According to credible reports, throughout the rest of the night following the attack, security forces clashed with civilians and may have killed scores of other villagers, students and Buddhist monks in the villages surrounding the attack site. The Government admitted that 4 people were killed and 48 were injured in the attack on the NLD convoy, but did not acknowledge the alleged killings in the surrounding villages. The Government subsequently rewarded Lieutenant General Soe Win, who was reportedly involved in planning the attack. The then SPDC Secretary-Two was promoted to Secretary-One, a very high-ranking position in the ruling junta. Regional commander Brigadier General San Neing, reliably reported to be responsible for executing the attack, was laterally transferred and made commander of the Irrawaddy Division, and was not prosecuted or reprimanded.

Organizations such as the Shan Human Rights Foundation (SHRF), which has been associated with armed ethnic resistance groups in the past, reported numerous cases throughout the year of military troops killing civilians in border areas and areas of ethnic resistance, often after confiscating property or torturing these individuals. Interviews by foreign observers documented similar abuses. SHRF reported that in March, two farmers working in their fields were accused of being or helping Shan soldiers. They were shot and killed by a patrol of Burmese Army troops at a farm in Nam-Zamg Township in Shan State. On 29 April, a patrol of soldiers shot and killed a displaced farmer on the road just outside Phuay Hai village in Lai-Kha town in Shan State, for being unable to sell his rice quota as demanded by government troops. On 5 May, a patrol of government troops beat to death a farmer who was working at a remote farm in Shan State. In August, the Karen National Union (KNU), an armed insurgent group, reported that on 16 July battalion commander Myint Htun Oo and company commander Moe Mung arbitrarily and summarily executed Karen village headman Saw Htoo Pwe Saw and Saw Kyaw Aaye Swe.

There were no reports that the Government took action to investigate or prosecute soldiers involved in the following 2002 killings: in April, the killing of 10 people, including 6 children, and the injuring of 9 people in Karen State; in July, the reported robbery and killing of 6 civilians near the Thailand border in Shan State; and in September, the killing of 10 villagers in Kholam, Shan State. There were no reports that the Government took action to investigate or prosecute soldiers involved in the 2001 shooting and killing of 11 prisoners conscripted into forced labour to build a frontline camp in Tenasserim Division. In addition to all this, citizens have continued to 'disappear' at levels that exceeded the well-known phenomenon in Argentina in the 1970s.

Myanmar's desperate health situation

According to an Australian TV programme broadcast on 22 January 2007 about the attempts of Australian-based NGOs to address Burma's primary healthcare crisis, 'Burma has one of the world's worst health records.'[7] Around 40% of the population have tuberculosis and almost 50% of all malaria cases in all of Asia occur in small isolated Burma. In addition, about 360,000 people are registered as having HIV/AIDS – and it is known that many HIV/AIDS cases are not registered. UN and NGO aid groups, armed with such appalling statistics, are warning of an impending health crisis in Burma, but of course, as Burma is run by an exceptionally severe military junta, humanitarian efforts – especially international ones – are routinely impeded. Previous attempts to fight malaria, TB and HIV/AIDS in Burma have been abandoned because of the regime's restrictions, along with huge levels of government corruption. As will be detailed later in this chapter, the latter is a major factor in creating conditions that actually prevent people from gaining access to the primary healthcare that the UN Universal Declaration of Human Rights identifies as one of their rights.

The ABC (Australian Broadcasting Corporation) broadcast, alluded to above, quoted the findings of an Australian medical worker who had recently returned from Burma, and his comments can be summarized as follows.

In a country where at least 1.3% of all adults are HIV positive, sex education could seem to be essential. Education about safe sex practices could mean the difference between life and death of many people who are now of primary school age. However, the military regime is relentless in exploiting the young – especially boys – as slave labour in remote areas in mining, agriculture, mine-clearance, etc. Large numbers of such youngsters are thus forced to live huge distances away from home or, if they are not put to work in this way, are driven to travel long distances in search of work to survive.

Such circumstances virtually guarantee that the young and inexperienced will become caught up in risky behaviour involving unprotected sex and easy access to drugs. These go hand in hand with severely compromised health and grinding poverty. In fact, Australia's own disease research agency, the Barnet Institute based in Melbourne, estimates that Burma's provision for primary healthcare is the second worst of any country in the world. However, official government agencies are reluctant to acknowledge the problems, especially with regard to HIV/AIDS, and offer little support to agencies that are attempting to ameliorate the situation.

Levels of government corruption are so high – with some government figures making huge profits from the illegal sale of teak wood and from international trafficking in both narcotics and young girls – that they routinely steal money from aid programs. In fact, in Australia itself many commentators have even expressed the belief that Australia's attempts to provide humanitarian assistance only serve to prop up the regime.

Hente Myent, a spokesperson for the NLD, has even called for an international monitoring system which would ensure that humanitarian aid resources are properly targeted. Various donor countries and the UN have promised to set up additional checks to help to mediate this aim. If the UN can organize the mediation of IMF Structural Adjustment Policies (SAPs) to protect capital investments in the Third World, it should be able to operate similar facilities to administer humanitarian aid funding.

As will be detailed in the next section, these health problems are further exacerbated by the sheer mobility of Burma's oppressed people. Thousands try to flee by crossing the borders into Thailand and China. This alone renders treatment and prevention of the spread of AIDS and TB much more difficult than it need be. Added to this is the fact that both Thailand and China, anxious to keep Burma on side, are becoming ever more vigilant in returning such refugees to Burma. All of these factors have more than once brought Burma's atrocious human rights record to the attention of the UN Security Council. However, that body is crippled in its ability to intervene by the existence of the veto system. As we have already seen, when the US representative to the Security Council tried to introduce a motion to call Burma to account for its human rights record on 13 January 2007, the attempt was nullified when both Russia and China vetoed it. Matters such as this will be considered in greater detail in Chapter 10.

Burma's ethnic minorities, especially the Karen and the Sham people, have been particularly exploited by the government, its ancillary objective being to crush any attempts by such groups to gain some kind of autonomy. As one would expect, therefore, their access to any kind of humanitarian and health aid is even more strenuously impeded by the military regime. An NGO called Aide Medicale International (AMI) has been particularly assiduous in its attempts to compensate for this calculated deficit in primary healthcare provision.[8]

Since 1984, AMI has provided medical and sanitary aid to Burma's ethnic minorities. Some of this has been through direct support in the field, but much more has involved the training of the medical staff who man such medical facilities as already exist. Another NGO that has been active in such human rights advocacy in Burma is Amnesty International. Their activities have mainly converged on the problem of Myanmar's creation of its own huge corps of refugees trying to flee the regime, as mentioned above.

Burma's refugee crisis

Few countries have ever generated such efforts of their own people to escape as Burma. Amnesty International has specialized in collecting details of the health and other human rights abrogations that this movement of refugees has caused. These have affected the ethnic minorities in particular.[9]

The routine military interference with the exercise of human rights includes forced labour, forcible relocation, extortion of food, money and other personal possessions, house destruction, and the denial of freedom of movement.

During May and June 2004, Amnesty International interviewed 115 migrant workers in seven locations in Thailand who were either working or searching for work. They were members of the Mon, Kayin, Kayah, Shan, Rawany, Tavoyan and Bama ethnic groups, and followed the Buddhist, Muslim or Christian faiths. They were employed mostly in the fishing, manufacturing, agricultural, construction and domestic service industries. The interviews were conducted confidentially with the assistance of an independent Bama (English interpreter). Both the men and the women who were interviewed were predominantly from rural areas, although some were from urban centres, including small towns, State and Division capitals, and Yangon.

In the last decade, hundreds of thousands of workers from Myanmar have migrated to neighbouring Thailand in search of jobs and other economic opportunities. Migrants interviewed by Amnesty International had left their homes in Myanmar for a variety of reasons, including the inability to find a job, confiscation of their houses and land by the military, and fear that if they remained they would be subjected to human rights violations, including forced labour. Many of the young people who were interviewed had come to work in Thailand in order to send money home, but were working there so as not to be a burden to their parents. Those who had fled from militarized areas in Myanmar were much more likely to have had direct experience of human rights violations at the hands of the Myanmar military.

In some areas the vast majority of young people have left their villages in order to work in Thailand. One Mon man from Hpa'an township, Kayin State, told Amnesty International about the situation in his village: 'Many people have been in Thailand for the last 15 years and many more are leaving now. Prices are going up, the population is growing, people are having a hard time feeding themselves and have decided to leave.'

However, as already mentioned, Burma is a member of ASEAN, and thus its government's indifference to internationally accepted humanitarian norms always had the potential to be a source of embarrassment to it in such transnational groupings. This finally turned out to be the case in 2005 at an ASEAN meeting.

During the ASEAN Ministerial meeting in Vientiane, Laos in July 2005, the SPDC Foreign Minister announced that Myanmar would postpone chairing ASEAN, a post which the country was due to assume in July 2006, amid reports that the SPDC had delayed the move in order to avoid further EU and US Government censure and potential conflict within ASEAN itself. The SPDC stated that it was deferring its chairmanship in order to deal with urgent domestic issues, including the implementation of the seven-point 'roadmap to democracy', beginning with the completion of the National Convention, convened in order to draw up a constitution. The National Convention – which was originally convened in 1993, adjourned in 1996, and reconvened in 2004 – comprises various groups, but does not include the National League for Democracy (NLD), the main opposition party led by the eponymous Daw Aung San Suu Kyi.

At the same time, widespread and reliable reports emerged of increasing SPDC restrictions on the UN Development Program (UNDP), the UN High Commission for Refugees (UNICEF), the World Food Program (WFP), other UN agencies, and international aid organizations working in the country. In addition, the activities of the ILO's Liaison Office have been constrained by a lack of cooperation from the SPDC, which severely curtails the ILO's efforts to combat forced labour of civilians by the military. Restrictions include those on the ability of the UN and other agencies to travel to rural areas, particularly in the ethnic-minority border regions, in order to assist the local population. Such prohibitions had already been in place with regard to access to internally displaced people (IDP), who are concentrated mainly in ethnic-minority counter-insurgency areas, and are thought to number hundreds of thousands.

In August 2005 the Executive Director of the World Food Program visited Myanmar, and reported that 15% of the population face 'food insecurity'[10] and 'About a third of the children . . . are chronically malnourished, eight percent are actually undernourished . . .'[11] The top WFP official commented further: 'I'm suggesting that the government would be well advised to make it easier for people to move about, to buy and sell agricultural commodities, without economic interference from the government.'[12] Other UN officials, including the Special Rapporteur on Myanmar and the Secretary General's Special Envoy, have been denied access to the country for over one year.

These increased restrictions and further repression are believed to relate to the overthrow of General Khin Nyunt, who was removed as Prime Minister by Senior General Than Shwe, SPDC Chairman, and put under house arrest in October 2004. General Khin Nyunt was generally viewed as pragmatic and relatively willing to engage with the international community. At the time of his arrest, Military Intelligence, the security apparatus that he headed, was largely dismantled. In this environment, political arrests have continued throughout the country, and Daw Aung San Suu Kyi remains under house arrest. Although some political prisoners have been released, at least 1,110 remain behind bars.

As discussed previously, Burma's population includes a number of geographically defined ethnic minorities, some of which have actively fought the central government and aspire to some degree of autonomy, if not outright nationhood.

Burmese migrants in Thailand generally come from four ethnic-minority states in eastern Myanmar, including the Kayin, Kayah, Mon and Shan states, and from Bago and Tanintharyi Divisions. Some of them live in areas of internal armed conflict, where the remnants of ethnic-minority-based armed opposition groups have been fighting against the central Myanmar Government for decades. Although such conflicts have greatly decreased in the last 16 years, there remain pockets of resistance in the south-eastern Shan State, and in small areas of Kayin, Kayah and Mon States and in the Tanintharyi Division. Migrants from these regions have often been victims of or witnesses to the Myanmar Army's counter-insurgency activities, which include forced labour and forced relocation. Others from conflict-free areas have left their homes because there were no jobs or other economic opportunities.

Since 1987, Amnesty International has extensively documented violations of ethnic minorities' physical integrity rights, including torture and ill-treatment, and extrajudicial executions by the Myanmar army in counter-insurgency areas where armed groups operate. Civilians living in these areas continue to be vulnerable to a wide variety of human rights violations, including ill-treatment or even killings by the army. Civilians who have been required to perform forced labour for the Tatmadaw (Burmese Armed Forces) are especially at risk. Civilians who are forced to contribute labour, particularly those seized for portering, are sometimes injured or even killed by the army if they fail to perform their duties to the satisfaction of the Tatmadaw.

Amnesty International has also documented human rights abuses in Myanmar by ethnic-minority-based armed opposition groups, including arbitrary detention, torture and unlawful killings. The organization has reported abuses against civilians by the Karen National Union (KNU) and an unidentified Mon armed opposition group, as well as other armed opposition groups.[13] One more recent case directly relates to the violation of economic and physical integrity rights of civilians by armed opposition groups. Armed opposition groups are almost entirely dependent on local villagers for rice and other supplies, which civilians routinely provide for them, reportedly because of their shared ethnicity. This can result in civilians being deprived of sufficient food, or being punished by the Tatmadaw if they believe that villagers are voluntarily giving rice to members of armed groups.

In May 2004, a Karen village headman from Kyaw-ein-seikyi township, Kayin State, told Amnesty International about the killing of the village secretary by the KNU in August 2003. Aung Kyaw Oo was killed by the KNU for failing to send them the village rice quota because the monsoon had flooded roads and there was no way to transport it. His family had witnessed his abduction the previous night by uniformed Karen-speaking KNU soldiers. The headman found his body the next day. He had been stabbed to death in the abdomen. The KNU had come to the headman to explain that they viewed Aung Kyaw Oo as pro-SPDC, because his job was to deal with SPDC demands, while the headman dealt with the KNU requests. The headman reported that at least three times per month the KNU sent him a 'shopping list' consisting of chicken, rice and other goods, which he was compelled to purchase for them. He routinely collected money from the villagers, but many of these had already fled to Thailand to avoid such harassment.

Burmese migrant workers represent approximately 80% of migrant workers in Thailand. Lao and Cambodian workers are the other two largest groups of migrant workers there. In addition, there are over 145,000 Burmese refugees in Thai camps near the border, mostly from the Kayin and Kayah ethnic minorities. Tens of thousands of Shan refugees are also in Thailand, but they are not permitted by the government to live in refugee camps. Most of the Shan refugees are migrant workers, but many of them have well-founded fears of persecution were they to be returned to Myanmar.

On 28 October 2005, a report was made to the UN by Paulo Sergio Pinheiro, a Special Rapporteur who had been commissioned by the UN to visit Myanmar and to report on conditions there. He wrote the following desolate statement:[14]

> Today, I address the General Assembly for the final time, as my mandate expires in April next year. I stand before you with a sense of frustration for not having been able to fulfil my duty as I wished. Indeed, the Government of Myanmar has not invited me to visit the country since November 2003. Similarly, the Special Envoy of the UN Secretary General has not been granted access since March 2004, which I deeply regret.
>
> The Government's pledge to democratic reform and respect for human rights was made and has been reiterated since the 1990 elections were cancelled. A first step was the convening of a National Convention, charged with drafting a new Constitution. This National Convention has been in place for over twelve years. In its last session of 17 February to 31 March 2005, it was convened, yet again, under a number of similar procedural restrictions. Many key political actors, such as the National League for Democracy, have been excluded from the process. Critical voices are not tolerated. Inclusion is dependent upon the participants' acceptance of the six 'objectives' that should serve as the basis for the future Constitution. One such objective is the participation of the military in the national political leadership of the state, with a quarter of seats in the national parliament and one third of the seats in the regional parliaments reserved for the military.
>
> Freedom of assembly and association are still not respected or guaranteed. Almost all of the offices of political parties such as the National League for Democracy have been shut down. Press censorship appears to be

worsening. Intimidation and detention of pro-democracy activists continues. Over 1,100 people are currently behind bars for their political beliefs, some with prison sentences of over 47 years. Many of those include MPs elected in the 1990 elections who were prevented from taking their seats, as well as poets, journalists, monks, students and teachers. Daw Aung San Suu Kyi, the Nobel Peace Prize Laureate, remains in a virtual solitary confinement in her house, with no visitors permitted, even without access to the ICRC, which otherwise has full access to all other prisoners in Myanmar. The General Secretary of the NLD has spent a total of 10 years in three separate periods of house-arrest from 1989–1995, 2000–2002 and from May 2003 until today. Elderly political prisoners such as the poet U Win Tin, the Vice-Chairman of the National League for Democracy U Tin Oo and the author and lawyer U Shwe Ohn are in their late seventies and early eighties. Many are in urgent need of medical care.

The Government's 'roadmap' to democracy has no time frame and no scale. The destinations are hazy, the road-signs keep shifting and the journey time between each place is anybody's guess. The loose mention of a referendum and political elections has not yet been clarified. The political transition process has become a long and winding road with no clear end in sight. Of grave concern is the level and consistency of abuses committed against Myanmar's ethnic communities. It is reported that some ethnic groups are re-considering ceasefire agreements as they have failed to bring about any improvement in their day-to-day life. In some instances, and despite those agreements, there has been an increase in Government military presence in certain ethnic areas. Moreover, the political concerns of ethnic communities appear to be unaddressed in the deliberations of the National Convention. There is a risk that, should the Government continue to ignore these ethnic concerns, including the alleged gross violations committed against ethnic communities and the duty to arrest and detain those responsible, these fragile agreements may unravel.

I stress in my report the record of widespread and systematic violations of human rights in Myanmar and the consistent failure of the Government to protect the citizens prevail throughout the country. The Government has shown little interest in examining allegations of serious human rights abuses by its forces against its own citizens. Successive requests for investigations to be conducted into allegations of rape of ethnic women in Shan State and the Depayin killings were met with inertia. The culture of impunity is such that complaints which are brought to the authorities' attention are frequently met with threats and reprisals. The machinery of law, order and justice, far from upholding the rights of citizens, has been employed as an implement of repression and silent dissent. Calls for reform and offers of technical assistance to train officials in international standards have been met with silence.

Widespread reports of forced labour are commonplace, where men, women, children and the elderly are obliged by authorities to carry out such duties as road construction, fencing of military barracks, mine-sweeping, portering of military supplies and cultivation of crops on civilian land for military use. Those who are unwilling or unable to carry out such orders are frequently exhorted to pay a fee, in lieu of their 'duties', or face punishment. Anyone found to have made what the Government deems as 'false' complaints to the International Labour Organization, according to a Government spokesman, faces prosecution.

Forced relocations of entire villages by Government agents continue, ostensibly to curb the activities of armed opposition groups. Such forced relocations have been described by one of my predecessors as being akin to a 'scorched earth policy.' It was estimated in October 2004 that since the end of 2002, 157,000 people have been displaced by armed conflict or human rights abuses and around 240 villages have been destroyed or relocated.

The resulting outflow of people fleeing such violations has produced several hundred thousand refugees, as well as a high number of displaced people. Many have become migrant workers in neighbouring countries. The number of people originating from Myanmar in Thailand alone is estimated to stand between 700,000 and 1 million. India, Bangladesh, Malaysia and other countries in the region are also playing host to people leaving Myanmar. Repeated calls for immediate economic reform have been unsuccessful. The economy continues to spiral downwards as the price of daily commodities rapidly increases beyond the affordability of citizens. Without fundamental economic and political reforms being instituted, there cannot be any improvement in these trends. To postpone the normalization of the political environment means arresting the development of the country and impeding the rich potential of Myanmar.

Trafficking is a pressing problem, which is having a major impact within the borders of Myanmar and its neighbouring countries. There is also now serious concern at the very rapidly increasing rate of HIV/AIDS infection within Myanmar, which is spreading across its borders to neighbouring countries. Unfortunately for the people of Myanmar, increased restrictions on the operations of the Global Fund led the Fund to take the very regrettable decision to withdraw from the country.

Let me stress this point. I believe that the increased scrutiny and excessive bureaucratic restrictions to which humanitarian organizations are being subjected should not deter the international community from its duty to respond to the humanitarian crisis within the country. The ability to provide assistance when and where it is required and to assess the needs is a key humanitarian value that all member states are bound to uphold. The peoples of Myanmar have a right to be supported.

A positive statement made by the 'Student Generations since 1988', which calls for cooperation among the Government, UN agencies, independent civil groups and international donors in addressing the critical humanitarian needs of the people of Myanmar, must be warmly welcomed. They point out the importance of establishing appropriate mechanisms in the country, which are open and accountable, to coordinate the flow of humanitarian aid to people in distress.

I urge the international community to step up its assistance and not to retreat from supporting the people of Myanmar. We have a duty to the hungry and suffering people to overcome these difficulties.

I have included so much of Pinheiro's statement because it so cogently addressed a number of the key issues which will be dealt with in the final chapter, in which we consider specific weaknesses in the UN's mediation of the Universal Declaration of Human Rights.

Not mentioned in detail so far in this chapter has been the issue of the military regimes' cynical exportation of the narcotics trade and the trafficking of people (largely women and children) through involvement with international criminal organizations. Furthermore, much of this high level of organized corruption is for the financial benefit of individual high-ranking military officials, and does not often redound to the financial benefit of the Myanmar government or its people.

Myanmar's growing dominance in narcotics trafficking

As we saw at the beginning of this chapter, when the military seized control of Burma's government, displacing a somewhat lacklustre democracy, it gained considerable international approval on the grounds that a military regime could crack down on such corrupt practices as Burma's rôle in the international narcotics trade. By the time a military regime again overthrew another popularly elected government in 1990, such illusions about the 'inherent honesty' of military government had faded. However, few could have predicted just how such corruption would flourish to unprecedented levels under the avarice, greed and lack of moral principles of the generals. Since 1991, Burma has succeeded in achieving hegemony in the globalization of the heroin trade, for instance, especially in cooperation with corrupt administrations in Singapore.[15]

The above-cited article quotes Professor Mya Maung, a Burmese academic now safely in the USA, as stating that 'Singapore's economic linkage with Burma is one of the most vital factors for the survival of Burma's military regime. This link is central to the global expansion of the heroin trade.' In fact, Singapore is now Burma's junior partner in the trade, which involves other illegal narcotics along with a host of other international criminal activities. Singapore's investment in Burma's trade in heroin in 1998 totalled more than US$1.3 billion. The person running the racket from Burma was – and still is – Lo Hsing Han, Minister for Trade in Burma's government. The link with Singapore is now proving of enormous benefit to the Burmese military dictatorship, because Singapore is a major force in Asian international commerce. In addition, Singapore now has a strong rôle in the WTO. Indeed, the Burmese dictatorship could hardly hope for a more advantageous link with respectability in the context of neoliberal global finance, for Singapore has become a financial trading base and a route for vast sums of money that flow in and out of Asia.

If the brutal Burmese dictatorship's international pariah status is of any concern to its more powerful partner, Singapore shows no sign of this. Following the visit of Singapore's Prime Minister Goh Chok Tong to Rangoon on 24 March, a Singapore spokesperson proclaimed that 'Singapore and Myanmar should continue to explore areas where they can complement each other.' As both countries continue to glory in their complementary relationship, the international community must also be aware of the immense support that this relationship confers on both Burma's illegitimate regime and its booming billion-dollar narcotics trade.

The Burmese regime – the State Peace and Development Council (SPDC) – depends on the resources of its drug traffickers. Since 1998, opium production has doubled, and by 1998 Burma had become the world's leading opium supplier. It was supplying the USA with 60% of its heroin and methamphetamine by 2001.[16] However, much worse has been Burma's rapidly increasing involvement in the trafficking of people – including children – for prostitution, domestic slavery, fieldwork, farming, etc. In fact, in 2005 the US State Department *Trafficking in Persons Report* listed Burma, along with North Korea and Cambodia, as Asia's worst human-trafficking violators.[17]

Both the Burmese generals and drug lords have been able to take advantage of Singapore's liberal banking laws and money-laundering opportunities. For example, in 1991 the SLORC laundered $400 million through a Singapore bank, which it used as a down payment for Chinese arms. Despite the large sum, Burma's foreign exchange reserves registered no charge either before or after the sale. With no laws to prevent money laundering, Singapore is widely reported to be a financial haven for Burma's elite, including its two most notorious traffickers, Lo Hsing Han and Khun Sa (also known by his Chinese name, Chang Qifu).

SLORC cut a deal with Khun Sa for his 'surrender' in early 1996, allowing him protection and business opportunities in exchange for retirement from the drug trade. Khun Sa now bills himself as a 'commercial real estate agent' who also has a foot in the Burmese construction industry. Already in control of a bus route into the northern poppy-growing region where the military is actively involved in the drug business, he is now investing $250 million in a new highway between Rangoon and Mandalay, an SPDC cabinet member confirmed. 'The Burmese government says one thing but does another', according to Banphot Piamdi, director of Thailand's Northern Region's Narcotics Suppression Centre. 'It claims to have subdued Khun Sa's group . . .however, the fact is that the group under the supervision of . . .Khun Sa's son has received permission from Rangoon to produce narcotics in the areas along the Thai–Burmese border.'

Khun Sa's son is not the only trafficker reaping benefits in the Shan State, which borders Thailand and China and serves as Burma's primary poppy-growing area. Field intelligence and ethnic militia sources consistently report a pattern of Singapore's investments in Burma as opening doors for the drug traffickers, giving them access to banks and financial systems.

Burmese military involvement with drug production persists in these remote areas. Government troops offer protection to the heroin and amphetamine refineries in the area in exchange for payoffs and gifts, such as Toyota sedans, pistols and army uniforms. The only access to the refineries is through permits issued by Burmese military intelligence. Without this, the heavily guarded areas surrounding the refineries are too dangerous to approach. The military is also involved in protecting the transport of narcotics throughout the region, which the authorities have sealed off from the outside world.

'There are persistent and reliable reports that officials, particularly army personnel posted in outlying areas, are involved in the drug business,' confirms the March 1998 US government narcotics report. 'Army personnel wield considerable political clout locally, and their involvement extends all the way to the top. The central government in Rangoon demands funds on a regular basis from regional commanders who, in turn, expect payoffs from rank and file. The soldiers get the money any way they can through smuggling, gambling or selling jade – with drugs being the most accessible source of revenue in Shan State. The officers in the field also "tax" refineries, drug transporters and opium farmers.'

At great risk, the intelligence sources – who go undercover to infiltrate troops in the field – collect painstakingly detailed data, including names, dates and places, such as drugs delivered in March 1998 from Shan State: 'On 10th Jan. 98, SPDC army no 5-65 stationed at Mong Ton, sent 40 troops to Nam Hkek village. Pon Pa Khem village tract collected 0.16 kilo of opium per household or (collected payment of) Baht 600. Then the troops sold the collected opium to the drug business men at the rate of Baht 6000 for 1.6 kilos.' Another report states: 'Troops from SPDC Battalion nos. 277 and 65 stationed at Mong Ton are still protecting heroin refineries situated at Hkai Ion, Pay Ion and Ho Ya areas, Mong Ton township. Those who can pay B.20,000 per month are allowed to run the heroin refineries.' And 'On 3rd of Jan. 98, Burma Army no. 99 collected opium tax in Lashio township. They charged 0.32 kilo per household. They arrested and beat seriously those who failed to give.'

These sources also report that Ko Tat, Private 90900 from SPDC Battalion No. 525, stationed in Lin Kay, recently defected from the Burmese army and said that his company had been giving protection to the opium fields around Ho Mong. While the lower-ranked officers struggle to meet their quotas in the field, the highest levels of the government in the capital city strike deals with Burma's two top traffickers, one of whom is the prosperous partner of Singapore.

In this context it should be noted that we are not discussing Burma alone, but also Singapore and even China. Yet the latter two countries are members in good standing of the WTO and, of course, they are signatories to all of the UN's humanitarian declarations and covenants. This opens up a whole raft of possible UN actions under the Universal Declaration of Human Rights. These will be discussed in the final chapter.

Burma's involvement in people trafficking

The report cited above lists Burma in a negative 'Tier 3' assessment, which includes countries that have failed to take important steps to fulfil the minimum standards for the elimination of human trafficking.

'Burma is a source country for women and men trafficked for the purposes of forced labour and sexual exploitation', the report stated. 'Burmese men, women and children (primarily from the country's ethnic minority populations) are trafficked to Thailand, China, Bangladesh, Taiwan, India, Malaysia, Korea, Macau and Japan for forced labour – including commercial labour – involuntary domestic servitude, and sexual exploitation.'

However, the Burmese government has claimed that it has prosecuted 474 cases related to trafficking for sexual exploitation and smuggling since July 2002. It has also claimed to have instituted new anti-trafficking laws and to have organized a special police unit in 2004.

Yet corruption has continued to be a major problem. According to the report, 'Although local and regional officials were suspected of complicity in trafficking, the Burmese Government reported no prosecutions of corrupt government officials related to trafficking.' The Burmese military continued to carry out trafficking abuses, including forced portering and other forced labour.

In its review of 150 countries and their efforts to combat human trafficking, the US State Department also cites the Cambodian government for its involvement in trafficking, as well as North Korea for its 'involuntary return' of North Korean refugees from China, who often faced 'serious abuses' by the Pyongyang government.

'Wherever the trafficking trade flourishes, the rule of law erodes, corruption thrives, public health suffers and organized crime threatens the security of entire communities', stated US Secretary of State Condoleezza Rice on the press release.

Closely linked with the international trafficking of people is a huge array of domestic exploitation of people in involuntary servitude under brutal and dehumanizing conditions. For example, Amnesty International has reported on such issues regularly over the last few years. Their 2005 report, *Myanmar – Leaving Home*, is particularly detailed.[18] From this report we learn that unpaid forced labour, forced relocation, house destruction or eviction, and confiscation of land, food and other personal possessions by the army deprives civilians of their right to an adequate standard of living. The practice of unpaid forced labour, including participation in public works under threat or penalty by the military, for prolonged periods of time, or without any remuneration, is a direct violation of the right to earn a living, as civilians often spend so much time working without payment for the SPDC that they cannot work to provide for themselves and their families. Forced labour also arbitrarily deprives them of their liberty through de facto detention by the military, and sometimes violates their rights to physical integrity, taking the form of ill-treatment or extrajudicial executions.

For several decades the military has taken tens of thousands of ethnic-minority civilians for forced labour duties, confiscated arable land, crops, livestock and other possessions, and prevented many ethnic-minority civilians from farming in an effort to break imputed support for ethnic-minority armed opposition groups. The army stepped up these practices from 1996 to 1997, when they were told by the central authorities to become more self-sufficient. At the same time the army was still expected by the central command to build infrastructure projects, including roads, but any additional funds which may have been directed to regional commanders did not appear to have reached troops in the field.

As a consequence, local troops took greatly increased numbers of civilians for compulsory labour duties on roads and other infrastructure projects. Soldiers extorted money from those civilians who could not or would not perform forced labour duties. The military also confiscated more land from civilians, and began forcing them to grow crops in what had previously been their own fields. Moreover, the military took all the harvested crops for themselves, leaving very little or no food for the civilians. Troops also lived off the civilian populace in other ways – for example, by stealing their livestock, possessions and money. The central government's policy of self-sufficiency for troops in the field has meant that soldiers have had to steal what they can from villagers.

Professor Paulo Sergio Pinheiro, the UN Special Rapporteur for Myanmar, has regarded economic, social and cultural rights as a central part of his mandate. In a recent report, he stated that 'With respect to economic and social rights, there are areas of concern which could be addressed by the Government, economists, political parties and other players, with assistance and advice from the United Nations, international agencies and neighbouring States, thereby paving the way for the integration of Myanmar into international financial and economic structures.'[19] In the same report he expressed concern that 'Civilians in those areas have reportedly witnessed widespread violations of economic, social and cultural rights, including the deprivation of means of livelihood through land and crop confiscation, the destruction of houses, excessive taxation and extortion.'[20]

Much but not all of these violations of the rural population's human rights, particularly unpaid forced labour, has taken place in the context of counter-insurgency activities by the Tatmadaw (the Myanmar armed forces). After gaining independence from Britain in 1948, many armed opposition groups, consisting primarily of ethnic minorities, took up arms against the central Bama-dominated government. Some of these groups, most notably the Karen National Union (KNU) in some parts of the Kayin State and Tanintharyi Division, and the Shan State Army-South (SSA-South) in the Shan State, continue to engage the Tatmadaw militarily. Shan and Karen civilians living in areas where the SSA-South and the KNU continue to operate are at risk of reprisals and collective punishment by the military if they cannot or will not perform forced labour duties. Such retaliation includes extortion of food and other possessions, and threats of physical violence. Civilians who are taken for forced portering – the most arduous form of forced labour in Myanmar – are often beaten or even shot dead if they cannot keep up with the military column. In addition, porters are not provided with adequate food, water or rest, and so often become weak and can no longer carry their loads.

In Southern Ye township, southern Mon State, civilians are also vulnerable to such violations at the hands of the Tatmadaw in the context of their counter-insurgency campaign against a small but disruptive Mon armed opposition group. In June 1995, the New Mon State Party (NMSP) agreed a ceasefire with the then SLORC, the provisions of which allowed NMSP troops to retain their arms in small 'ceasefire' areas. Shortly before this ceasefire was agreed, thousands of Mon refugees in Thai camps near the border were forcibly returned to Myanmar by the Ninth Infantry Division of the Royal Thai Army, in the absence of international monitoring. Many of these returnees continue to live in ceasefire areas, with no land or means of earning a living. Some disaffected NMSP members subsequently broke away from the NMSP, forming the Hongsawatoi Restoration Party (HRP) in November 2001, led by former NMSP Colonel Nai Pan Nyunt. Its armed wing, the Monland Restoration Army (MRA), fields very few troops and engages in skirmishes with the Tatmadaw in some townships of southern Ye township and in small areas of Tanintharyi Division further south.

Over and above general human rights considerations, many actions of the Burma regime in exploiting its own people violate specific UN conventions and codes of its associated agencies. Amnesty International has been particularly astute in documenting these. Citing further evidence,[16] let us briefly analyse this dimension of violation of international law.

As has been reported by Amnesty International and many other organizations, the security forces continue to take thousands of civilians for forced labour duties in Myanmar, especially in ethnic-minority states. Forced labour, whether paid or unpaid, contravenes the International Labour Organization (ILO) Convention Concerning Forced or Compulsory Labour (No. 29), to which the Myanmar Government acceded in 1955. It also contravenes the right, enshrined in the UDHR, to work, free choice of employment, and just and favourable conditions of work.[16] For many years the ILO has raised its concerns about this practice with the Myanmar Government. In 1999 and 2000 the SPDC issued two orders which outlawed the practice of forced labour of civilians by both civilian and military authorities, making it a punishable offence. However, despite these prohibitions, the security forces continue to take ethnic-minority civilians for forced labour duties on a regular basis.

From 21 to 23 February 2005, in accordance with the ILO Governing Body's recommendations, the ILO dispatched a very High Level Team (vHLT) to Myanmar in order to examine the SPDC's compliance with ILO Convention No. 29 and with its own regulations against forced labour. The vHLT reported its findings about its trip to Myanmar – during which the SPDC Chairman Senior General Than Shwe was not available – to the March 2005 Governing Body. They had sought this meeting with the Senior General as a matter of urgent priority, as only he is believed to have the authority to ensure that the Tatmadaw chain of command functions properly. In the vast majority of cases, civilians are seized for forced labour by the army despite the prohibition of this practice under both international and domestic law. In its report to the Governing Body, one of the vHLT's recommendations was that the SPDC should issue direct orders to all its commanders forbidding the practice of forced labour by the military.

In its March 2005 meeting, the ILO Governing Body invoked the resolution adopted in 2000 by the International Labour Conference (ILC), which called upon all ILO members, including governments, employers, workers and all international organizations, to review their relations with the SPDC to ensure that the latter 'could not perpetuate or extend the system of forced or compulsory labour' in Myanmar. On 21 April 2005 the Director-General of the ILO wrote to all these parties asking them to ensure that their relations with the SPDC did not foster the use of forced labour in Myanmar. On 4 June 2005 in Geneva the ILC considered Myanmar and concluded that 'the extent of forced labour had not significantly changed in most areas, including ethnic areas, and its worst forms – including forced labour for the army and forced recruitment of child soldiers – continued.' Furthermore, Order 1/99 and Supplementing Order 1/99, which provide for judicial punishment of civilian and military officials who are found to be responsible for forced labour, was 'not effectively implemented', according to the ILO.[21]

Some of the most egregious violations of health rights involve the routine use of civilians as porters for the military. The Tatmadaw exploits a common family practice among certain tribes, in which children are expected to 'help out' with work needed by the family to support itself. This tradition has been cynically abused by the army, especially in zones in which the Burmese forces encounter ethnic opposition to them. Civilians – including children – are forced to carry heavy loads for days at a time, often resulting in death or injury. Such 'portering' includes building barracks, working on roads and railways, and agricultural labour on military farms, which had often been 'confiscated' from the very people who were forced to work on them. Most of these 'portering' violations of global health rights are imposed on ethnic minorities, especially the Shan and Karen people.

A 24-year-old Bama Buddhist man who worked six days per week in a rock quarry in Kya-ein-sei-kyi township, Kayin State, and one day per week in forced labour duties making charcoal for the military to sell, told Amnesty International that he was required to perform forced portering in March 2004. He was taken by Tatmadaw Division 45, and forced to carry rice and other supplies weighing 35 kilos. He was with 13 other village men, who were all forced to walk to Kyeikdone, near Three Pagodas Pass on the Thai-Myanmar border, with no rest during the day or night. After three days he managed to escape with some others to Thailand, and although he was not beaten, he found it extremely difficult to carry such a heavy load with no rest and very little food. A 25-year-old Karen woman from Myawaddy township, Kayin State, told Amnesty International that her husband had to porter for the military in April 2004. He also escaped after a few days and fled to Thailand. Neither of these townships in the Kayin State are areas of intense counter-insurgency activities by the Tatmadaw.

A 35-year-old Shan rice farmer, who had been relocated from Kunhing township to Nam Kham relocation site, told Amnesty International that he had been taken as a porter in January 2004. He was camping at his old village in order to grow rice when the Tatmadaw seized him, forcing him to carry food and equipment to another village. He was tied with his hands behind his back and pulled by a rope, and when he could not move quickly enough, soldiers hit and kicked him around the waist. In addition to portering, he also had to perform on a regular basis other forced labour tasks, including clearing the road and breaking rocks every 5 to 10 days, for 2 to 5 days at a time. He was never paid for any of this work, but he and his fellow villagers were told by their community leader in June 2003 that the practice was illegal in Myanmar.[22]

One could go on at length, but Burma's violations of elementary human rights are thoroughly documented in a variety of other international reports. However, we should not leave the matter without referring to Burma's rôle in one of the worst forms of abuse known, as well as flagrant violation of the UN Declaration of the Rights of the Child. The author is referring to the use of children of both sexes, some as young as 5 years of age, as soldiers or as objects of sexual gratification by soldiers. In 2005 the Tatmadaw was continuing to recruit large numbers of child soldiers, despite government statements prohibiting this. Human Rights Watch estimated that children may account for 35–45% of new recruits into the national army, and 70,000 or more of Myanmar's estimated 350,000 soldiers. Children, some as young as 11 years, were forcibly recruited, brutally treated during training, used in forced labour by the army, and forced to participate in armed conflict.

Burma acceded to the Convention on the Rights of the Child in 1991. Since then, however, there has been little progress towards the implementation of the convention, and the underlying problems which impede implementation have not changed. These include a total lack of the rule of law and accountability of the government, as well as draconian restrictions on freedom of expression, association and peaceful assembly, which prevent local reporting and monitoring of the human rights situation with regard to children.

As the reader has seen, the above account of human rights and the widespread neglect of the right to primary healthcare in particular has revealed a rather different variety of inadequacy on the part of the UN in promoting its own declarations. These will be discussed in full in the final chapter of this book, but there are at least two other areas that need to be analysed before a wide enough range of deficiencies in the way in which the UN conducts its rôle as an international arbiter of global human rights can form a minimal basis of a useful critique. These include the conflicts in nations whose territories are extraordinarily rich in terms of natural resources, but whose people are grindingly poor and heavily exploited as other parts of the world exploit the nation's riches. There is a variety of examples, but this author will consider Liberia in the next chapter.

References

1 *Democratic Voice of Burma*, 30 January 2007; http://english.dvb.no/letstalk.php?id=22 (accessed 3 February 2007).
2 Aung San Suu Kyi biography from Whoz.com; www.whoz.com/aunsansuukyi.htm (accessed 3 February 2007).
3 Burma Lawyers Council. The case for humanitarian intervention. In: *Legal Issues on Burma Journal* No 7. December 2000; www.ibiblio.org/obl/docs/LIOBO7_humanitarian_intervention.htm (accessed 3 February 2007).
4 Bureau of Democracy, Human Rights and Labour. *Country Reports on Human Rights Practices – Burma*; www.state.gov/g/drl/rls/hrrt/2003/27765.htm (accessed 4 February 2007).
5 Health Unlimited. *Burma*; www.healthunlimited.org/Burma/index.htm (accessed 5 February 2007).
6 Bureau of Democracy, Human Rights and Labour, op. cit., p. 2.
7 Australian Broadcasting Corporation (ABC). *Australia helps Burma Tackle Health Problems.* Broadcast 22 January 2007; www.abc.net.au/7:30/content/2007/51831456.htm (accessed 6 February 2007).
8 Aide Medicale Internationale (AMI). Advertisement for an HIV/AIDS doctor for Myanmar; www.unjobs.org/vacancies/1167835436.99 (accessed 10 February 2007).
9 Amnesty International. *Myanmar: leaving home*; http://web.amnesty.org/library/index/engasa 160232005
10 Agence France Presse. UNICEF Report: Burmese military government blocks UN programs. *International News*, 5 August 2005, p. 13.
11 BBC (Radio) World Service from Bangkok, Thailand, 5 August 2005.
12 Amnesty International, op. cit., p. 12.
13 Amnesty International. *Lack of security in Burmese counter-insurgency areas.* London: Amnesty International; 2002. pp. 30–34.
14 United Nations Commission on Human Rights. *Statement on the Human Rights Situation in Myanmar by Special Rapporteur Paulo Sergio Pinheiro*; www.burmanet.org/news/2005/10/28/united-nations-statement (accessed 8 February 2007).
15 Kean L, Berstein D. The Burma–Singapore axis: globalizing the heroin trade. *Covert Action Quarterly*; www.thirdworldtraveller.com/global_secrets_lies.htm (accessed 8 February 2007).
16 Amnesty International. *Myanmar: leaving home*; http://web.amnesty.org/library/index/engase 1602300.htm (accessed 4 February 2007).
17 Irrawaddy. *Burma Among Asia's Worst Human Trafficking Violators*; www.irrawaddy.org/aviewer.asp?a=46928z=153 (accessed 2 February 2006).
18 Amnesty International, op. cit., p. 4.
19 United Nations Commission on Human Rights, op. cit., p. 12.
20 Ibid., p. 13.
21 Amnesty International, op. cit., p. 13.
22 Amnesty International, op. cit., p. 13.

Chapter 5

Human rights in the context of conflict

Some broad comparisons

When considering the human rights situation with respect to Sudan, and to Darfur in particular, we confront a combination of long-lasting racial tensions and the determination of the Khartoum leadership to hold on to its vested economic privileges, while doing as little as possible to improve the general welfare of its own people. Like apartheid South Africa, present-day Zimbabwe and a number of other countries, with regard to the issue of human rights within its own borders it does its utmost to frustrate intervention by the international community and by the UN in particular.

In Burma many of the same factors also prevail, but there are important differences. Burma had some experience of political democracy in its not too distant past, and its total abrogation in 1990 by a corrupt and self-serving military regime has, even domestically, robbed the government of moral authority. This has created the foundations for civil war, much exacerbated by the military junta's open exploitation of the nation's ethnic minorities. In Sudan, the Khartoum government may attack people in Darfur, rob them and gravely violate their human rights, but there is little evidence that it is actually using Darfur civilians as slave labour, or that the Khartoum administration is being run by individuals using government power to further such international crime as the trafficking of narcotics or of people as a source of individual financial gain.

Turning our attention to a country like Liberia, we again do not confront a set of circumstances unique to that one country, but some representing a different context for the widespread violation of human rights to that seen previously in Sudan or Burma. Liberia, in some ways paralleling the case of Israel, was arbitrarily established in a country already occupied by an indigenous people, and many of its current problems with regard to human rights stem from that history. This author has found that nothing is more effective in imbuing ordinary people with a commitment to and an interest in their country's history than a perceived ancient wrong.

During the US war in Vietnam, I spent some time in North Vietnam and was amazed at the passion even barely literate peasants, and school children as young as 7 or 8 years of age, had about their country's history. In one instance, two young children and their elderly (but illiterate) grandmother were describing a great battle that the Vietnamese had fought against an invading Chinese army. They described in detail how the Chinese ships were sunk in the Mekong River by a brilliant combination of forethought and tactics. Their description had all of the emotional urgency of a recent event. I therefore asked when it had happened. 'In the early spring of 1206', answered the 8-year-old! Conversations with Liberians at all levels are often of this character.

Historical background to conflict in Liberia

Liberia has the distinction of being the first republic in Africa, and it was founded as such in 1847 by freed African slaves from the USA. They had been repatriated by various anti-slavery philanthropic foundations then extant in the USA. The major contributor to this effort was one such foundation – the American Colonization Society.[1] At that time, almost all of the rest of the African continent had been colonized by various European nations. Sadly, the freed slaves from the USA did not behave noticeably differently to the most rapacious of these European colonists. The descendents of these freed slaves maintained this tradition by excluding the indigenous people from the benefits of economic development and from access to political power in their own country. For instance, only in 1946 did native Liberians gain the right to vote. Extraordinarily, exclusionary policies persisted at a local level, thereby affecting most of the population, despite the efforts of two presidencies in favour of making all citizenship rights universal. These presidencies were those of William V Tubman (1944–1971) and William R Tolbert (1971–1980).

Effective resistance to this state of affairs really began when, in 1980, Samuel K Doe, a sergeant of the Liberian Army who had indigenous roots, organized a coup d'état and took power after brutally assassinating President Tolbert and some of his collaborators. This coup ushered in an era of violence in Liberia. Corruption, mismanagement and repression were characteristics of the 10 years during which Samuel Doe ruled, before he was overthrown by a rebellion launched in 1989 by Charles Taylor.

Sharing a similar fate to his predecessor, Samuel Doe was tortured and murdered in 1990 by a former lieutenant of Taylor's militia. The civil war, made infamous by massive human rights violations and the systematic recruitment of child soldiers, involved about half a dozen factions fighting for control over the Liberian government and its resources. A semblance of peace returned to Liberia in 1996 with the intervention of a peace-keeping force sent by the Economic Community of West African States (ECOWAS).

Largely through fear and intimidation, Charles Taylor won the elections organized in 1997, ushering in years during which terror and a high level of corruption reigned over the country. In 1999, a rebellion began in northern Liberia, led by a group known as the Liberians United for Reconciliation and Democracy (LURD), armed and supported by Guinea. A group called the Movement for Democracy in Liberia (MODEL), allegedly backed by the Ivorian government, emerged in southern Liberia and achieved rapid successes. By the summer, Taylor's government controlled only about a third of Liberia, namely Monrovia and the central part of the country.

This new phase of violence and abuses ended in August 2003 when Charles Taylor, indicted for war crimes by the Special Court of Sierra Leone, was forced to step down and agreed to leave for exile in South Nigeria. The peace agreement signed in Accra in August 2003, which put an end to a conflict that had resulted in the death of 150,000 Liberians, was followed by the deployment of peacekeeping forces of the United Nations Mission in Liberia (UNMIL). UNMIL, then the largest UN mission in the world, with 15,000 soldiers, was mandated to secure the country and lead the Disarmament, Demobilization and Reintegration (DDR) process of the rebel groups. The Peace Agreement also put in place an interim government, the National

Transitional Government of Liberia (NTGL), led by a Liberian businessman, Charles G Bryant. Despite accusations of corruption, the NTGL accomplished its main objective by guiding the country towards elections within 2 years' time.

On 23 November 2005, Liberians chose Ellen Johnson-Sirleaf as president of Liberia in credible and peaceful elections. The election of 67-year-old Johnson-Sirleaf as the first female president of an African country has brought great hope for the stabilization of Liberia, although the tasks that she faces in order to bring durable peace and sustainable development to the country are numerous.

However, these apparently smooth and peaceful developments need to be seen in the context of Liberian politics and the level of animosity that prevails between the indigenous people and the 'aristocracy of former American slaves' – one of the kinder euphemisms one still encounters in some Liberian newspapers! As this author sees it, a major problem is the extraordinary strength that is accorded the office of President in modern Liberia. The previously mentioned presidents, Tubman and Tolbert, did not have such a high level of authority as was, for instance, accorded Charles Taylor, who came to the presidency in 1996. He only assumed that position after a brutal 7-year civil war. In 1997, his National Patriotic Party (NPP) won three-quarters of the seats in the legislature. The elections were administratively free and transparent, but were conducted in an atmosphere of intimidation, as most voters believed that Taylor's forces would have resumed fighting if he had lost. Most other leaders of the former warring factions subsequently left the country. The bicameral legislature exercises little independence from the executive branch. The judiciary is subject to political influence, economic pressure and corruption.

The regular security forces include the Armed Forces of Liberia (AFL), the Liberian National Police (LNP), which has primary responsibility for internal security, the Anti-Terrorist Unit (ATU), also called the Anti-Terrorist Brigade (ATB), and composed of an elite special forces group, and the Special Security Service (SSS), a large, heavily armed executive protective force. The ATU absorbed Taylor's most experienced civil war fighters, including undisciplined and untrained loyalists. There are also numerous irregular security services attached to certain key ministries and parastatal corporations, the responsibilities of which appear to be poorly defined. The national army, which fought against Taylor's faction during the civil war, has yet to be downsized and restructured as required by the Abuja Peace Accords, due primarily to a lack of funding. In late 2000, a commission to downsize and restructure the army was established with allocated funding of approximately US$ 100,000. Several thousand troops deployed in northern countries were fighting armed dissidents. However, there were few troops deployed to maintain security in other rural areas of the country. During the year, fighting intensified between the security forces and the Liberians United for Reconciliation and Democracy (LURD) rebels. President Taylor called up 15,000 former fighters from the faction he had led during the civil war to combat the growing rebel threat. In 2000 the Government revived the National Bureau of Investigation (NBI), which had become defunct during the civil war. Security forces frequently acted independently of government authority, particularly in rural areas. Members of the security forces committed numerous serious human rights abuses.[2]

Liberia, which has a population of approximately 3,164,000, is a very poor country, with a market-based economy that has yet to recover from the ravages of the civil war. Average annual per capita income is estimated to be less than US$ 200. An estimated unemployment rate of 70%, a literacy rate of 30%, the internal displacement of civilians in Lofa and Nimba counties, and the absence of infrastructure throughout the country continued to depress productive capacity, despite the country's rich natural resources, which are often siphoned off for personal benefit by government officials. Extortion is widespread at all levels of society.

The Government's human rights record has remained poor, and there were numerous serious abuses in many areas. The security forces committed many extrajudicial killings, and they were accused of being responsible for the disappearance of numerous individuals. Security forces tortured, beat and otherwise abused or humiliated citizens. The Government investigated some of the alleged abuses by the security forces, but offenders were rarely charged or disciplined. Prison conditions remained harsh and sometimes life-threatening. Security forces continued to use arbitrary arrest and detention at times, and lengthy pre-trial detention remained common.

The judicial system, hampered by political influence, economic pressure, inefficiency, corruption and a lack of resources, was unable to ensure citizens' rights to due process and a fair trial. In some rural areas where the judiciary had not been re-established, clan chieftains administered criminal justice through the traditional practice of trial by ordeal, and the authorities tacitly condoned this practice. Approximately 20 political prisoners remained in jail, although some were released during the year. Security forces violated citizens' privacy rights, conducted searches without warrants, engaged in harassment and illegal surveillance, and looted homes. The Government restricted freedom of speech and of the press, and it detained, threatened and intimidated journalists. Police forcibly dispersed more than one student demonstration. Security forces restricted freedom of movement, using road-blocks to extort money from travellers and displaced people who were fleeing the fighting, primarily in Lofa County.

Security forces frequently harassed human rights monitors. For instance, violence and discrimination against women remained a problem. The welfare of children remained widely neglected, and the practice of female genital mutilation (FGM) continued to increase. Societal ethnic discrimination remained widespread, and today ethnic differences continue to generate violence and political tensions. The Government continues to discriminate against indigenous ethnic groups that had opposed Taylor in the civil war, especially the Mandingo and the Krahn ethnic groups. Forced labour persists in rural areas. Child labour remains widespread, and there have been reports of forced child labour. Ritualistic killings also persist. All of this has set an appalling standard with regard to the provision of primary healthcare (PHC) and recognition of all other human rights, and the situation has not been helped by rebels in the north of the country who routinely commit torture and extrajudicial killings.[3]

Prevalence of extrajudicial killings

As recently as 2001 it was reported that the security forces continued to undertake extrajudicial killings on a large scale, with various human rights organizations estimating the number of such executions to be of the order of hundreds.[4] Guinea also became involved as anti-government dissidents launched a series of cross-border incursions from that country. It is significant that no perpetrators were arrested for any of these killings. In late October, members of the ATU reportedly detained and tortured two Nigerian men, and both men died as a result of their injuries. On 2 November 2001, Deputy Minister of Labour Bedall Fahn and five members of the ATU were arrested. They remained in detention awaiting trial at the year's end, and two ATU suspects remained at large at the year's end. Fahn had reportedly accused the men of stealing jewellery from his house.

On 7 December in Gbarnga, a police commander shot and killed a fourth-grade boy. The police officer said that the boy was a thief, and announced the shooting publicly. Students rioted to protest at the killing, and on 10 December police killed two more students during a demonstration in front of the police station. The National Chief of Police ordered the arrest of the police commander who shot the fourth-grade student. The Government reported that the police commander remained in detention at the year's end. However, human rights NGOs were not granted access to the police commander, and were unable to confirm his arrest by the year's end.

There were credible reports that government forces as well as members of the Lorma ethnic group continue to harass, intimidate and kill members of the Mandingo ethnic group in Lofa County. Human rights monitors reported that hundreds of Mandingos were killed during the year. In May 2002, Amnesty International reported that security forces, especially the ATU, committed widespread abuses, including killings, torture and rape, against civilians suspected of supporting armed dissidents in Lofa County. The Minister of Information, Reginald Goodridge, stated that he was unaware of any abuses committed by the security forces, and he asked Amnesty International to provide more information about the abuses committed by the armed dissidents. No action was known to have been taken against the police officers responsible for the killings of Nyanqui Luoh in 2000.

At the year's end, the Government had not released a report on its November 1999 investigation of the reported killing of as many as 30 Mandigos in Lofa County in August 1999. There was no investigation into or action taken about the death of a security officer, allegedly while in detention, in May 1999. In August, unknown individuals killed the Chief Finance Officer of the Police Training Academy outside Monrovia. Police officers were suspected of involvement, but no reported action had been taken against the individuals responsible by the year's end. On 30 January, Defence Minister Daniel Chea reported that a Guinean helicopter gunship had attacked Solumba, a northern border town, killing at least 10 people. There continued to be reports during the year of attacks on Guinean border towns by fighters based in Liberia, which caused numerous deaths. These attacks were generally perpetrated by a combination of government security forces, Revolutionary United Front (RUF) rebels from Sierra Leone, and some Guinean rebels. However, some attacks were also launched by armed Liberian dissidents based in Guinea. In January there was at least one attack reported on a Guinean town close to the Sierra Leonean border.

Rebel forces fighting the Government in Lofa County killed, tortured and raped civilians. In April, in Lofa County, armed dissidents killed Youth and Sports Minister Francois Massaquoi when they shot at his helicopter. There were no further developments following the November 2000 attacks reportedly in north-eastern Nimba, which resulted in numerous deaths. It was even unclear whether the rebel incursion was from Guinea or Côte d'Ivoire. There were no reported developments in the October 2000 case of 12 men arrested for the burning of a mosque and other buildings, and the death of 4 people in a property dispute in Nimba County. The 12 men reportedly remained in detention pending a trial at the year's end.

To add to all this, there has been regular reporting of 'ritualistic killings' in which body parts of the victim have been removed. The police routinely report these as 'accidents' in order to avoid awkward questions. Relatives who have persistently raised such questions have themselves 'disappeared.'[5]

Involvement of the security forces

There is ample evidence that the security forces themselves are very much involved on a day-to-day basis with such 'disappearances' and other gross violations of human rights. The above-cited US Department of State document links many examples for the years 2001 and 2002, but other more recent reports suggest that there has been little or no effective action by the UN or its agencies to prevent or even to monitor such events. Much of this responsibility has been left to NGOs and to individuals who report anonymously on their behalf. Even when reporting to this author by email, many NGOs have requested that they remain unnamed.

For example, a human rights organization reported that security forces detained 24 individuals from a truckload of internally displaced people who were fleeing fighting in Lofa County in May. It was suspected that they were transported to the Gbatala military base in Bong County. However, they have not been seen since. The whereabouts of seven refugees who were arrested on their return from Guinea in June 2000 remained unknown at the year's end. The authorities claimed that they were members of an armed dissident faction based in Guinea and were plotting to overthrow the Government, and they charged them with treason. The men have not been seen since their arrest, and NGOs and relatives believe that they were killed. Security forces produced suspects whom they had held without charge when the courts issued writs of habeas corpus on the application of human rights organizations. Their disappearance was often the result of prolonged illegal detention at the Gbatala base. There were no indications by the year's end that the Government had carried out its promised investigation of the reported disappearance of Mandingos following the violence in Lofa County in 1999,[6] and no UN agency has followed this up.

Use of torture to support prosecutions

Obviously this practice violates various UN declarations and is totally illegal under Liberia's own constitution, but it is widely used. Moreover, this practice is fairly 'open' in that most Liberians seem to be aware of it. There have been many cases in which security forces produced suspects in court who had been held in prison for months, even when courts had issued writs of habeas corpus on the application of both domestic and international human rights organizations.[7] The detainees themselves testified that they had been tortured, especially at the Security Forces detention centre in Gbatala. Both victims and witnesses reported beatings, torture, killings and sexual abuse at the base. Despite calls by human rights organizations for the closure of the base, it remained open at the year's end. A local NGO, the Catholic Affiliated Justice and Peace Commission, tried to investigate the claims. However, the Government blocked its efforts and continued to deny it access to Gbatala. There were also continued reports of beatings and torture by both government security personnel and armed dissidents in Lofa County.

On several occasions, government security personnel harassed, assaulted and arrested journalists. According to Amnesty International, the security forces targeted and sometimes tortured critics of the Government, including students, journalists and human rights activists.[8]

Law enforcement personnel, including the security forces, have been implicated in numerous reports of harassment, intimidation and looting. According to Amnesty International, security forces tortured criminal suspects. In May and June, police personnel fired on vehicles at security checkpoints in Monrovia, and at least one person was shot and injured. In July 2005, in Monrovia, officers of the Police Special Operations Division beat and attempted to rob marketers. The National Director of Police intervened and apologized to them. In July, the commander of the Kakata town police and another officer were arrested for murder and armed robbery following the ambush of a rubber plantation vehicle. In August, in separate incidents, police beat and flogged Congresswoman Ellen King and Senator Armah Jallah, two members of the legislature. Several policemen were arrested after the August incident, but no further action had been taken against the policemen by the year's end. In September, in response to the high incidence of abuse by police, the Government held special training seminars on officer conduct and public relations. Also in September, the Security Forces commander publicly demanded that officers improve their behaviour towards civilians at checkpoints, and stated that offenders would be punished. However, there was no subsequent improvement in police behaviour at checkpoints, and no action was known to have been taken against any police officers responsible for such abuses.

Ameliorative rôle of the UN

Despite all of the above, UN agencies have had some positive effect on the catalogue of abuses in Liberia. For instance, there have been some signs of progress over the past 3 years, but abuses are still common.

The peace agreement signed between the Liberian government and two rebel groups in August 2003 ended more than 3 years of internal armed conflict and provided for a transitional government, largely made up of members of the three former warring parties, to guide Liberia to elections in 2005. In 2004, the deployment of some 15,000 UN peacekeepers and 1,000 civilian police, and the disarmament of more than 90,000 combatants, contributed to a marked decrease in abuses against civilians and attacks against human rights defenders. However, the human rights situation remains precarious as a result of frequent criminal acts by ex-combatants in the face of inadequate police and civil authorities, as well as striking deficiencies within the national judicial system, infighting and allegations of corruption within the transitional government, serious shortfalls in financing the programme to reintegrate and train demobilized combatants, and continued regional instability, most notably in neighbouring Côte d'Ivoire and Guinea. There has been little discussion on how to ensure accountability for past human rights abuses. The selection of commissioners for the Truth and Reconciliation Commission mandated by the 2003 peace agreement lacked transparency. The Nigerian government, which offered former president Charles Taylor a safe haven in August 2003 when rebels threatened to take the capital Monrovia, has refused to hand him over to the Special Court for Sierra Leone, which indicted him for war crimes connected with his support for rebels in Sierra Leone. Meanwhile, several of Taylor's close associates have been implicated in plans to attack neighbouring Guinea, which once served as a haven for the rebels which led to his removal from power.[9]

One of the most appalling deficiencies has been the increasing use of children as soldiers by contending Liberian armed groups, including the government. Human Rights Watch reported[10] that, at the height of the civil war, more than 15,000 child soldiers were involved in active military rôles. In fact, many units were comprised primarily of children. This Human Rights Watch report cites details of many abuses committed against child soldiers, and the violations of international human rights laws which they were required to commit against civilians. What must be emphasized in this context is that, even when (and if) conflict ends, the re-integration of these children into normal childhood will pose immense psychosocial problems for Liberia for generations to come.

Use of child soldiers in Liberia

International law itself, as well as UN declarations as the Rights of the Child and the Universal Declaration of Human Rights, absolutely forbid the use of children under the age of 15 years as soldiers. However, many thousands of children were used in this way during the civil war itself, and this practice has continued. The main rebel forces towards the end of 1994, namely Charles Taylor's National Patriotic Front of Liberia (NPFL) and the United Liberation Movement of Liberia for Democracy (ULIMO), have both been prodigious in their use of children under the age of 15 years as armed fighters. Standing apart from this practice have been those forces loyal to the former government of Samuel K Doe. They have scrupulously avoided recruiting anyone under the age of 18 years. However, the Armed Forces of Liberia (AFL) have never observed any such compunction.

The widespread use of child soldiers has ensured that many thousands of children in Liberia have suffered exceptional cruelty. Many child soldiers have been killed or wounded, or have witnessed terrible atrocities in a period in which thousands of other children have died. Moreover, many children have themselves taken part in the killing, maiming or rape of civilians, including other children, or the looting of civilian homes. Many have staffed military checkpoints throughout the country where they have harassed and sometimes killed civilians. Some were only 10 years old when they joined in the fighting, and sometimes the weapons they carry are as tall as the children. As one Liberian working with former combatants expressed it, 'It's the climax of abuse of children's rights.'[11]

The use of children as soldiers presents grave human rights problems. Many of these children have been killed during the conflict, and thus have been denied the most basic right – the right to life. Others have been deprived of their liberty – forcibly conscripted by warring factions, and separated from their families against their wills. Many have been tortured and otherwise treated inhumanely by the warring factions with which they have served. Some have been forced to kill or torture others, with consequent severe psychological effects on these children. All of them have been denied a normal childhood.

Lack of relevant information about child soldiers

No one knows the exact number of children who have been used in the civil war in Liberia. Even the total number of fighters used by all factions is unknown. It is estimated that 40,000 to 60,000 fighters are involved in the conflict. UNICEF estimates that 6,000 of the fighters (or 10%) are children under 15 years of age. In general, most observers agree that all of the factions are largely made up of very young people. Some estimate that another 20% of the fighters are between the ages of 15 and 17 years.

People who work closely with child soldiers believe that the factions use children because they are obedient and do not question orders, and because they are easier to manipulate. As one Liberian working with former combatants expressed it, 'Adults need a good reason to take up arms. It is easier to convince kids to fight for almost nothing, with small promises of money and loot. . . . They are easy prey for the factions.'[12]

Some observers told Human Rights Watch that children are used because they do not know what they are doing and do not realize that they are actually killing people. Counsellors who work with former child soldiers do not believe this is true. Several of them told Human Rights Watch that once children have built up a relationship of trust with a counsellor, they often reveal the guilt, horror and nightmares they suffer because of the appalling atrocities they have committed.

All of the warring factions have forcibly recruited children, but some children have joined voluntarily, usually because they saw no other way to survive. Children say they joined for various reasons – to avenge the killings of parents, other family or friends, to protect their families from the warring factions, or to get food for themselves and their families. In some cases the children's families had been killed, there was no one left to take care of them, and they took up the only option that they thought they had, namely to join a fighting force.

Children have played many rôles in the conflict, ranging from carrying ammunition and cooking to serving at the front in major battles. Some have been used as spies, some as executioners, and some as cannon fodder to draw the fire of adversaries. Many young boys (as young as 9 or 10 years) staff checkpoints, where they have killed or terrorized civilians for no apparent reason. Almost all of the child soldiers are boys, although observers have reported girls among the child soldiers.

The educational level of the boys interviewed by Human Rights Watch ranged from no education (one boy could not read or write his own name) to fifth grade. A UNICEF official reported that before the war only 34% of Liberian children completed first grade.

Psychological damage caused to child soldiers

Child soldiers reported training that lasted from one week to several months. Several described being taught how to shoot, how to put together and take apart weapons, how to 'walk a far distance with a heavy load', how to take cover, how to carry out an ambush, how to 'dodge bullets', and how to crawl, squat and jog.

All of the child soldiers interviewed by Human Rights Watch had been armed. Most of them told us that they had carried AK47s – fully automatic Kalashnikov assault rifles designed and manufactured in the former Soviet Union and the former eastern bloc. One boy said that he had carried and used a G3 (a German-designed assault rifle used by NATO troops). With either of these weapons, one pull on the trigger can release as many as 20 (in the case of the G3) or 30 (in the case of the AK47) bullets.

Child soldiers report being treated cruelly by the factions to which they belonged. They have been beaten, flogged, and subjected to a form of torture called tabay – in which a person's elbows are tied together behind his back, causing severe pain and often leading to nerve damage in the arms. Many children report being drugged with a mixture of cane juice and gunpowder, or with 'bubbles', an amphetamine, to make them 'strong and brave' for fighting at the front. Many child soldiers also report having been subjected to a cruel initiation rite on joining a warring faction, in which the child is forced to kill or commit some other atrocity in order to demonstrate that he would be a reliable fighter – and to mark a turning point from which there would be no going back.

Many former child soldiers suffer from symptoms of post-traumatic stress disorder, including sleeplessness, nightmares, flashbacks, bedwetting, anxiety and depression. Reintegrating these children into their communities is an immense task. The parents of some children have been killed. In some cases children's families have fled, and no relatives can be found. In others, families have refused to take their children back because of the abuses they have committed. Efforts are currently under way to rehabilitate and reintegrate those children who have been captured or demobilized – by examining and counselling them and attempting to reunite them with their families. These efforts have been spearheaded by UNICEF and by a Liberian organization known as the Children's Assistance Program (CAP).

Human Rights Watch believes that children under 18 years of age should not take part in armed conflict, killing and being killed. Human Rights Watch supports international efforts to raise the minimum permissible age for participation in armed conflict from 15 to 18 years. All warring factions have been urged by NGOs to disarm and demobilize immediately all fighters under the age of 18 years, and to refrain from any further exploitation of children. They also urge the current government, the Liberian National Transitional Government (LNTG), to do everything in its power to prevent the warring factions from using children as soldiers. The government is obliged to take all possible steps to ease the former child soldier's transition from war to a peaceful and productive life. Programmes for this transition should start immediately, with long-term planning for the period after the war.

The war's violation of the rights of the child

Life for children caught up in the civil war in Liberia was filled with random violence and acts of sickening cruelty. The war spared no one. The World Health Organization reported in February 1994 that nearly two-thirds of high-school students in Monrovia, the capital of Liberia, had seen someone killed, tortured or raped during the civil war:

> The survey, of 334 pupils in grades nine to twelve, showed the war had caused serious psychological damage to young people in the capital. It showed that 61 per cent of students had seen someone being killed, tortured or raped, six per cent had said they had taken part in violence themselves, and 77 per cent had lost a close friend or relative killed in the war. . . . Some of the students said

their experiences were constantly on their minds. Half said they had nightmares, trouble sleeping and were more easily frightened. Sixteen per cent were
using the tranquilliser Valium without medical supervision.[13]

The children who were caught up in the war within the very ranks of the opposing
forces experienced additional horrors beyond those faced by the rest of the nation's
children. People who work closely with former child soldiers told Human Rights
Watch many stories of the appalling experiences through which these children have
lived.[14]

The four accounts which follow (and the author has 15 others) were shared by the
victims with counsellors and social workers in Monrovia in the last 2 weeks of April
1995. The names and affiliations of these informants cannot be divulged, as the author
was told that if this was done, the NGOs would be expelled from the country, if not
prosecuted. All of the accounts given here are included in the Human Rights Watch
item cited above.

Before considering these accounts, the reader is given a list of the acronyms which
describe various agencies that are active in the Liberian situation. Throughout his
work in a number of African contexts, this author has constantly been amazed (and
often amused) by the way that even children refer to various agencies and commercial
concerns by their acronyms. Whatever language they are speaking, they almost
invariably use the English acronyms as well, which can sometimes be most confusing.
However, the following tragic accounts are heavy with the following acronyms in
common use. They are listed as follows:

AFL – Armed Forces of Liberia
ECOMOG – Economic Community Ceasefire Monitoring Group of ECOWAS
ECOSOC – Economic Community Economic and Social Council
ECOWAS – Economic Community of West African States
IGNU – Interim Government of National Unity
INPFL – Independent National Patriotic Front of Liberia
LDF – Lofa Defence Force
LNTG – Liberian National Transitional Government
LPC – Liberian Peace Council
NPFL – National Patriotic Front of Liberia
OAU – Organization of African Unity
ULIMO – United Liberian Movement for Democracy in Liberia
UNDP – United Nations Development Program
UNICEF – United Nations Children's Fund
UNOMIL – United Nations Observer Mission in Liberia

Four testimonies given to NGOs

FW, aged 15 years, came from a small village in the interior of Liberia. His father was a
diamond digger and his mother sold small items in a local market. FW's parents
divorced, and he subsequently lived with his father and stepmother. He attended a
mission school through the first grade, where he did learn to read.

When the conflict reached FW's area in 1990, his father left to find accommodation
for the family in Guinea, but was not able to return for his family. FW was afraid, and

left his stepmother to look for his mother. During his search he came into contact with the Independent National Patriotic Front of Liberia (INPFL – the rebel group headed by Prince Johnson) fighters at a checkpoint. They 'arrested' him and asked him to join the INPFL, but he refused. He was told to kill a captured AFL soldier who was being beaten. He refused. The INPFL fighters told him that he would be killed himself if he did not kill the soldier. With regret, he carried out the order.

After this incident, FW was trained to be a soldier. He fought with the INPFL from 1990 until October 1992. He says that he was given 'bubbles' (an amphetamine) to keep him 'strong and brave' when he fought. When his commanding officer was killed in an ambush, he was assigned to Prince Johnson's camp. During the 1992 October crisis (operation Octopus – the INPFL attack on Morovia) he was seized by Economic Community Ceasefire Monitoring Group (ECOMOG) soldiers and taken to their base.

FW was sent to a transitional home for war-affected children and was seen regularly by a counsellor. His counsellor reported that the most significant part of his treatment was the opportunity for him to retell his killing of the AFL soldier. FW was filled with guilt, shame and continuous memories of the event. He vividly described how he was forced at knife point to kill another man. He continually explained how he had begged the INPFL soldier to let him go, so that he would not have to kill another person.

Forgiveness was essential for FW. He longed for forgiveness from his mother, and spoke repeatedly of his wish to see her and the rest of his family, all of whom remain behind the lines of the conflict.

BH grew up in the Buchanan area and attended school there through first grade. Later he moved to Monrovia to live with an aunt. In August 1990, when he was 14 years old, he left his home in Monrovia to search for food. When he returned his aunt had left, so he lived with friends for a time. He and his friends stole items from the port area. One day he was captured by the Independent National Patriotic Front of Liberia (INPFL), Prince Johnson's armed opposition group. BH said:

> The people tied me up until all the bones in my chest were showing, and they laid me down and told me to look at the sun. I stayed there the whole day. I was begging them to loosen me. They said the only way they could loosen me was if I agreed to join them. So I agreed because I did not want to die.

BH was trained for 3 weeks, and was then sent to the front to fight. He fought for some time and said that he felt scared when he saw others die from their wounds and hunger. He said that he felt pained and frightened when he learned that his only sister also died of hunger.

In 1990, when TL was 13 years old, fighters from the National Patriotic Front of Liberia (NPFL – the group headed by Charles Taylor) came to his town, called his father a Mandingo (an ethnic group considered to have collaborated with the Doe regime), and beheaded his father in front of TL's two brothers. When TL and his mother returned from looking for wood, they were told what had happened. TL's mother refused to believe it, and told TL to go and see whether it was true. TL went to the edge of the town where the incident had taken place and found his father's body, which he recognized by his clothes, but not his father's head. TL says that he looked and looked for his father's head, crying all the while.

He returned home and told his mother, who was pregnant with her seventh child. His mother fainted, and when she came to, she did not know her own name or her children. She stayed that way for 2 weeks, during which time she lost the baby she had been carrying.

After 2 weeks, the NPFL came through again and everyone in the town ran away. TL and his older brother became separated from their mother and brothers and sisters, but managed to find some distant relatives and stayed with them in another village. To this day, TL has no idea where his mother and his other brothers and sisters are.

TL's older brother left the relatives to join ULIMO. TL's relatives did not allow him to join. He bitterly resented this, and looks forward to the day when he can join ULMIO, too, which he believes is the 'manly' thing to do. Now he lives with cousins in a camp for displaced people. He sells cigarettes to make some money, but is eager to go back to school. He says that he has a deep hatred for Gios and Manos (the ethnic groups that were predominant among the early supporters of the NPFL), and says 'They killed my pa.'

TL says that he daydreams a lot, and that the daydreams are always the same. He joins ULIMO and carries out great military exploits. He wants desperately to find his mother and brothers and sisters. He suffers from recurring nightmares in which men are running after him to kill him and there is no one to help him and nowhere to hide. He wakes up just as he is caught, and finds himself sweating and crying.

UE is 15 years old and reports:

> In July 1990, five Armed Forces of Liberia (AFL) soldiers came to my house and knocked on the door at about 11.00 pm. My dad went to the door and asked who it was. They said, 'We are friends and want to tell you about something.' My dad said, 'Let it be in the morning.' Then the soldiers broke the door down and came in. My mother came running. My sister was sound asleep and I was hiding behind a cushion.
>
> The soldiers tied up my mother and father, and said, 'Do you have any money here?' They said no, and the soldiers said, 'You are lying. You Mano and Gio people are dogs, but we will get rid of you one by one.' My parents were screaming. The soldiers took out their knives and beheaded them. Then they ran away.
>
> I woke my sister up and we ran to our neighbour's house. We never saw our parents again until they were put into the ground. My uncle heard the news and came for us and took us to his house.

Child soldiers have themselves committed serious atrocities, sometimes against total strangers, but often targeting people they knew. As one social worker commented, 'It is a fratricidal war. A poor or low-status villager joins, say, ULIMO. Then he kills the teacher who flunked him, the man who beat him. Often women were raped by friends of their sons.'

One international relief worker told Human Rights Watch:

> Some of the boys were forced to kill. Others did horrifying things and you just don't understand why. One boy, about seventeen, described to me what he did to women at checkpoints – how he raped them – and exhibited no remorse. But he's the exception, not the rule. Other kids followed orders, or followed what the adults did.

The Lutheran World Federation, among other agencies, has noted a gradual improvement in some aspects of the human rights situation in Liberia since 2000.[15]

However, human rights, especially those relating to child and maternity PHC and civilian healthcare generally, are still widely ignored. Levels of corruption on a grand scale are among the worst in Africa, and various government agencies and individuals – with many parallels to the situation in Burma – are involved in such practices as people trafficking and other violations of international trading rules. It is instructive to now address some of these.

Continued violation of the right to health

The reader could be forgiven for believing that by 2004, with the civil war officially at an end, we would see in Liberia an increasing improvement in human rights. This has not in fact happened and, on reflection, it is not difficult to see why this is so. Post-war confusion, crippling poverty, multiple displacements and continuous war have decimated Liberia's health infrastructure, which prior to June 2003 was composed of only 32 registered doctors and 185 registered nurses. The intensification of the fighting since early 2003 further pressured the already crippled healthcare system. Prior to the recent escalation, most of the communities did not have functional health facilities, and in Monrovia the JFK and Catholic hospitals operated only with a minimum staff and the support of NGOs such as the ICRC and MSF. Overcrowding, deplorable sanitary conditions and limited access to safe drinking water and food have led to an increased incidence of malnutrition, diarrhoea, cholera and vaccine-preventable diseases. In the aftermath of the June onslaught on Monrovia, MSF officials reported that on average 350 cases of cholera were treated weekly, and there was a significant rise in severe malnutrition. This is further complicated by the fact that at the height of the recent attacks on Monrovia there was not a single public hospital functioning in the whole of Liberia. In addition, the continuing conflict and looting of relief items have greatly reduced the capacity of the humanitarian community to respond to the current challenges in the health sector.

The above clearly illustrates the magnitude of the human rights problems found in post-conflict Liberia. However, unless such human rights problems are urgently addressed, it is difficult to see how the equity discrepancies which had caused much of the conflict can be resolved. Over and above health per se, a host of related human rights challenges must be met. These include the need to abolish any existing mechanisms of impunity, establishing functioning and high-profiled human rights institutions, and inculcating broad public support for the levels of tolerance on which human rights are based. Given Liberia's recent background of personal and institutional violence, this will be no easy matter. After all, the atrocities committed against the civilian population of Liberia since 1989 – including widespread systematic killings and rape – constitute crimes against humanity, grave breaches of the Geneva Convention and serious violations of human rights and humanitarian law. They must not be allowed to continue or to go unpunished. The conflict in Liberia and the wider sub-region has been exacerbated by the inability of the international community to respond to continuing violations in Liberia. This culture of impunity cannot be allowed to persist. We owe it to the people of Liberia to provide them with the same remedies that are now available to victims of similar crimes in other countries. The investigation and documentation of the atrocities in Liberia are critical to any peace and reconciliation process in the country.

Rôle of official agencies in human rights abuse

It is not surprising, then, that the low esteem in which human rights are held should lead to antisocial behaviour based on opportunism and criminality. In addition to ordinary muggings and other street crime, levels of organized crime have likewise increased. Among these is a growing prevalence of trafficking of people from outside the country, and sexual abuse at the domestic level. For instance, by October 2004, various NGOs were reporting to this author an increase in the trafficking of Ukrainian and Moroccan women into Monrovia. There they served as prostitutes in popular bars that were in effect brothels. What is even worse is the evidence that their custom is largely foreign, and a large proportion of that comes from expatriate UN personnel. The UN Mission in Liberia (UMIL) is taking the problem seriously. As mentioned earlier, this particular violation of what should be a sacred trust is not confined to Liberia.

Human trafficking, which is essentially a modern form of slavery, is one of the most widespread violations of human rights in the world. Its main victims are women and children. The International Organization on Migration has estimated that approximately 700,000 women around the world are transported over international borders each year to work as prostitutes. Human trafficking undermines the rule of law and supports the corruption of power structures, thus impacting on efforts to build sustainable peace. It is often closely tied to the arms and drug trades, and has strong links to organized crime.

The 'wild west' environment of post-conflict countries is particularly conducive to trafficking, especially when international peacekeepers are present, as in Liberia. The humanitarian community has criticized previous UN peacekeeping missions for not taking the issue of trafficking seriously. Since peacekeeping operations introduce thousands of unattached men into a chaotic and conflict-ridden environment, mission planners should expect to find trafficking and exploitation emerging in its areas of operations.

The UN Department of Peacekeeping Organizations (DPKO)[16] has stated that it is committed to confronting trafficking in peacekeeping missions, despite the fact that peace operations are generally neither well suited nor directly mandated to deal with the challenges of combating human trafficking. The Special Representative of the Secretary General (SRSG) in Liberia, Jacques Paul Klein, told Refugees International, 'I have the most aggressive program. In Bosnia, we did raids. We have five investigations going now. I declared two clubs off limits (to UN personnel). I have no qualms about doing that. I will investigate. My trafficking (officer) is tough.' A senior CIVPOL officer told us that 'there are seven officers assigned to [the CIVPOL trafficking officer] who arrived only two weeks ago. She is working with my support and not putting up with any nonsense.' Paradoxically, however, this approach may in fact be exacerbating the problem. UN policy on trafficking baldly states:

> Trafficking cannot be addressed in a template fashion. It must be structured to ensure close integration with existing local and national enforcement agencies. In particular, the adoption of an overly aggressive law enforcement policy, without deep and subtle insight into the complexities of trafficking people from other countries, is not a model to be recommended.
>
> UN (2007) *Policy on Trafficking Drugs and Humans.*
> www.unodc.org/undoc/index.html

The director of CIVPOL, Liberia's anti-trafficking department, is not acting in accordance with this policy. According to people interviewed by Refugees International, and Liberian news reports, the trafficking officer and her staff raid nightclubs and 'rescue' trafficked women, who are then dropped off with NGOs with no prior warning or preparation. According to a Liberian who was interviewed by Refugees International, 'The people who own the brothels in Liberia are the same ones who are drug runners and arms dealers. You need to investigate these things together.'

By engaging in high-profile raids of clubs and 'rescues' of trafficked women, UNMIL may actually be putting these women at greater risk. 'Rescued victims' of trafficking are often expected to provide information to police or even to testify in order to receive assistance. In many of the countries of origin of the victims, there is no adequate witness protection for women who choose to testify against traffickers. Criminal networks involved in trafficking extend from origin to destination countries, and threats against the victim and their family members back home are very common and very real. After a failed raid (or a successful raid in which the girl chooses to return), brothel owners may punish women whom they think tipped off the police. High-profile raids can also drive the industry further underground, making it more difficult to get to the root of the problem. As UNMIL has made some clubs off limits to UN personnel, brothels are reported to be moving from public clubs to private homes.

How should victims of trafficking be treated?

Victims of trafficking often require special counselling, safe accommodation, and medical and social support. Effective counter-trafficking programmes are extremely complex, and success requires a high level of coordination with the different organizations that are involved. Once the victim is 'rescued', who becomes responsible for this very vulnerable person? If there are no services available for the victim, then the 'rescued' person may get dropped at the border or repatriated to an unsafe environment, a situation that result in their returning to the very place from which they were 'rescued.' Providing services requires the cooperation of other organizations beyond the CIVPOL trafficking team – organizations that CIVPOL is not consulting with prior to the raids. NGOs point out that CIVPOL expects them somehow to repatriate the trafficked women and protect them from the organized crime racketeers who sold them in the first place. This is a job which they are currently unprepared to do.

Refugees International is also concerned about the lack of female officers available in the CIVPOL trafficking taskforce to interview victims. Apart from the woman who leads the anti-trafficking taskforce, all of the officers assigned to the unit are male.

Liberian women are working alongside foreign nationals in these clubs. The number of Liberian women who are working as 'forced prostitutes' is unknown, but Refugees International is concerned that this may be a major problem. It urges CIVPOL to work with other organizations to ensure that Liberian women who are forced into prostitution have access to protection services from health and social services as well as law enforcement.

Refugees International recommendations

This important issue will be dealt with in the final chapter when the author considers ways of making minority human rights legislation more systematically organized at the international level. However, Refugees International suggests the following approach for Liberia.[6]

- UMIL needs to modify its law enforcement approach to human trafficking by workers in collaboration with local NGOs and human rights organizations, rather than primarily with local law enforcement agencies. This could be much more easily aligned with UN policy.
- In the Liberian context, the pivotal UN contact should be the Special Representative of the Secretary General (SRSG). The SRSG can then instruct the CIVPOL (Civilian Police) trafficking officer to follow explicitly UN rules with regard to people trafficking. Consideration of the 'moral status' of Liberia in the eyes of the international community, and the knowledge that they are definitely in the international eye, would make CIVPOL much more amenable to cooperation.
- UMIL needs constantly to involve CIVPOL in discussions about the international criminal networks which run the trafficking from out of the country.
- CIVPOL must ensure that any interviews with victims are conducted in a safe and secure environment by a female police officer. In addition, CIVPOL should recruit many more women officers to its trafficking team.
- CIVPOL on its part needs to begin to work with organizations to address the issue of Liberia's working brothels, and to provide them with equal access to protection.

Changing attitude among expatriate staff

The issue of badly behaved UN and NGO workers in former conflict zones, and in poorer countries in general, keeps raising its head and has been alluded to above. However, from what this author has been able to find out, the severity of this problem varies greatly from one country to another. Liberia, Côte d'Ivoire and the Democratic Republic of the Congo, probably because the destruction of the infrastructure of civil society has gone on for so long, seem to attract much more than their share of such instances. For instance, when working in Haiti during the post-Duvalier interregnum (1986–87), this author was struck by the low incidence of such reports, and it is interesting to note that Refugees International raises the same issue in its 2007 report, and attributes it to the attitude of senior management in the UN peacekeeping mission. In this author's view it was because the senior officers were largely resident in the USA and Canada, and were thus close to home, that their stays in Haiti tended to be punctuated by frequent visits home, and they thus would have felt a stronger psychological pressure to behave well.

In Liberia, former SRSG Jacques Paul Klein spoke forcefully and publicly about the issue of sexual exploitation and abuse, but his actions appeared to contradict his words. UNMIL was very slow to put the proper mechanisms in place to report, investigate and prevent sexual exploitation and abuse. One telling example was Klein's handling of the issue of the trafficking of women in Liberia.

Prior to serving as the SRSG for the UN Mission in Liberia, Klein served as head of the UN peacekeeping mission in Bosnia–Herzegovina (UNMIBH), where he was criticized for his handling of the problem of UN peacekeepers and trafficking of women, and overlooking the rôle of UN personnel in this. One of the programmes initiated in UNMIBH was called the Special Trafficking Operations Programme (STOP). This programme was notorious for conducting media-laden high-profile raids on brothels that were frequented by UN peacekeepers in Bosnia. Although STOP initially gained support because it drew attention to the issue of trafficking, the programme eventually drove trafficking underground, making it more difficult to stop the practice. Women's groups were highly critical of the media-driven approach, which did not take into account the safety and protection of the victims of trafficking. Against the protests of many women's organizations who worked on the issue of trafficking in the UN peacekeeping mission in Bosnia, Klein appointed a former reporter with no experience as his focal point on trafficking of women and sexual exploitation and abuse in Bosnia. Although those who have worked with her agree that she cares passionately about trafficking and the victims of this, she lacks formal training in the complex criminal investigations that are necessary for human trafficking. She was roundly criticized in Bosnia for exacerbating the problem of trafficking and overlooking the rôle of the UN in this. 'She led the STOP raids on brothels in Bosnia with cameras in tow', stated one expert on trafficking, 'The women were terrified. Sometimes the police officers who were involved in the raids were the very clients of the brothel.'

However, this observation by Refugees International in their 2007 report[17] suggests that even the senior staff (both male and female) need a longer specialized training in the issues before being assigned to such work. The report takes up this theme as detailed below.

The Zeid Report addresses this problem specifically, urging the UN to 'have access to professionals who have experience in investigating sex crimes.' It warns that 'complex and sensitive investigations into allegations not be undertaken by "enthusiastic amateurs."' Yet Refugees International found that some of the same problems that plagued the mission in Bosnia were occurring again in Liberia. Rather than listening to and learning from the criticism, Klein side-stepped DPKO and appointed the same woman to head up her trafficking unit in Liberia. When this came to light, Klein defended her work against the protests of different UN agencies and NGOs working in Liberia and in Bosnia. When Refugees International visited Liberia in December 2004, UNMIL personnel told us that, as in Bosnia, the brothels had gone underground. 'The women are still there but, thanks to the aggressive actions taken by UNMIL, it's a lot harder to find them now.' Again, rather than responding to this problem and removing her from her position, Klein then appointed her to be the focal point for sexual exploitation and abuse allegations.

Although Klein said that she was aggressively addressing sexual exploitation and abuse, she also complained vociferously that she had no way of punishing perpetrators except to repatriate those found in violation. However, there were other actions that could have been taken to show that she took the problem seriously. Advocates for the victims complain that they never heard about the results of any investigations that were reported directly to the SRSG. The issue of lack of concern about reporting back to the local population was echoed by her employees. 'There is no accountability in this mission', one UNMIL employee said to Refugees International. 'The SRSG sweeps it all under the carpet. No one will talk about this openly.' A member of an international NGO who works closely with women's groups in Liberia also complained to Refugees International that 'They just don't take [sexual exploitation] very seriously. I've had UNMIL people tell me that some prostitution is not exploitative, and that the Liberian women choose to be prostitutes. This attitude is unacceptable.'

In general, UNMIL employees did not evidence the same knowledge about the consequences of sexual exploitation and abuse that MINUSTAH (United Nations Stabilisation Mission in Haiti) employees did. In March 2004, Refugees International reported that UNMIL lacked a clear and transparent process for reporting sexual exploitation incidents. Refugees International interviewed representatives of local NGOs and women's groups, international NGOs and other UN agencies, as well as many different members of UNMIL's staff. At that time there was no individual who was formally assigned to be the sexual exploitation focal point. No two people that Refugees International interviewed could identify the correct focal person whom they should contact in the event of having to report such incidents. Reference was made above to the fact that not only has human trafficking increased since the civil war, but also the domestic abuse of women has shown few signs of declining. We shall conclude this chapter with a brief analysis of this.

Abuse of women civilians within Liberia

Although domestic abuse of Liberian women has always been extensive in Liberia, during the civil war it was very much a part of the widespread brutality that affected both sexes. This concealed the cultural and social 'permanence' of brutality against women in particular. It is only since the end of the civil war that this 'fixedness' of much routine violation of the rights of women has become more evident. Refugees International reported on the situation in 2007.[18]

They report, for instance, a resurgence of the practice of female circumcision of girls and young women. Female genital mutilation (FGM), which is widely condemned by international public health experts as damaging to both physical and psychological health, was traditionally performed on young girls in northern, western and central ethnic groups, particularly in rural areas. Prior to the onset of the civil war in 1989, approximately 50% of women in rural areas between the ages of 8 and 18 years were subjected to FGM. A local organization, Human Rights Watch Women and Children, which does not receive government funding, launched a campaign during 1990 to eradicate FGM. The Association of Female Lawyers of Liberia (AFELL) has also spoken out against FGM.

Social structures and traditional institutions, such as the secret societies that often performed FGM as an initiation rite, were undermined by the war. Although many experts believe that the incidence of FGM dropped to as low as 10% by the end of the war, traditional societies are re-establishing themselves throughout the country, and the incidence of FGM is increasing. While the most extreme form of FGM, known as infibulation, is reportedly not practised, the Government has taken no action against FGM itself, nor has any UN agency.

The status of women varies according to region, ethnic group and religion. Before the outbreak of the civil war, women held a quarter of the professional and technical jobs in Monrovia. On the whole, women have not recovered from the setbacks caused by the civil war, when most schools were closed, and they could not carry out their traditional rôles in the production, allocation and sale of food.

Women who are married under civil law can inherit land and property. However, women who are married under traditional laws are considered to be the property of their husband, and are not entitled to inherit from their husband or to retain custody of their children if their husband dies. Women's organizations continued to press for legislation on behalf of inheritance rights in traditional marriages. There continued to be few programmes to help former combatants reintegrate into society, and there were none specifically to benefit former female combatants. However, several women's organizations advanced family welfare issues, helped to promote political reconciliation, and assisted in rehabilitating both former female combatants and women who were victims of the civil war. The Liberian chapter of the Mano River Women's Peace Network visited neighbouring countries during the year to promote regional peace and stability.

Throughout the year, professional women's groups – including lawyers, market women and businesswomen – remained vocal about their concerns regarding government corruption, the economy, security abuses, rape, domestic violence and children's rights. Government officials often responded negatively to public criticism. There were credible reports of harassment and possible surveillance of outspoken critics. In March 2004, the Government created the Ministry for Gender and Development, whose mandate included the promotion of the well-being of women and girls.

As one would expect, such a cavalier lack of concern for women's rights has been reflected in the rights of young children, especially girls. The latter are – even in 2007 – still often denied access to primary education, although the latter is enjoyed increasingly by male children. This, of course, does not augur well for the future of a democratic Liberia. It is no accident that universal access to primary education by 2015 was designated as one of the Millennium Development Goals (MDGs),[19] but there is also the clear realization that civil development depends on the participation of all citizens in the knowledge of their inalienable human rights.

References

1 Jesuit Refugee Service (JRS) *Six Months after the Official Closure of the IDP Camps. JRS assessment of the IDP (internally displaced people) return process in Liberia*; www.jesuit.org/faithandjustice/jts.htm-10k (accessed 3 February 2007).

2 Wikipedia. *History of Liberia*; http://memorg.loc.gov/ammem/gmdhtml/Liberia.htm (accessed 2 March 2007).

3 Human Rights Watch (2005) *Overview of Human Rights Record in Liberia*; http://hrw.org/English/docs/2005/01/13/liberia9879.htm (accessed 2 March 2007).

4 US Department of State. *Country Reports on Human Rights Practices – Liberia*; www.state.gov/g/drl/rls/hrrpt/2001/af/8388.htm (accessed 2 March 2007).

5 Ibid., p. 5.

6 Refugees International. *Must Boys be Boys?*; http://refugeesinternational.org/section/publications/pk_attitudes.html (accessed 3 March 2007).

7 Ibid., pp. 2–4.

8 Amnesty International. *AI Report in Liberia*; http://web.amnesty.org/report2003/lbr-summary-eng (accessed 3 March 2007).

9 Human Rights Watch. *Overview of Human Rights Issues in Liberia: essential background*; http://hrw.org/English/docs/2005/01/13/liberia9879.htm (accessed 2 March 2007).

10 Human Rights Watch. *Liberia: how to fight, how to kill*; www.eldis.org/static/DOC13981.htm (accessed 3 March 2007).

11 Human Rights Watch. *Liberia: human rights abuse by the Liberian Peace Council and the need for international oversight*; www.hrw.org/reports/1994/Liberia (accessed 28 February 2007).

12 Ibid., p. 16.

13 Reuters Information Services, Inc. *Sierra Leone Liberian News*; www.einnews.com/sierraleone/newsfeed.html (accessed 16 February 2007).

14 Human Rights Watch. *Liberia: human rights abuse by the Liberian Peace Council and the need for international oversight*, op. cit., p. 19.

15 Lutheran World Federation. *Situation of Human Rights in Liberia*. Address to the 61st Session of the UN Commission for Human Rights, 19 April 2005. www.lutheranworld.org/News/IWI/EN/1437-EN.html-20k (accessed 4 March 2007).

16 Refugees International. *Liberia: UMIL's crackdown on trafficking puts women at risk*; www.refugeesinternational.org/content/article/detail/960 (accessed 4 March 2007).

17 Refugees International. *Must Boys be Boys?*; www.refugeesinternational.org/section/publications/pk_attitudes (accessed 17 February 2007).

18 Ibid., pp. 7–8.

19 MacDonald T (2007) *The Global Human Right to Health: dream or possibility?* Oxford: Radcliffe Publishing; 2007. pp. 11, 12, 180.

Chapter 6

The Palestinians

Israel and the Palestine Territories

In entitling this chapter 'The Palestinians', the author is alluding to the fact that there is no such 'nation' as Palestine, but Palestinians do exist. Moreover, no analysis of breaches of the human rights of Palestinians could possibly be complete without reference to the State of Israel. However, that immediately confronts us with the internal conflict of the UN's rôles, as alluded to earlier. Israel is a state, and has been recognized as such by the UN since 1948. As such, the UN is committed to mediating its relationships with other nations, and vice versa. 'Palestine' is not a nation recognized as such by the UN but, under the mandate of the UN's Universal Declaration of Human Rights, the UN is committed to protecting the rights of Palestinians to human rights, such as access to primary healthcare (PHC). This represents an almost impossible tight-wire act for the UN to perform, because citizens of Israel have the status of nationhood to defend their national integrity, whereas the Palestinians do not. This difference alone does not result *ipso facto* in Palestinians having a lesser claim to human rights than do Israelis, but the fact that Israelis and Palestinians have been in protracted conflict as to how to share the small territory they occupy means that the technical difference of nationhood and non-nationhood becomes absolutely crucial as far as the UN's capacity to protect the human rights of Palestinians is concerned. It also means that we cannot properly analyse the issue without constant reference to Israel. The two are inseparable in that context.

Even a cursory glance at a map of the region (*see* Figure 6.1) illustrates yet another problem. The territory occupied by the Palestinians is not contiguous. Palestinians, for instance, are restricted in their ability to move from the West Bank to Gaza without having to enter Israeli territory when they leave the West Bank and then leave it when they get to Gaza. Given the level of conflict between the two peoples (both of them Semites, by the way!), this raises immense problems of passport control, rights of passage, etc.

Very brief conspectus of the roots of the conflict

A virtual library of scholarly books has been written about this, and hundreds of kilometres of newsprint and years of time in total devoted to media comment on it. The reader needs some contextual knowledge about these events in order to even begin to appreciate the analysis of human rights violations in Palestine and the international response to it. In the following very brief account, the author has tried to be impartial, but would recommend the reader to check other sources as well. In this account, the need for brevity has, I am sure, interfered substantially with both balance and detail. Despite this, the details of political, military and diplomatic convolutions have been so involved that even the briefest sketch given here will involve several pages of discourse. The reader may rest assured that it will all be necessary to sustain the focused human rights detail that follows.

Foundations of the Palestinian Territory

One cannot help but be amazed at how physically tiny the land area of Israel–Palestine is, when compared with the countries surrounding it. And yet it has assumed an importance in international affairs that can hardly be overstated. Many commentators have stated that all of the issues of contention in Iraq, Syria and the Middle East in general cannot be solved until a workable solution to the Israel–Palestine issue has been achieved. In total we are speaking of a land area of about 28,042 km^2. In 2006, Israel accounted for 22,072 km^2 of this, and the Palestinians controlled 5,970 km^2.

However, in the 1880s all of that territory was a part of the Ottoman Empire, referred to by the Ottomans as 'The Land of the Palestinians.' Yet it did not have the status of a nation in its own right. If it had done, things would certainly be different today.[1] For the sake of brevity, let us move forward to the twentieth century. The information that follows in this contextual introduction has been derived from a variety of easily accessible sources. One of the most comprehensive summaries is provided by the Middle East Research and Information Project (MERIP).[2]

At the start of the twentieth century, the Ottoman Empire ruled much of the Arab world, including the territory that is now Israel, the West Bank and Gaza. With the Allied victory in World War One, the area came under the control of the British and French, which both made contradictory promises to Arab and Zionist leaders about how – and by whom – the Mandate of Palestine was to be governed. At the time, 90% of the population were Arab. The Jewish community included long-time residents and new immigrants who were fleeing persecution in Russia and, later, in other parts of Europe. A 3-year uprising in the late 1930s against British rule and increased Jewish immigration resulted in a British proposal to partition Palestine into Jewish and Arab states. UN General Assembly Resolution 181 reaffirmed partition in 1947.

To gain some insight into the changing proportions of Israeli–Palestinian populations in 'Palestine' during those years, the reader is referred to Table 6.1.[3]

Initially, the trickle of Jewish immigration emerging in the 1880s met with little opposition from the local population. However, in the 1920s and 1930s, as anti-Semitism grew in Europe, Jewish immigration began to increase markedly, causing Arab resentment of British immigration policies to explode. Zionist agencies legally purchased land from absentee landlords and replaced the Arab tenants with European Jewish settlers. The influential Jewish trade union Histadrut demanded that Jewish employers hire only Jews. In 1929 and 1936 Arabs rioted in various cities, including Hebron, and murdered Jews.

From MERIP[2] we learn that the war that followed led to the establishment of the State of Israel. Part of the area that was designated for the Palestinian state was conquered by Israel, leading to the displacement of around 750,000 Palestinians. Gaza came under the control of Egypt, while Transjordan occupied and later illegally annexed the West Bank. Less than 20 years later, in the June 1967 war, Israel gained control of the rest of the former Mandate of Palestine (the Gaza Strip and the West Bank, including East Jerusalem, which Israel annexed in 1980), the Egyptian Sinai

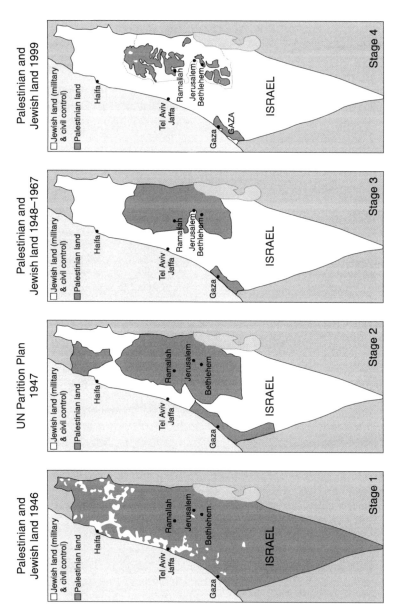

Figure 6.1: Jewish immigration to Palestine from 1946 to 1999 (Jewish areas are in white).

(since returned to Egypt), and the Syrian Golan Heights. UN Security Council Resolution 242 (22 November 1967), still not implemented, affirmed 'the inadmissibility of the acquisition of territory by war' and called upon Israel to withdraw 'from territories occupied in the recent conflict.' The 1970s and 1980s saw Arab–Israeli wars in 1973 and 1982, the 1978 Camp David Accords between Israel and Egypt, the outbreak of the first Palestinian Intifada in December 1987, and Yasser Arafat's condemnation of terrorism and recognition of the state of Israel in December 1988.

The Madrid peace conference followed the Gulf War in October 1991. A year later, secret Israeli–Palestinian talks began in Oslo, Norway, culminating in the September 1993 Declaration of Principles (DoP) on interim Palestinian self-government, signed by Arafat and Israeli Prime Minister Yitzhak Rabin. The DoP set out a process for transforming the nature of the Israeli occupation but left numerous issues unresolved, including the status of Jerusalem, the right of return for Palestinian refugees, the disposition of Israeli settlements (whose expansion continues until today) and final borders between Israel and a Palestinian state.

Under the DoP, Israel relinquished day-to-day authority over parts of the Gaza Strip and the West Bank to the Palestinian Authority, headed by Arafat, who returned to Gaza in 1994. However, ultimate power remained with Israel, which exercised its control by frequently sealing off the Palestinian-governed areas from the rest of the Occupied Territories and from Israel. Subsequent agreements in 1995 (Oslo II), 1998 (Wye River I) and 1999 (Wye River II) failed to resolve these issues. With Palestinian–Israeli negotiations stalled, US President Bill Clinton called a summit at Camp David in July 2000. After 2 weeks of intensive negotiation, the talks ended without a deal.

The rôle of Ariel Sharon

The infamous Ariel Sharon, whose predilection for violence against Palestinians had already been established by his attempts in 1971 to 'pacify' the population of Gaza by a combination of military repression and wholesale expulsion of Palestinians, was elected. He was first elected to the Knesset in 1977. Sharon was defence minister during the June 1982 Israeli invasion of Lebanon. An Israeli tribunal found Sharon indirectly responsible for the September 1982 massacre (by Lebanese militias under Israeli control) of thousands of Palestinian and Lebanese civilians living in the Sabra and Shatila refugee camps. As a result, Sharon was removed as defence minister but

Table 6.1: Jewish immigration to Palestine from 1870 to 1946

	Palestinians	*People of Jewish Faith*	
1870	367,224 (98%)	7,000 (2%)	Small native Jewish population; others from Europe started immigrating in the 1880s
1912	525,000 (93%)	40,000 (6%)	Prior to Balfour declaration
1925	598,000 (83%)	120,000 (17%)	Mass increase in Jewish immigrants entering Palestine
1946	1,237,000 (35%)	608,000 (35%)	Just before partition plan

retained a rôle in the Cabinet as 'minister without portfolio.' Survivors of the massacre filed briefs with a Belgian judge calling for indictment of Sharon and Lebanese militia commanders for war crimes. This effort came to nothing.

In the early 1990s, while serving as housing minister in Yitzhak Shamir's Likud government, he promoted a massive construction drive to increase Israeli settlement in the occupied West Bank and Gaza Strip. Sharon was a vociferous critic of Prime Minister Ehud Barak's decision to negotiate with the Palestinians. His provocative visit to al-Haram al-Sharif on 28 September 2000, and the harsh Israeli response to the protests that followed, helped to ignite the Palestinian uprising. When Barak resigned and called for new prime ministerial elections, Sharon won with 60% of the vote.

Assuming office in February 2001, Sharon increased repression against Palestinians, several times sending Israeli troops and tanks into Palestinian-controlled cities, villages and refugee camps, including the full-scale invasions of West Bank population centres in March and April 2002. Since the September 11 events in the USA, Sharon had ratcheted up rhetoric that pinned the blame for Israeli–Palestinian violence on the person of Yasser Arafat, and equated Israeli offensives in the Occupied Territories with George W Bush's 'war on terrorism.' At that time, the Bush administration and Sharon's Labour coalition partners restrained him from expelling Arafat from Palestinian lands altogether and completely dismantling the Palestinian Authority (PA).

Sharon had clearly articulated his refusal to compromise over Jerusalem or to withdraw Israeli forces from more than the 42% of the West Bank and 60% of Gaza now under nominal PA administration – should negotiations begin again. He had also refused to discuss return or reparations for Palestinian refugees who were expelled in 1948. The reader no doubt realizes that Ariel Sharon's stroke on 4 January 2006, and the election of the Kadilla Party under Ehud Ohmet's leadership on 8 April 2006, profoundly changed the Israeli political scene. This and the electoral victory of Hamas in the Palestinian Occupied Territories are issues that will be dealt with below.

The rôle of Yasser Arafat

From the beginning, the Palestinian uprising expressed cumulative popular anger at both the violence of the Israeli occupation and the compromises that Yasser Arafat seemed to be willing to make on basic Palestinian national rights – such as the establishment of a viable sovereign state, the right of return for Palestinian refugees displaced in 1948 and 1967, and Palestinian sovereignty in East Jerusalem. The Palestinian protests following Sharon's visit to al-Haram al-Sharif were spearheaded by Islamists and students – the sectors of the population among whom Arafat enjoys the least influence. Since September 2000, Arafat had followed the uprising and guerrilla war, not led it.

Of course, the PA was not a national government,[4] but it did provide municipal services and attempted to maintain order in the areas under its control. Before and during the Intifada, Palestinians had repeatedly complained about the PA's inadequate services and uncertain leadership. The PA's top ranks, including Arafat, mostly belonged to Fatah, the largest faction of the Palestine Liberation Organization (PLO). Many junior officers of the PA security services were also Fatah members. However, Fatah was independent of the PA, and Arafat did not control the entire faction through a single chain of command. The uprising pushed militant local leaders of

Fatah to the forefront. The Fatah militants' demands – full Israeli withdrawal, removal of settlements, a sovereign state with its capital in Jerusalem, and the right of return for refugees – are the demands of the Intifada.

When Palestinian resistance began to be punctuated by Israeli incursions into and reoccupation of Palestinian-controlled areas, even Palestinians who were critical of PA rule rallied behind Arafat. Palestinians feared that Israel sought to replace Arafat – still their elected leader despite his shortcomings – or to destroy the PA altogether. Apart from Palestinians' resistance to the idea that their leader should be chosen by outside forces, no other figure back then had emerged as a potential replacement. Arafat's ever-tightening 'isolation' in his Ramallah headquarters since December 2001 further enhanced his popularity, in contrast to Israel's apparent intentions.

Sharon demanded, with US backing, that Arafat stop the uprising and publicly forbid all forms of 'violence', not just suicide bombings. However, Israeli assaults destroyed many PA security installations and pushed many security personnel in the direction of the militants. Even if the PA had been able to maintain 'absolute calm', to do so would have strengthened the voices that described the PA as a proxy police force for the Israeli occupation, and once again endangered Arafat's status as leader of the Palestinian cause.

In early 2002, a splinter from the secular Fatah movement called the al-Aqsa Martyrs Brigades began carrying out suicide bombings inside Israel, probably in retaliation for Israel's assassination of one of its leaders, Raed Karmi. Evidence purporting to show a direct link between this group's suicide bombings and Arafat is so far inconclusive. Other Palestinian factions have expressly forsworn attacks on civilians inside the 1967 borders of Israel, although they have conducted suicide operations targeted at settlers and soldiers in the West Bank and Gaza.[5]

Throughout 2001 and into 2002, following the election of Ariel Sharon. Israeli operations increasingly targeted the infrastructure of the PA and its police and security forces, and eroded the boundaries separating PA-ruled areas from areas of full Israeli military control. The Israel Defense Forces (IDF) carried out armed incursions into PA-controlled areas, bulldozed Palestinian houses and crops, conducted systematic assassinations of key Fatah and Hamas militants, and fired rockets at PA police stations from F-16 warplanes. These incursions resulted in the wholesale violation of Palestinian human rights.

Following several suicide bombings in early December, Ariel Sharon declared that Arafat and the PA were no longer partners for negotiations, and placed Arafat under virtual house arrest in Ramallah. The IDF began a series of deeper military incursions into PA-controlled areas, repositioned its tanks and troops to new positions and conducted mass arrests.

The growing Israeli military encirclement of and penetration into PA-ruled areas entered a new phase in March and April 2002, when Israeli forces responded to suicide bombings with two massive invasions of Palestinian towns and refugee camps.

On 29 March 2002, Israel launched its largest military operation since the invasion of Lebanon in 1982 by sending armoured divisions into Ramallah and fully reoccupying the city. Israeli forces attacked the presidential compound, and held Arafat hostage with no electricity, water or telephone lines. The IDF then invaded and reoccupied nearly all of the PA self-rule areas, including the cities of Bethlehem, Jenin, Tulkaram, Qalqilya and Nablus. Soldiers imposed tight 24-hour curfews and cut the electricity and water supply to the population. Palestinians – both militiamen and some policemen given arms by Israeli–Palestinian peace agreements – resisted the offensives with force, particularly during pitched battles in Nablus and Jenin.[6]

The Israeli operation has been characterized by massive tank deployments and intensive shelling of PA and civilian buildings, house-to-house searches, confiscations of arms and mass arrests of Palestinian men between the ages of 14 and 45 years, who were rounded up, stripped, blindfolded and taken away to undisclosed detention centres.

Forcible intimidation, including several IDF shootings, prevented journalists, observers and medical personnel from gathering full details of this offensive. However, multiple reports confirmed instances of ambulance workers being unable to reach wounded Palestinians, Israeli soldiers raiding hospitals, and troops using Palestinians as human shields – all contraventions of the Geneva Conventions. Numerous Palestinian civilians were shot dead during the invasions or in violation of Israeli-imposed curfews.

In mid-April 2002, the Red Cross warned of a severe humanitarian crisis in West Bank towns and refugee camps due to the lack of food, water and electricity, and army restrictions on the movement of residents and rescue workers.[7]

Impact of Israeli occupation

Throughout the 2002 uprising (referred to as the Second Intifada) and war of attrition, Israel used much greater force than it generally employed during the First Intifada (from 1987 to 1993). Numerous respected human rights organizations, including Amnesty International, Human Rights Watch and Physicians for Human Rights, conducted studies that showed IDF soldiers employing excessive force in their suppression of Palestinian demonstrators. Their reports cited (among other violations) the use of live ammunition against unarmed civilians, attacks on medical personnel and installations, the use of snipers with high-powered rifles, and attacks on children.[8]

Israel has regularly closed its borders to over 125,000 Palestinian workers – especially Gazans – who rely on jobs inside Israel for their modest incomes. The UN estimated that Palestinian workers lost between US$ 2.4 and 3.2 billion in income between October 2000 and September 2001 due to closures. Cautious statements by the UN and the World Bank in April 2002 put the unemployment rate across the Palestinian Territories at 50%. Israeli blockades around Palestinian towns, even those that were not reoccupied during the invasions, sometimes cause severe shortages of necessities such as flour, sugar and gasoline. These 'internal closures,' enforced by a series of checkpoints, disrupt normal civilian life and prevent ready access to workplaces, hospitals and schools even in times of relative quiet.[9]

What are settlements?

The Mitchell report – the centrepiece of current US diplomacy on Israel–Palestine – called for a complete freeze on building of Jewish settlements in the Occupied Territories. However, Peace Now, an extra-parliamentary Israeli activist group, had documented the establishment of 34 new settlements in the West Bank and the Gaza Strip under Sharon.[10]

Settlements are scattered throughout Palestinian lands that were occupied by Israel during the June 1967 war, including East Jerusalem. Since 1967, successive Israeli administrations have expanded the settlements in the name of both ideology and 'security.' In ideological terms, historically endorsed by the Likud Party, settlements secure Jewish sovereignty over the entire biblical 'Land of Israel', demonstrating the power of Jewish nationalism. In security terms, historically endorsed by the Labour Party, settlements ensure Israel's permanent military control west of the Jordan River. Regardless of rationale, settlements have been used to alter the demography of the Palestinian Territories and preclude Palestinian self-determination. In effect, this means that thousands of Palestinians have been displaced, their olive groves destroyed and their human rights compromised on the basis of biblical history, the geographical details of which are not even regarded as reliable by most theological scholars!

The first wave of state-sponsored settlement began in 1967 under the Labour administration. Settlement growth was limited during this period, but the ground-work was laid for more. Labour used 'security' arguments to justify settlement, but allowed messianic groups such as Gush Emunim to establish claims in the Palestinian Territories. Intensive development began in 1977 under Likud, which used the ideological biblical rationale to justify heavy investment in the settlement infrastructure. Construction increased again in the early 1990s, during which time the settler population rose by around 10% annually. Since the Oslo 'peace process' began in 1993, the settler population has nearly doubled. Under the Labour administration of Yitzhak Rabin, settlements grew at a rate unprecedented in Israel's occupation. Ariel Sharon's government vowed to support the 'natural growth' of settlements – a term that belies both the magnitude and the political context of the planned expansion that is occurring. Currently, around 400,000 Israeli Jews live in the Occupied Territories – approximately 200,000 in the West Bank, 200,000 in East Jerusalem and 6,000 in the Gaza Strip.[11]

Religious nationalists represent the minority among settlers. The majority was lured to the settlements by government stipends and favourable mortgages. For them, the settlements are like suburbs within commuting distance of Israel's major cities – with commuting made possible by restricted-access roads that bypass Palestinian towns. Public opinion polls show that most Israelis support a freeze of settlement activity in return for a ceasefire. Such polls are misleading, because settlements in the 'Greater Jerusalem' area (which house the majority of settlers) have been deemed virtually 'non-negotiable' by most secular Israelis, as well as by Labour and Likud. Most so-called 'settlements' are actually outposts consisting of no more than a cluster of mobile homes set up near more substantial settlements. The commitment of successive Labour governments to dismantling settlements has often focused solely on these ad hoc units.

It is important to note that all settlements in the Occupied Territories violate international law and continuously infringe on Palestinian human rights. Article 49 of the Fourth Geneva Convention prohibits an occupying state from transferring parts of its own civilian population into the territory that it occupies. International humanitarian law prohibits permanent changes within an occupied territory that are not intended to benefit the local population. Israel blatantly discriminates between Jews and Palestinians in its planning and building policies in the Occupied Territories. Throughout the Oslo 'peace process', the USA accommodated Israel's refusal to halt settlement growth. George W Bush called for the removal of settlements in a Rose Garden speech in April 2002, but stopped short of classifying them as illegal.[12]

Rôle of the UN

Since Israel's 1967 occupation of the West Bank, Gaza and East Jerusalem, there has been an almost unanimous international consensus on how to resolve the crisis – an international conference based on international law and UN resolutions. However, Israel disagreed, and this was backed by the USA. In fact, as the reader will see, Palestinian authorities have on several occasions actually made it clear that they would welcome UN peacekeepers, or even observers, into the area. Israel has always refused.

The USA, while continuing to mention UN resolutions, has kept Israel–Palestine diplomacy under its own control for most of the period since 1967. Washington – Israel's major financial, diplomatic and military backer – claimed the rôle of the 'honest broker.' The actual requirements of international law and existing UN resolutions (such as 194, ensuring the right of Palestinian refugees to return and receive compensation) were sidelined in favour of US-brokered talks between Israel – the strongest military power in the Middle East and the 17th wealthiest country in the world – and the stateless Palestinians living under occupation or in exile.

As far back as 1991, in the Madrid Talks, the US–Israeli Memorandum of Understanding stated explicitly that the UN would have no rôle. Nor was the UN involved in the Oslo process that began in 1993. The failed 2000 Camp David summit ignored the UN altogether.[13]

In October 2000, when 14 out of 15 members of the UN Security Council voted to condemn Israel's use of excessive force against civilians, it was the USA alone that abstained. The then US Ambassador Richard Holbrooke threatened to veto any further resolution. The Israeli government rejected any fact-finding commission that might be authorized by the UN, insisting that it would be nothing but a 'kangaroo court', and instead demanded an investigation led by the USA. Shortly thereafter, the parties agreed to accept a fact-finding commission led by former US Senator George Mitchell, not under UN auspices.

During the last months of President Bill Clinton's administration, UN Secretary General Kofi Annan assumed an unprecedented, albeit significantly constrained rôle in negotiations. At the Palestinian–Israeli negotiations at Taba in early January 2001, European and UN officials were far more visible than the US diplomats hovering in the background.

Further US diplomatic involvement

When George W Bush's administration took over, there seemed to be even more potential for a greater UN (and perhaps European) rôle. The Bush foreign policy team asserted its intention to avoid Clinton's micro-management of the peace process. However, on 28 March 2001 the USA vetoed a Security Council resolution that would have established a UN observer mission to provide international protection for the Palestinians, as well as an end to closures of the territories and full cessation of settlement activity.

As the war of attrition ground on, and especially during Sharon's major invasions of

Palestinian-controlled territory, there was mounting domestic and foreign pressure on the Bush administration to 're-engage' in controlling the conflict. The administration responded in part by endorsing, for the first time, the idea of a Palestinian state. However, the missions of General Anthony Zinni and Secretary of State Colin Powell, like most of the Bush administration's diplomacy, have focused only on ending the immediate violence.

Until the spring of 2002, public and official attention focused on the US-backed Mitchell report. The Mitchell report called for 'ending violence' and returning to the 'normal' conditions of 27 September 2000, before the uprising began. Later confidence-building measures were to include a complete freeze on Israeli settlement construction, but Mitchell said nothing about occupation overall. While both Israel and the PA accepted the Mitchell recommendations 'with reservations', Israel explicitly rejected the complete settlement freeze.

Following the suicide bombing on 1 June 2001 that left 21 young Israelis dead, the two sides agreed to new security talks led by CIA Director George Tenet. The Tenet agreement called for increased Palestinian efforts to clamp down on resistance activities, while asking Israel simply to redeploy tanks and heavy weapons back to the positions occupied before 28 September 2000. Both the Mitchell report and the Tenet 'ceasefire' plan explained the current conflict as a security crisis – rather than a political crisis of the occupation, and one that requires a political solution.

Heeding strongly pro-Israel officials in the Defence Department and the Vice President's office, the Bush administration described both Israeli invasions of PA-controlled territory in March and April 2002 as 'self-defence.' On both occasions, the administration only called for a halt to the offensives when it feared that Israel would cross the 'red line' of expelling Arafat and completely destroying the PA.

Several administration actions belied the media's representation of Bush's response to the invasions as 'tough on Israel.' US ambassador to the UN John Negroponte blocked the passage of a Security Council resolution demanding that Israel withdraw from West Bank towns 'immediately', substituting the words 'without delay' in the final draft. This phrase was interpreted by Israel as permission to continue the operation. A Defense Department official was quoted in the *Boston Globe* as saying that Powell's arrival in Jerusalem on 11 April 2002 was postponed for several days to allow Israel time to complete its offensive. Certainly Powell's lackadaisical itinerary undercut Bush's belated use of the term 'immediately' in his calls upon Israel to withdraw from reoccupied West Bank cities.[14]

> The best hope for lasting peace is the insertion of UN peacekeepers invested with a mandate to implement international law's requirements of ending occupation, along with UN-led negotiations over refugees, Jerusalem and other outstanding issues. A growing international consensus supports this option, but so far, the Bush administration has said only that US observers might be deployed to enforce a ceasefire. Though Powell has spoken of coupling implementation of the Tenet and Mitchell plans with a 'political' initiative, the outlines of the administration's ideas are murky at best. The Bush administration continues to view the 'storm of violence' in Israel–Palestine as a security problem, rather than a political one.[2]

As 2002 drew to a close, both Israel and the USA had lost faith in Arafat, and both refused to negotiate with him. They tended to favour a rising star in Palestinian diplomacy, Mohamoud Abbas, who was one of the few remaining founder members of the Fatah Party. Pressure was brought to bear on Arafat to appoint him as Prime Minister, and Arafat did so on 19 March 2003.

However, Arafat repeatedly tried to undermine Abbas' authority, and in October 2003 he resigned as Prime Minister, citing internal incitement against his government. Much of this had come from another Palestinian grouping, Hamas, which virtually opposed any cooperation with Israel. However, Abbas was not out of politics for long. As has already been mentioned in this chapter, Yasser Arafat died in November 2004, and in January 2005 new elections were called. Fatah, under Abbas, was elected.

The political situation today

This result greatly alarmed Israel, and also the USA, because – in keeping with his Fatah background – Abbas did not even recognize Israel's right to exist. This rendered further negotiations rather difficult. Moreover, Israel – backed by the USA, Russia, the EU countries and NATO (known as 'The Quartet') – froze Palestinian access to funding from outside the territory. In a very real sense, this constituted a bald attempt to starve out a democratically elected government, and it puts the UN in a most difficult position. It has done nothing to enforce the release of Palestinian money and, as of now, there is no funding for much of Palestinian social and civic infrastructure. Medical care cannot be sustained, nor can education. This constitutes a blatant violation of human rights.

The foregoing 'contextual material' has been kept as brief as possible. It has left out a great deal, including the destructive 'civil conflict' in the Palestinian Authority between Fatah and Hamas and many other retrograde developments caused largely, in this author's view, by the refusal of Israel and the USA to recognize the legitimately elected Hamas Government and the funding of Abbas (of the Fatah faction), while withholding legitimate funding from the PA. This surely in itself constitutes an international crime, and is certainly a violation of many of the human rights supposedly protected by the UN's own Universal Declaration. The situation has been made worse by the efforts of the USA to bring the EU and other individual nations into line with this policy of withholding external funding from the Palestinians. Whatever objections one may have to the Palestinians' choice of Hamas, it was legally and fairly elected. It was therefore up to Israel, the USA and their backers to then use all legitimate means available to persuade Hamas to act in accordance with the peace process. The UN could have played a major rôle in this. Let us now finally turn our attention to the human rights issues in Palestine for which this lengthy discourse so far has only set the context.

Access to PHC and other health services in the Palestinian Territories

As of mid-2007, the situation can only be described as dire, and worsening. In fact, on 15 November 2006 the International Commission of the Red Cross (ICRC) stated that there had been a sharp decline in Palestinian health services since 2003, when it had already been described as 'seriously deficient.'[15] So acute has the situation become, in late 2006, due to Israel and the Quartet running a campaign of withholding foreign funding, that the ICRC found itself financing – but only to a severely limited extent – some critical PHC services. It was able to give some support to four hospitals and 30 clinics, and to pay the salaries of some Palestine Red Crescent Society (PRCS) medical staff. It has pushed its disposable finances to the limit in an attempt to alleviate serious financial deficit in the supply of drugs and disposables to Ministry of Health (MoH) sectors. The situation has become very much exacerbated by the fact that, after 6 months without pay, most branches of the PA health services went on strike on 23 August 2006.

One report issued by the ICRC on 15 November 2006 dealt explicitly with the growing collapse of government health services in the West Bank.[16] ICRC health teams visited 10 surgical MoH hospitals between 22 September and 11 November. In addition, all PRCS hospitals, the sole UN-funded hospital, and selected private and charitable hospitals were also visited in order to understand where patients currently go in order to receive essential hospital services. The report presents a qualitative account based on observations and interviews with hospital staff. Quantitative analysis compares 2005 hospital activities and other activities since the onset of the strike. Although the MoH has provided some statistics, the limits of its contribution are indicative of the system's breakdown. Whenever MoH statistics could not be obtained, the ICRC sought to obtain the relevant information directly from concerned hospitals. It cross-checked this information with whatever had been received from the MoH.

The ICRC report is of limited use in analysis because it was restricted to hospitals. However, we are able to get a more comprehensive view of the whole PHC situation by virtue of the fact that the ICRC asked all of the hospital staff whom they questioned about the broader issues in considerable detail. The effect of the strike was clearly evident at all levels. It resulted in a decline in service provision, both in hospitals and in outside PHC. For instance, on 23 August 2006:

- all outpatient departments (OPD) closed
- all elective surgery ceased
- only life-saving emergencies were admitted to hospital
- most PHC provision stopped. Within 2 weeks, some of the staff agreed to work on alternate Wednesdays, and immunizations were provided on alternate Saturdays in some clinics.

By mid-September the situation had deteriorated further:

- normal maternity services stopped
- only late-stage labour (cervix dilated 5 cm or more) were admitted for delivery
- all elderly and chronic patients were discharged
- certain critical specialized services, such as oncology and haemodialysis, continued to be offered only in major referral hospitals.

By 15 October 2006, only 'top-level' life-saving emergencies were being admitted. The category 'top-level' was decided solely by the healthcare professional receiving the patient – there were no specific criteria! In addition, only 'on-call' staff were permitted in the hospitals. Those patients who did attend government hospitals had to receive treatment with greatly reduced staffing levels. Obviously this has implications for the safety and efficacy of the treatment. Only 3 weeks later, by 7 November 2006, matters had worsened further. Hospital emergency rooms were ordered to close and to stop receiving maternity patients, and all remaining PHC services were closed.

The ICRC report also documented the following 'extraneous' effects of the financial crisis.

- Staff transport to and from hospitals was problematic due to the staff's reduced ability to pay for transportation. Coping mechanisms included use of ambulances, staff grouping, and sharing of travelling expenses.
- Contractors without payment provided food for the hospital patients and the staff on duty on a credit basis. In some hospitals, the community provided additional support.
- Staff were present in all emergency rooms (ERs). However, some ERs had their lights turned off and their doors closed. In one hospital, emergency equipment was locked away.
- All but one of the ERs visited were empty of patients. On one occasion, an emergency case came in and the staff reacted quickly.
- Staff in 4 out of 10 hospitals were threatened by relatives and patients over patients being turned away from hospital.
- There was a high level of tension among staff in some hospitals. This was due to disagreement over the category of top emergency cases allowed for admission. No clear definition of 'top-level emergency' was made available to the staff.
- Relatives damaged one PRCS ambulance when a patient was denied admission.
- Adequate supplies of drugs and disposables were available in all hospitals, because of the very low level of activity. When specific emergency items were needed, ambulances referring patients passed by the Central Medical Store (CMS) in Ramallah. The CMS had not delivered supplies since the strike began.
- Six hospitals reported problems with maintenance and repair of equipment. In many cases, spare parts were unavailable, or technicians were not present to make routine repairs or carry out urgent maintenance. In one hospital, the staff had reported a problem with a ventilator in use in the morning. By the afternoon, during the ICRC visit, no technician had yet arrived.
- In most hospitals, electricity and fuel for generators were available. However, many hospitals raised concerns over the availability of fuel for heating over the winter months.
- Community support was instrumental in keeping some hospitals functioning.

In the light of all the above, the question must arise as to where people from the community could go for explicit medical intervention or even for more routine PHC. Most do not now bother trying to go to the government hospitals. Those who can afford it try the NGO-run facilities, but very few people can afford the fees. In the Palestinian Territories as a whole, it is estimated by the health professionals who were questioned that as much as 70% of the population lives below the poverty line![17] Typical fees charged by private hospitals for common services are US$ 70–186 for a normal delivery, US$ 300–700 for a Caesarean section, and even US$ 5–12 for a private consultation. As well as the cost barrier itself, most charitable hospitals and clinics only have a licence for obstetrics, gynaecology and paediatrics, but not for overnight stays, internal medicine or surgery. There are private hospitals, of course, but these charge much more than the NGO-run or charitable hospitals.

As if all of this does not represent a sufficiently egregious violation of basic human rights, people seeking urgent medical services are routinely restricted by Israeli checkpoints and by the West Bank Barrier itself. In fact, the birth of babies at checkpoints is sufficiently common for this author to have seen several birth certificates stating a specified checkpoint as the place of birth.

The situation prior to the strike

Even prior to the strike, PHC in the Palestinian Territories was seriously restricted, but after the Hamas election victory, the refusal of Israel and the Quartet to allow funding into the territory has rendered an already bad situation critical. The following WHO details describe healthcare provision in the Palestinian Territories prior to the cutting off of funds and the subsequent strike 6 months later.[18]

In 2005, the Ministry of Health (MoH) served a population of about 4 million in total, with 2.7 million in the West Bank. It operated more than 60% of PHC facilities, 60% of beds in general hospitals and 47% of all maternity beds. In total, it covered approximately 65% of all health needs. Every month around 35,000 people were admitted to hospitals and, of these, the MoH dealt with nearly 65%, and 85,000 people or more received specialist outpatient care, about 74% of them in MoH hospitals. A total of around 11,000 people underwent surgical operations, nearly 75% of them in MoH hospitals, and around 9,000 women delivered babies, more than half of them in MoH hospitals and clinics.

As far as NGO facilities were concerned, the WHO as cited above provides the following information. NGOs provide 31% of beds in general hospitals and 26% of maternity beds. The UN Work Relief Agency (UNWRA) manages 1.8% of hospital beds and 2% of maternity beds. In addition, NGOs look after about 12% of household health services in the occupied territories. In the West Bank, the rate of use of NGO health services is just over 13%. NGOs account for 30% of PHC services. NGO health services seem to be favoured by wealthier Palestinians, and private hospitals accommodate the remaining 20%.

The strains thus imposed on restricted resources seriously compromise the basic human right to PHC. For instance, it has now become common for emergency patients, even after struggling to get through Israeli checkpoints, to be denied access to emergency services when they do get through. Although there had been a considerable increase in normal deliveries in Palestinian Care's hospitals and charitable hospitals, these facilities cannot possibly cope with the usual demand. If they are wealthy enough, patients may try private clinics, but these have much poorer maternity safety records than MoH hospitals. Alternatively, there is the option of home delivery. However, especially under present conditions of seriously restricted access to electricity, safe water supplies, etc., home births can be fraught with danger.

All of this will inevitably result in unnecessary increases in maternal and child mortality. For instance, an increase in mortality rate was recorded at two MoH hospitals in September 2006, from 2.1% to 3.7% in one and from 1.3% to 3.6% in the other. The strike has greatly increased waiting times for surgery, and this has increased mortality and morbidity rates. Overworked doctors forced to work in over-crowded facilities have been far more likely to perform Caesarean section rather than waiting an unpredictable time for normal birth. For instance, one charitable hospital doubled its rate of Caesarean sections during September 2006, with 220 normal deliveries and 59

Caesareans (compared with 120 normal deliveries and 13 Caesareans before the strike).

As a result of closures, the provision of routine monitoring of chronic illnesses, and antenatal and postnatal care, has been stopped. The facilities of the NGOs UNWRA and PRCS together cannot possibly provide an adequate substitute for MoH hospital services. They do not offer enough beds, for one thing, to say nothing of inadequate resources for obstetric-gynaecology work or paediatrics. Obviously the inability of potential patients to pay the fees is a further deterrent. However, matters grew even worse, for on 7 November 2006 the labour unions made further cuts in the provision of services. Such PHC services as vaccinations and drug dispensing for the chronically ill were stopped. Inpatient figures in 10 government hospitals during 2006 in the West Bank steadily dropped from 223 on 7 November to 144 on 12 November!

Table 6.2 lists the 10 hospitals concerned, and also shows how the figures compared with those for 2005.

Table 6.2: Inpatient numbers at 10 West Bank hospitals, comparing November 2006 figures with those for November 2005[19]

Date/hospital	7 Nov	8 Nov	9 Nov	11 Nov	12 Nov	Average number of in-patients in November
Amira Alia	57	36	30	24	20	185
Rafidia	19	17	15	12	20	142
Khalil Suliman	17	14	8	0	0	103
Jericho	20	7	5	6	6	24
Ramallah	63	61	57	54	70	132
Al Hussein	35	25	22	27	23	98
Salfit	8	1	2	0	1	8
Qalqilya	1	1	0	3	3	6
Yatta	3	1	0	3	1	14
Thabet Thabet	?	7	5	5	?	67
Total	223	170	144	134	144	779

In 2003, the estimated child immunization rate was 98%, and by 2005 it had increased to 100%.[15] By September 2006, it stood at 98% again. However, given the lack of immunization provision, even if it is restored within a few weeks, this will bring about a recurrence of preventable diseases. Moreover, this recurrence will occur in a context of acute deprivation, which means that there will be a legacy of mortality and mobility of far greater proportions than would prevail in less fraught circumstances. Likewise, what about the chronically ill, such as those with diabetes (types 1 and 2), cancer patients, people in need of regular dialysis, etc.?

Attendant upon all of the above, ordinary civil life will be jeopardized by the fact that no births are currently being recorded. Water supplies have been heavily polluted because of the Israeli destruction of the electrical infrastructure, and water is no longer routinely tested for potability. The core infrastructural damage has prevented safe storage of meats, dairy products, etc., and there is no longer any systematic public health surveillance.

The following three brief accounts exemplify the grievous impact of all that has been described above. They are drawn from the ICRC West Bank report cited above.[20]

Case 1

After a home delivery, a newborn was admitted to a private hospital after developing breathing problems. The baby was treated and taken out of the hospital against medical advice hours later. The family could not afford to pay the hospital fees. A day later, the baby was returned to the hospital in breathing distress. The baby suffered respiratory arrest and developed brain damage. The baby spent a few days in the hospital and was discharged with a feeding tube. The family did not have to pay. However, days later the baby was readmitted after aspirating (milk entered the lungs) days previously, and later died.

Case 2

Two pregnant women were turned away from the emergency department, but they arrived back at the emergency department hours later. Both had developed complications during this waiting time. Both women had emergency Caesarean sections, and both babies died.

Case 3

A 75-year-old woman died 15 minutes after she was denied access to the emergency department.

As the reader will appreciate from previous chapters, and as the present author has explicitly demonstrated in a previous book,[21] the link between domestic life, financial security and health is a fundamental one. We shall now consider this critical contextual aspect to health in the Palestinian Territories.

Household economy and health

As we have seen above, the lives of people resident in the Occupied Territories of Palestine were already difficult, but became much more so with their election of Hamas to government, and the reaction of Israel and the Quartet in restricting the Palestinian Authority from accessing its out-of-country sources of income. To set the broader context, though, the author invites the reader to briefly retrace events from 2002. Details of all of this are available in the ICRC Report on Economic Assessment in the 2006 Palestinian Territories,[22] and a summary of those findings follows.

In 2002, the situation deteriorated further in the West Bank. The deployment of the Israel Defense Forces (IDF), curfews, closures and other restrictions on movement had a severe impact on every facet of Palestinian life. In response, in 2003 the ICRC launched its Rural Relief Programme in the West Bank. This provided assistance to 30,000 households in rural areas, and set up a voucher programme for 20,000 households in urban centres. A total of 50,000 households, or approximately 300,000 individuals, were helped.

The years 2004–2005 saw some improvement in the overall situation, although many specific areas, such as Nablus City and Jenin District, continued to suffer economically. As a result of continuing restrictions on movement, areas south of Nablus City have developed smaller urban centres to minimize the overall effects of the closures on trade and access to essential services. These emerging urban centres cater largely to the agro-trade, but also provide warehouses for large traders. Reference documents and key informants indicate that these small urban centres cannot replace the services offered by Nablus City.

The measures taken by Israel and the international community following the election of the Hamas government on 1 April 2006 had a negative effect on the economy. According to a World Bank study in April 2006, the suspension of revenue transfers by Israel in March, the tightening of Israeli security measures (including closures), the increased restrictions on the movement of people and goods, and the reduced flow of aid observed in 2006, have already caused severe economic damage in the Palestinian Territories in 2007. By 2006, the real Gross Domestic Product (GDP) per capita had declined by 27%, and personal income had decreased by 30%. This abrupt contraction of economic activity is, by definition, equivalent to a deep economic depression.

Until the recently imposed financial restrictions, Value Added Tax (VAT) and customs transfers and donor payments accounted for up to 75% of the PA's budget. The loss of these sources of income, together with the refusal of banks to transfer funds to the PA as of March 2006, have seriously undermined the functioning of the PA's institutions, and the consequences in humanitarian terms have been severe. The loss of PA salaries has had a direct impact both on the cash-starved local economy and on society as a whole. Throughout the Palestinian Territories, adverse socio-economic conditions are now identified as the primary cause of insecurity, ill health and death. Collectively, they constitute so many breaches of the Universal Declaration of Human Rights that the lack of international concern or action is an issue. It is all meeting the political and ideological needs of Israel and the Quartet at the proximal level and, one suspects, of the neoliberal agenda at the distal level. Israeli military damage alone has been pivotal, for instance. In Gaza, the extensive damage caused by Israeli military operations in the summer of 2006 has further undermined development. For instance, the destruction of its power plant has increased Gaza's requests to Israel for electricity. Similarly, the reduction in Gaza's exports to Israel has weakened local production capacity, cut revenues and increased dependence on imports from Israel.

According to the World Bank, achieving a desirable level of economic growth will depend on Israel resuming its transfer of fiscal revenues, rolling back the current system of restrictions on movement, and maintaining or increasing labour access to Israel, as well as sustaining high rates of donor and private investment. Whether all this will happen by the end of 2007 is at best doubtful.

In summary, the ICRC analysis tended to focus on two 'zones', namely agricultural (or 'Agro', as they call it) and urban.

1 *Agro zone:* This zone consisted of all agricultural areas in the four districts assessed. The areas are not geographically contiguous. Agriculture is the main source of livelihood in this zone. Additional economic activities include trade, day labour and other paid work in both the private and public sectors.
2 *Urban zone:* The areas that make up this zone are also not contiguous. Most

income opportunities are linked to trade, commerce and employment in the formal and informal sectors. Some agricultural activities play an important rôle in Salfit and Beni Naim.

In both cases, it can readily be appreciated that the impacts on health, security, education and all human rights have been, and continue to be, immense. As the report explains, the assessment was conducted in four locations in the Gaza Strip, namely Beach Refugee Camp in Gaza, Alqarara and Al Mawasi in Khan Yunis, and Arayba in Rafah. With the exception of the camp, all of these areas depended largely on either fishing or agriculture. Other sources of income included public-sector employment and small-scale trading activities.

Analysis of the ICRC findings

Even the most superficial analysis of the ICRC findings shows how desperate the situation has become, not only for the poor Palestinians, but for the health and human rights infrastructure of the Palestinian Territories as a whole. The following is a brief summary.

In the West Bank, 'poor' (as defined by local agencies) households account for approximately 48–56% of the population in the agricultural zone and 42–49% of the population in the urban zone. The corresponding figures for 'very poor' households were 14–18% and 14–17%, respectively. Their definitions of 'poor' and 'very poor' were as follows. 'Poor' households earned US$ 116–232 per month, whereas 'very poor' households were defined as earning less than US$ 116 per month, with US$ equivalencies calculated at prevailing international banking rates.

Generally, households in the Gaza Strip are even more economically deprived – with conditions deteriorating by the day – than those in the West Bank. And in the latter, conditions already represent unacceptable compromises with basic health rights. The ICRC Reports showed that for Gaza the following applied:

Households categorized as 'better-off' in Gaza had an income greater than US$ 232–348. A similar threshold was used for 'middle' households in the West Bank, while 'better-off' households in the West Bank were described as earning more than US$ 464 per month. Meanwhile, 'middle' households in Gaza had similar cash income levels to 'poor' households in the West Bank (i.e. US$ 116–232 per month). In all the areas that were assessed, the majority of the households were either 'poor' or 'very poor.' They represented approximately 58–64% of the community and earned less than US$ 116 per month. These earnings do not include support from relatives, or formal or informal assistance, which constitute additional sources of income both in cash and in kind.

Directly threatening not only PHC but also health generally is the fact that hygiene expenses are being steadily cut back throughout the Palestinian Territories. Educational expenses are also increasingly being curtailed. In the urban zones, housing is a critical consideration, but it is a less acute problem in the rural areas, where 90% of households own their own dwellings, however rudimentary. Yet the habit of the Israeli Defence Forces (IDF) of routinely uprooting olive groves – often several generations old – has imposed drastic economic restrictions. In some areas – for example, Tabad – 21 'poor' households had already had their electricity supply completely disconnected by November 2006.

The situation for the 'very poor' is even more perilous. At the time of the ICRC Report (late 2006), the very poor households were unable to meet their needs at the current income levels and to maintain minimum health and hygiene standards. The ICRC Report for 2006 showed that the rate of household impoverishment was increasing, with most households in both the West Bank and the Gaza Strip falling within the 'poor' or 'very poor' categories. However, in Gaza the situation is made worse by the fact that the economy is much more dependent on external factors, rendering it more easily disrupted by restriction of movement imposed by Israeli checkpoints, etc. These factors can be summarized as follows.

1 Increased restrictions on the movement of people and goods, with the following consequences:
   - reduced access of Palestinian workers to the Israeli labour market
   - limited marketing outlets for agricultural produce, both inside and outside the West Bank and Gaza, which pushed prices down. This culminated in farmers becoming unable to repay loans and reducing the use of land to grow crops.
2 Irregular payment of wages to civil servants following the suspension of funds to the PA in March 2006.
3 Increased restrictions on fishing. According to the Fishermen's Union in Gaza and Al Mawasi, the area in which fishing was permitted had been reduced to less than 1 nautical mile from the shore. The previous limit was 8–10 nautical miles.

These factors had seriously undermined the ability of households to meet their basic needs without outside assistance. Wherever that assistance was irregular or inadequate, they had been forced to cut back on their basic expenses to levels that could threaten their well-being in the long term. Households with an income below US$ 116 had difficulty meeting their basic needs.

Even without considering other categories of human rights abuses prevailing in the Palestinian Territories, one can appreciate that international intervention is long overdue. However, the occupation has greatly exacerbated a number of other specific categories of human rights violations, and some of these will now be considered.

To end this section on the violation of the basic health rights of Palestinians, the author cannot do better than to quote directly from the World Health Organization's 2007 statement:

> The Occupied Palestinian Territory (OPT) is facing a three-layered humanitarian crisis: five consecutive years of Intifada, the financial crisis of the Ministry of Health (MoH), and the escalation of the security and humanitarian situation – especially in Gaza – are precipitating a further deterioration of the health crisis.
>
> As MoH facilities provide more than 60% of health services, problems within the MoH, around which all other health actors revolve, affect the entire health system. This may increase the risk of avoidable morbidity and mortality, especially from non-communicable diseases.
>
> Palestinians still have relatively stable health indicators, but with worrying social and economic trends. Life expectancy is 72 years, the fertility rate is 4.6, and the infant mortality rate is 24.2 per 1,000 live births.
>
> Access to health care services remains one of the main constraints, both for health care workers as well as for patients. Curfews and the increasing number

of checkpoints and roadblocks aggravate the situation. In the West Bank, as a consequence of the strike of MoH staff, only critical medical cases are received at governmental hospitals and health clinics and hospital wards.[23]

Violence against women and children

Generally speaking, women's rights in many Arab societies do not occupy the high profile to which many readers of this book will be accustomed. In what follows, then, it must be appreciated that not all of the violations of the rights of women and children in the Palestinian Territories are due to the occupation. However, the fact that the occupation has greatly exacerbated the impact of such violations cannot be denied. In 2005, Human Rights Watch made clear the high level of such abuse that prevailed prior to the arbitrary cutting off of expatriate funding and the consequent collapse of much of civil society in the Palestinian Territories.[24]

They point out that the Palestinian Authority has not created an internal social or legal infrastructure for responding to this level of violation of human rights. They suggest a number of actions that the PA could take to ameliorate the situation which would not be affected by the occupation itself. These findings and recommendations are based on field research conducted in the West Bank and Gaza in November 2005 and early 2006, and document dozens of cases of violence, ranging from spousal and chid abuse to rape, incest and murders committed in the name of family 'honour.' There is increasing recognition of the problem, and some PA officials have indicated their support for a more vigorous government response, but the PA has taken little action to prevent these abuses. As a result, violence against women and girls often goes unreported, and even when it is reported, it usually goes unpunished.

Farida Daif, one of the Human Rights Watch researchers, states in the above-cited source that PA officials generally view security 'only within the context of the ongoing conflict and the occupation, and all but ignore the very real threats to the security of their women and children in their homes.'

A huge body of discriminatory gender-based legislation in the domestic context perpetuates levels of violence that leave Palestinian women and girls with very little protection. Women regularly pay a high price for officials to act, because the latter are frequently unwilling to respond to incidents of gender-based violence. The Human Rights Watch report goes on to point out that the discriminatory criminal legislation in force in the West Bank and Gaza has led to virtual impunity for perpetrators of such violence, and has deterred women and girls from reporting abuse. These laws include provisions that reduce penalties for men who kill or attack female relatives who have committed adultery, relieve rapists who agree to marry their victims from any criminal prosecution, and allow only male relatives to file incest charges on behalf of minors.

With some exceptions, Palestinian police lack the expertise and the will to address violence against women in a manner that is effective, sensitive to the needs of the victim and respectful of their privacy. As a result, police officers often resort to informal measures rather than serious investigations. When questioned, many were unapologetic about their efforts to encourage marriage between a rapist and his victim, sometimes with the assistance of influential clan leaders. They see intervention as a means of 'solving' these cases. In addition, police often force women to return to their families even when there is a substantial threat of further harm.

Lucy Mair, one of the Human Rights Watch observers, pointed out that when the Palestinians' own criminal justice system is confronted with violations of the human rights of girls or women, it is often more interested in avoiding community scandal than in mediating justice. In other words, it regards a woman's basic right to life and bodily integrity as a secondary concern at best.

In addition, there is little advice available to doctors, nurses, teachers and other societal agents on how to respond to such incidents appropriately or how to report them.

The absence of medical guidelines for doctors also seriously affects the quality of treatment that is given to female victims of violence. The healthcare system is typically the first and sometimes the only government institution with which victims of abuse come into contact, yet doctors are ill-equipped to deal with such cases. The Ministry of Health has no medical procedures or protocols to guide medical professionals or ministry staff in their treatment of domestic violence cases. Doctors lack specialized training and guidance on how to treat women victims of violence, preserve evidence of the abuse and maintain confidentiality.

Although the availability of shelters has increased during 2005 and 2006 in the West Bank, movement restrictions within and between the West Bank and Gaza make it impossible for some victims of violence to reach these shelters, so that they are left without a refuge. Sometimes the lack of shelters and socially acceptable living arrangements for single women has forced Palestinian women's organizations and the police to house victims in police stations, governors' offices, private homes, schools or orphanages.

It is obvious that Israeli military violations of Palestinian human rights, including attacks on PA medical, educational and social services, have made matters much worse. In particular, Israel's refusal – with the backing of the Quartet – to pass on tax revenues has significantly undermined Palestinians' capabilities. However, this is no excuse for inaction. Despite its political and economic challenges, the PA has built important new institutions and reformed and unified some laws, such as those governing the justice system and children's rights. The same must be done to protect women and girls from family violence.

It is therefore important, if the Palestinians are to attract the international support that their struggle for justice so richly deserves, that they take their own breaches of human rights seriously and address them. In this regard they need to establish guidelines for responding to domestic violence, or even suspicion of it, and to ensure that these are widely disseminated and understood. They also need to instruct all government employees – teachers, health workers, police, etc. – to respond sympathetically and supportively to victims of violence. Above all, PA legal authorities must promote laws that specifically criminalize gender-based discriminatory practices and violence. Only such a line of action will sustain strong commitment among all Palestinians to the rightness of their cause.

This necessarily lengthy disquisition on such a crucially important topic has, as the reader will appreciate, added a raft of issues of appropriate transnational responses to the issue of protecting human rights. The Israeli–Palestinian conflict in particular exposes the UN's compromised position with regard to national rights vs. human rights, and these issues will be considered in the final chapter. However, to emphasize the point that not all unaddressed violations of the global human right to health, and other human rights, take place either in conflict zones or in less developed countries,

Chapter 7 will consider the UK's glaring failures in this regard. The author could have selected any of several wealthy developed countries to make the point, of course, but the situation in the UK is in many ways representative.

References

1 Kimmerling B, Migdal J. *The Palestinian People: a history.* Cambridge, MA: Harvard University Press; 2003.
2 Middle East Research and Information Project (MERIP). *Primer on the Uprising in Palestine*; www.merip.org.new_uprising_primer/primer_all_text.htm (accessed 8 March 2007).
3 Palestine Monitor. *Palestine Fact Sheets;* www.palestinianmonitor.org/factsheets/history_june2002.htm (accessed 8 March 2007).
4 Ibid., p. 3.
5 Oren M. *Six Days of War and the Making of the Modern Middle East.* Oxford: Oxford University Press; 2002. pp. 20–29.
6 Wikipedia. *History of the Israeli–Palestinian Conflict*; http://en.wikipedia.org/wiki/history_of_the_Israeli-Palestinian_Conflict (accessed 8 March 2007).
7 International Committee of the Red Cross (ICRC). *Declining Health Services in the Palestinian Territories;* www.icrc.org/web/eng/siteengo.nsf/html/Palestinian-report (accessed 3 March 2007).
8 Morris B. *Righteous Victims: a history of the Zionist–Arab conflict 1881–1999.* New York: Knopf Publishers; 2002. pp. 16–28.
9 Wikipedia, op. cit., p. 2.
10 Peace Now; www.peacenow.org.il/site/he/peace.asp?pi=2128decid=2194 (accessed 1 March 2007).
11 Middle East Research and Information Project (MERIP), op. cit., p. 14.
12 Middle East Research and Information Project (MERIP), op. cit., p. 15.
13 World Health Organization. *Addressing the Health Situation in the Occupied Palestinian Territories.* Geneva: World Health Organization; 2006. p. 19.
14 'US gives Israel more time to fight.' *Boston Globe* (Section I. World news), 30 April 2002, p. 4.
15 International Committee of the Red Cross (ICRC), op. cit., p. 10.
16 International Committee of the Red Cross (ICRC), op. cit., p. 12.
17 World Health Organization. *Country Profiles: Palestine*; www.embro.who/int/emirinfo.index.usp?ctry=pa (accessed 2 March 2007).
18 World Health Organization, op. cit., p. 5.
19 Middle East Research and Information Project (MERIP), op. cit., p. 6.
20 World Health Organization, op. cit., p. 5.
21 Human Rights Watch. *Occupied Palestinian Territories: authorities must address violence against women and children*; www.hrw.org/English/docs/2006/11/07/palab14496.htm (accessed 2 March 2007).
22 International Committee of the Red Cross (ICRC), op. cit., p. 14.
23 World Health Organization. *Resource Mobilization for Health Action in Crisis in the Occupied Palestinian Territory;* www.who.int/disaster (accessed 1 March 2007).
24 Human Rights Watch, op. cit., pp. 3–7.

Human rights violations in the UK

The UN and the developed world

At the time of the formation of the UN, the world had just emerged as victorious from a calamitously destructive war. The UN was seen as our major guarantee that such conflicts would be prevented in the future. As we have seen, the UN addressed two pivotal issues to carry out this mandate. On the one hand, it would act to protect the integrity of nations in such a way as to mediate differences between them and thus prevent war. On the other hand, it would act as the protector of 'human rights.' These have taken decades to define in detail – and the task is by no means complete yet – but the basic ideas about the inviolability of human dignity and the worth of each person were enshrined in the Universal Declaration of Human Rights. In the euphoria of our hard-won peace back in 1945, most of us did not notice that, in applying itself to these two issues, the UN had already put itself in a difficult if not impossible position. Also it tended to give people in the developed world, particularly in the UK and the USA, the impression that the issue of 'human rights' was largely about 'victimhood', and that the developed world comprised the 'benefactors' while the less developed nations constituted the 'victims.' That is, human rights were violated in poorer foreign countries but not in the victorious nations, especially the English-speaking ones.

The UK and violations of children's human rights

That, of course, is not the case. One could select the USA, Canada, Australia or any of the EU nations to make the point. Many of them embody gross violations of human rights domestically and cause them abroad in one way or another. How does the UK stack up? Most thinking British people were horrified when, on 14 February 2007 (Valentine's Day, no less!), a UNICEF Report – based on 5 years of research and analysis – was released which showed that the human rights of British children were more seriously violated than those of children in any of the other 21 developed nations studied.[1] The USA itself was the second worst. The same story was featured equally prominently, even in the UK tabloids and by all of the other media. 'How could this be?', shocked Britons across the country asked themselves. However, the research findings were incontrovertible – 16.2% of British children live below the poverty line, 35.5% of 15-year-olds only aspire to the lowest levels of employment, and 30.5% of young people have been drunk more than twice.

The report indicates that children in the UK suffer greater deprivation in a range of areas – affection, materially, educationally and socially – than children in other developed-world countries. They are more at risk of exposure to alcohol, drugs and unsafe sexual practices. Moreover, the report unambiguously shows that countries which have a narrower range of disposable income overall achieved much better child development results than did countries with wide income differences. Unsurprisingly, too, the evidence persistently indicates that children who grow up in poverty are much more vulnerable. They are more likely to be in poor health, to have learning difficulties and to display behavioural problems. They are more likely to underachieve in school and to leave formal education as early as possible. Girls from such backgrounds frequently become pregnant at an earlier age. Collectively, such children have fewer skills and more limited aspirations, and they more often grow up unemployed – often unemployable – and welfare-dependent.

The observation about the link between narrow and broad ranges of income distribution and the welfare of a country's children ties in precisely with a study by Dr Dennis Raphael, the Canadian authority on health promotion, and reported to the Politics of Health Group (POHG) on 14 September 2006.[2] The findings, which were published in the *British Medical Journal,* support the hypothesis that the political ideologies of governing parties affect some indicators of population health. The article establishes an empirical link between politics and policy, by showing that political parties with egalitarian ideologies tend to implement redistribution policies, which redound positively to improved child welfare. In fact, the study concludes directly that policies aimed at reducing social inequalities, such as a welfare state and labour market policies, have a salutary effect on such health indicators as infant mortality and life expectancy at birth.

Sarah Bosely's above-mentioned article in the *Guardian*[1] includes a figure from the UNICEF study which makes the point tellingly (*see* Figure 7.1).

Netherlands	4.2
Sweden	5.0
Denmark	7.2
Finland	7.5
Spain	8.0
Switzerland	8.3
Norway	8.7
Italy	10.0
Belgium	10.7
Germany	11.2
Canada	11.8
Greece	11.8
Poland	12.3
Czech Republic	12.5
France	13.0
Portugal	13.7
Austria	13.8
Hungary	14.5
US	18.0
UK	18.2

Figure 7.1: Ranking position for child well-being.

Notice that the countries ranking at or near the top of the list are known to have policies that are egalitarian. As far as human rights are concerned, all of the above raises important questions. Neoliberal policies tend to promote financial development as their dominant principle. Momentarily leaving aside the fact that this can often be shown to financially benefit corporate stockholders and banks in the developed world while impoverishing poor countries to which such policies are applied, that scale of values also impacts negatively on civil society in the developed countries themselves. In those countries, the 'work ethic' (be it Protestant or otherwise!) is now a dominant social theme. As the UNICEF study makes clear, this leads to serious levels of neglect of the emotional needs of children and their effective socialization as happy and fulfilled participants in their communities.

However, as we move beyond the issues raised in the UNICEF study, we discover that the UK violates a whole gamut of human rights both domestically and – by its neoliberally driven policies – internationally. One of the most obvious examples is the UK's dominant rôle in the arms trade.

The UK arms trade and the violation of human rights

The whole purpose of the arms trade is to promote more effective ways of killing people. It should therefore come as no great surprise that it is often associated with egregious levels of violations of human rights. For instance, on 8 June 2005, Amnesty International, through its Control Arms Campaign, released a report entitled 'G8 arms exports fuelling poverty and human rights abuses.'[3] The UK's political leaders, of both major political parties, frequently comment on their commitment to poverty reduction, stability and human rights. However, at the same time they have been assiduous in promoting the UK's position as a major arms provider with irresponsible arms exports to such countries as Sudan, Myanmar, the Republic of the Congo, Colombia and the Philippines. Of course, the rationale for this unscrupulous but highly profitable behaviour invariably is that it provides employment for British workers (and voters!). However, arms manufacture is not particularly labour intensive. For instance, it is not nearly as labour intensive as such public services as healthcare, manufacture of domestic goods for export, etc. In any case, the huge profits mentioned go mainly to a small and already obscenely wealthy elite.

Irene Khan, Secretary General of Amnesty International, had this to say:

> Each year hundreds of thousands of people are killed, tortured and displaced through the misuse of arms. How can G8 commitments to end poverty and injustice be taken seriously if some of the very same governments are undermining peace and stability by deliberately approving arms transfers to repressive regimes, regions of extreme conflict or countries who can ill afford them?
> web.amnesty.org/library/Index/ENGIOR30002102?open&of=ENG-316-21k

The reports from Amnesty International, Oxfam International and the International Action Network on Small Arms (IANSA) make a clear case for the G8 to support the call from the UK government and 10 other countries for an international Arms Trade Treaty.

'This research shows that, as well as the G8 being responsible for more than 80% of the world's arms exports, they persist in selling weapons that oppress the world's poorest and most vulnerable people. G8 foreign ministers meeting this week must back the Arms Trade Treaty and agree a process to make it happen', said Barbara Stocking, Director of Oxfam.

The UK's rôle in all of this is disproportionably larger, as reflected in the lack of control on UK equipment that can be used for torture, and the UK's increased use of 'open licences', which allow companies to make multiple shipments without any kind of public scrutiny or monitoring. Rebecca Peters, Director of the International Action Network on Small Arms (IANSA), has stated: 'In view of the massive loss of life and destruction of property and livelihoods fuelled by irresponsible arms transfers, the G8 must turn rhetoric into reality and push for negotiations to start on an Arms Trade Treaty by 2006. To do anything less would be a disgraceful betrayal of the millions of men, women and children subject to human rights violations and fear of armed violence every day.' Needless to say, no such Arms Trade Treaty has emerged as of 2007!

Arms sales and UK governments

However, let us look specifically at the rôle of the UK as a leading player in the arms trade scandal – for that is really what it is. The arms trade in the UK, even when the actual sales are really mediated through private companies, is mediated by government in the shape of the Defence Export Services Organization (DESO). Its rôle is to actively seek out potential opportunities for arms sales. It then coordinates other elements of government, and private British firms, to promote business. The fact that its activities support actual wars and human rights abuses, and that it in fact causes primary healthcare (PHC) to be withheld from vulnerable people, does not worry DESO in the least. In fact it seems to operate just as well under Labour or Conservative governments. It cannot even claim to be primarily concerned with either international security or the defence of the UK. Its focus is entirely on gaining maximum profits from the sale of arms. In total, DESO's net operating costs for 2004–2005 were £16.9 million, and for 2005–06 were £14.4 million.[4]

DESO employs nearly 500 civil servants in the Ministry of Defence (MoD). Any industry would be grateful for a complementary staff of this size dedicated to selling its output. And to have this staff based in a government department and have an official remit to coordinate government support for its exports is a marketing executive's dream come true. The value of DESO's staff goes far beyond the cost of their salaries.

The 500 civil servants are placed entirely at the service of arms companies. They are headed by a seconded arms industry executive, currently (in 2007) Alan Garwood, who has the formal rôle of advising government ministers on arms exports. This access goes right to the top – in his biography, Charles Masefield (Head of DESO from 1994 to 1998) at BAE Systems plainly stated that he enjoyed 'direct access to Major and Blair.'[5]

There is no ambiguity as to the nature of the post of Head of Defence Export Services. While the Heads receive a civil service salary, it is 'topped up' by the arms industry. When Tony Edwards (Head of DESO from 1998 to 2002) was asked about any potential for conflict of interest resulting from this, he stated 'I can say openly I am beholden to the industry and grateful to them for this top-up, but then I am working for them openly and overtly anyway.'[6] DESO provides pure insider influence for arms companies.

Many industries have trade associations, such as the arms industry's Defence Manufacturers Association and the Society of British Aerospace Companies, and these are readily understandable as private groupings that represent companies. Even though they are often influential, they are separate from government. DESO is different. It merges the major arms companies and UK government in a formal, institutionalized and profoundly undemocratic relationship. The resulting influence is of an entirely different level and nature to that of normal lobbying or political persuasion.

Moreover, its activities impact directly and adversely on human rights in at least 28 countries, namely Brazil, Brunei, Bulgaria, Canada, Chile, Czech Republic, Greece, Hungary, India, Italy, Japan, Kazakhstan, Kuwait, Malaysia, Oman, Poland, Qatar, Romania, Saudi Arabia, Singapore, Slovak Republic, South Africa, South Korea, Switzerland, Thailand, Turkey, United Arab Emirates and the USA.[7]

To illustrate the point, despite the UK government's frequent comments on 'justice and human rights' and even 'an ethical arms trade policy', DESO has no qualms about selling arms to both sides of the same conflict! For instance, China, Taiwan, India and Palestine each receive UK arms through DESO.[8] In 2005, the Human Rights Annual Report – produced by the UK's own Foreign and Commonwealth Office (FCO) – identified 20 'major' countries of concern in which there were serious and prolonged breaches of human rights. Yet in 2004, UK arms export licences were approved for 13 of these countries, namely Afghanistan, Belarus, China, Colombia, Indonesia, Iraq, Israel, Nepal, Russia, Saudi Arabia, Turkmenistan, Uzbekistan and Vietnam. In passing, it is interesting (if not puzzling) to note that most of the remaining seven did not qualify for such concern. These were Burma, Cuba, Democratic Republic of the Congo, Democratic People's Republic of Korea, Iran, Sudan and Zimbabwe.[9]

Of course, arms sales do not only violate basic human rights by sustaining actual military activity. They also divert huge sums of money that could otherwise be spent on health, education and other civil development projects. For instance, in 1998 South Africa spent £3 million on arms from the UK alone. It also purchased arms from other countries. In 2005 the UK deepened its military relationship with Pakistan through the signing of a Memorandum of Understanding on 'Defence Collaboration', and in 2006 the DESO published a briefing entitled 'Doing Business with Pakistan.' All of this was despite the fact that before either of these deals with the UK, Pakistan was in 2004 already spending more on the military than on health and education combined![10]

One could cite numerous other examples, such as persuading cash-strapped Tanzania to purchase a radar defence system that was already out of date, and in any case was completely superfluous to its defence needs. But perhaps the most noteworthy case involves the now infamous deal that British Aeronautics Engineering (BAE) struck with Saudi Arabia for the purchase of fighter aircraft. So much corruption accompanied the deal that the UK Serious Fraud Office (SFO) started to investigate it. This action had at first been advised by the Attorney General Lord Goldsmith (that the SFO investigation should go ahead). What happened subsequently shows how complicit the UK political establishment is in human rights abuses for profit. However, before dealing with that we shall first consider how Saudi Arabia ranks worldwide in its record on human rights.

The Saudi Arabia case

Amnesty International describes the overall human rights situation in Saudi Arabia as 'dire.' There are no political parties or trade unions, nor is there freedom of association, freedom of expression, or independent local media. Women are denied the vote and the chance to stand for election, and face severe restrictions on movement. Harsh repression of all forms of opposition is commonplace. There is ongoing concern over allegations of torture and mistreatment of prisoners. Flogging remains a routine state punishment, and the use of the death penalty continues. In the first 4 months of 2005, 40 people were beheaded.[11] There has been an escalation of killings by both security forces and armed groups, and the status of hundreds of prisoners of conscience remains shrouded in secrecy.

Saudi Arabia became DESO's main focus after the fall of their previous leading customer, the Shah of Iran, and it remains the priority today. An estimated 40% of current DESO staff work to provide the country with weaponry[12] (a third of them, those in the Saudi Arabian office, are paid for by the Saudi government).

In 1986 and 1988, the UK signed massive arms deals with Saudi Arabia, known as Al Yamamah ('the dove' in Arabic) I and II. The deals revolved around Tornado fighter and ground-attack aircraft, along with associated weaponry, spares and extensive support contracts. Mrs Thatcher and British Aerospace (now BAE Systems) were the main actors on the UK side, but the deals also involved notorious figures such as Jonathan Aitken, Mark Thatcher, Adnan Kashoggi and Wafic Said. The Al Yamamah deals have formed the basis of the arms trade relationship between the UK and Saudi Arabia ever since, including the current location of 5,000 BAE Systems staff in that country.

Over the past few years, however, Al Yamamah had begun to run down, and BAE Systems and DESO put their efforts into securing a further phase for the deal. This centred on the sale of the Eurofighter Typhoon, an aircraft that was noticeably failing to secure significant export orders, other than a small contract with Austria. The sales drive had the full support of the UK government, including, in July 2005, Tony Blair and Defence Secretary John Reid travelling to Riyadh to lobby for the deal.[13] In December 2005, the efforts of ministers and DESO bore fruit with the military agreement between the Saudi Arabian and UK governments, which included the commitment to buy at least 24 Eurofighters. The deal is thought to be worth more than £6 billion,[14] although the MoD has declined to provide information on prices.

This latest phase of Al Yamamah ensures that Saudi Arabia will remain the key focus of DESO's work.

To return to the issue of corruption, not least on the part of the UK government, in furthering the deal, much more information has since emerged. A story by David Leigh and Rob Evans appeared in the *Guardian* newspaper on 1 February 2007 to the effect that the UK's Prime Minister, Tony Blair, forced Lord Goldsmith to drop the fraud investigation and instructed the SFO to discontinue its investigations.[15] Lord Goldsmith had denied any pressure from the government, simply saying that on reconsideration he had changed his mind! In emergency meetings in late December 2006, he had agreed with lawyers from the Crown Prosecution Service that the SFO could bring corruption charges against Sir Dick Evans, the former head of BAE. In particular, the allegations involved backdoor gifts to the then head of the Saudi Air Force, Prince Turki-bin Nasser.

The *Guardian* article[15] revealed the following:

> Having reviewed the SFO's files, Lord Goldsmith agreed that BAE could, in effect, be offered a plea bargain in which investigators would drop further potentially politically embarrassing inquiries if the company agreed to plead guilty to these relatively minor charges.
>
> However, within 48 hours the agreement was countermanded after decisions taken in Downing Street, Whitehall sources said.
>
> The director of the SFO, Robert Wardle, was forbidden to make the approach to BAE. Instead the attorney general told Parliament the entire Saudi investigation was to be halted, and that there was insufficient evidence for it to succeed. Lord Goldsmith also said in the Lords that MI5 and MI6 believed national security was in danger. The heads of the agencies have refused to endorse his claim. The attorney general is supposed to act in an impartial, quasi-judicial rôle, to protect the public interest. But since the prime minister's elevation of Lord Goldsmith to the post in 2001, he has caused increasing controversy.

The *Guardian* article also pointed out that the human rights advocate, Lord Lester, even called for Lord Goldsmith to be stripped of his political powers. The conflict of interests in which the scandal had involved him rendered his position untenable, and Lord Lester went on to say that Goldsmith's terminating of the BAE investigation had gravely eroded public confidence in the integrity of the government. According to the *Guardian*,[15] the SFO case would probably have revealed staggering levels of corruption by UK government figures, to say nothing of Saudi ones. Indeed they initially acquired, on the Prince Tuski aspect of their Saudi case, the close involvement of a senior fraud barrister, Timothy Langdale QC, who regularly acts for the government as Treasury counsel.

The legal view was that adequate evidence existed to bring charges and to open a Crown case against BAE in court, although their defence to the allegations has so far never been heard.

On 28 February 2007, BAE said the suggestion that there was enough evidence 'directly contradicts the position of the attorney general and the SFO.' They stressed that Lord Goldsmith had said 'I consider, having carefully examined the present evidence, that there are obstacles to a successful prosecution so that it is likely that it would not in the end go ahead.'

Asked whether Sir Dick Evans and the company denied making payments to Prince Turki, BAE responded: 'The fact that we have not commented specifically on any statements made by the *Guardian* should not be taken as any kind of admission.'

The SFO refused to comment, but Lord Goldsmith's office said: 'The decision to discontinue the [Saudi] investigation was made by the director of the SFO. . . . The final decision was his alone. The prime minister gave his views on the national security implications.'

Having considered the full public interest case, the SFO concluded that pursuing the case, either as a full investigation or on some more limited basis, created the same risk to national and international security. In view of those risks to national and international security, the director of the SFO decided to halt the case.[16]

The Saudi case is far from over, and no doubt despite Lord Goldsmith's action in so suddenly going back on his previously argued reasons for proceeding with a fraud query. It all does much to besmirch the high international regard with which British law and government are held. However, there are other, less esoteric areas of human rights violations in which the UK has played a dominant rôle. We have already dealt briefly with Britain's poor record with regard to child care. One aspect of this concerns British treatment of 'children' (aged 16 years or less) who enter the UK as asylum seekers. Some of these have been trafficked, but we shall deal with that issue later. By whatever route children have arrived in the UK, what kind of treatment can they expect if they seek asylum?

Children seeking asylum in the UK

One case with which most British people are familiar, because it even attracted international media attention, was that of the Ay family from Turkey. The story was a good one for a media that feeds, as it does, on 'poignancy' (a word now beloved of reporters) and self-indulgence. However, two horrible facts have to be borne in mind by the reader. First, the Ays' experience of violation of human rights generally, and of the rights of the child in particular, was far from unique. Secondly, the media simply could not exaggerate the story – it was every bit as bad as the most lurid description, sentimentality and bad taste that media editors could contrive. In every sense, then, what befell the Ay family is emblematic of the miseries endured by all asylum seekers, both adults and juveniles, who are trying to survive in the UK.

Their story featured in all the broadsheets and many of the tabloids. The following summary is drawn from an account by Diane Taylor and Simon Hattenstone, which appeared in the *Guardian* on 20 January 2007.[17]

The family – father, mother and four children – are Turkish Kurds and because of their father's alleged link to the Kurdish cause, the entire family felt threatened. They travelled first to Germany, a society not altogether friendly to the Kurds, and on that account found it difficult to get by. Several months later they made their way to the UK. The account given in the *Guardian*, like all of the other accounts about this family that this author has read, is based largely on the testimony of now 14-year-old Beriwan, their eldest daughter. She developed a reasonable command of German and an absolutely fluent command of English, and she has for the last 4 years served as the spokesperson for the entire family. It is she who had to argue their case before UK immigration officials, social workers, health visitors and the like.

On arrival in the UK, the family settled in very quickly. Three of the children (the youngest was not yet old enough) enrolled at the local school in Gravesend, and excelled academically. According to Beriwan, the three peaceful and productive years they spent in Gravesend were unimaginably happy – 'the happiest in our entire lives. We all loved to play football, and Mum was a great goalie.' Their success in school encouraged the children to plan their future with optimism. Beriwan, paradoxically, dreamed of becoming a human rights lawyer.

What they couldn't know is the degree to which the UK government wanted to keep in Turkey's good books. Turkey is one of their best customers for arms. The sacrifice of a few troublesome Kurds was a small price to pay. It is at this point that the relationship that the Ay family had with the Turkish authorities before they left needs to be elucidated.

In some ways theirs is a typical story. Like many asylum seekers, Beriwan's parents were so terrified of their fate in their native country that they risked their lives in travelling to Germany and then later, with the children, to the UK to make a new start. Like others before them, they didn't tell the German authorities everything in case they were sent back to Turkey and punished yet more severely for speaking out. And, like others, despite the misery they have experienced in the west, they cling to the belief that the UK is the place that will ultimately allow them to be free.

Yurdagul and Salih, Beriwan's mother and father, married when she was 16 years old and he was 21. They came from the village of Nerinjin, in the Sirnak area of south-east Turkey, and were proud of their Kurdish identity. The couple refused to change their Kurdish names to Turkish ones, and spoke Kurdish rather than Turkish. For this, Salih was jailed six times and Yurdagul three times, usually for several weeks. Yurdagul's father was jailed for three years when she was small because he couldn't speak Turkish. Salih was repeatedly beaten for the same crime when he did his national service. First his arm was smashed, and then he was forced to clean floors one-handed.

'They would come looking for Salih, and if he wasn't at home they'd put me in jail instead', Yurdagul said in Kurdish.

On listening to her mother make that comment, Beriwan explained that even now the Turkish authorities wanted to get hold of her father. She thought he was safe in the UK because all that the Home Office required him to do was to report at regular intervals to the local police station, where a few boxes would be ticked on his papers and he would be sent on his way. Then, in March 2002, everything changed and their world was turned on its head yet again. This time, when Salih went to the police, instead of the usual bureaucratic ticking of boxes and a nod signifying that he was free to go, he was arrested and deported to Germany. The rest of the family were left behind in a state of shock. 'No matter what happened to us, we always assumed we'd be together', Yurdagul said.

Salih spent three months in Germany, most of it in jail awaiting deportation to Turkey, but he did make a visit to the Turkish embassy in Germany and overheard two officials say that the rest of the family would be arrested and deported soon. 'He called us and urged us to go into hiding to avoid deportation', Yurdagul said. The family hid with friends, but this was no life. The children were unable to go to school or show their faces in the community. After two months, they gave themselves up to the police. Detention swiftly followed.

'They came for us early in the morning', Yurdagul said. 'We had only 20 minutes to pack.' They were incarcerated in June 2003 in a Home Office detention centre in Scotland, known as Dungavel, on the border between Lanarkshire and Ayrshire. The family was locked indoors for 22 hours a day, had limited access to education and healthcare, and few other children to mix with.

Dungavel was once an ordinary prison and, according to Taylor and Hattenstone's report, has not been changed significantly for its new use for what is, after all, temporary accommodation for people who have not been accused of any crime in the UK. At the time of their interviews, the Ay family had been there for almost a year – without schooling for the children and with very little access to such outdoor pleasures as playing football together.

In Dungavel, they lived with the constant fear that they would be returned to Germany and from there to Turkey – a place which would hardly welcome them. After a year in Dungavel, their father was returned to Germany and eventually to Turkey. To cut a long story short, the rest of the family had their asylum application rejected and they were all sent to Germany, where they are now. However, the children especially have suffered immense psychological damage. Not as fluent in German as in English, their progress in school has been badly affected. They cannot visit their father and he cannot access them. Altogether this amounts to serious derogations of the rights of the children (under the UN Declaration) to security, adequate healthcare and appropriate education.

They are housed in a flat in Kirchen, in Germany, where the children attend a school involving a 45-minute walk each way. However, the fear of deportation to Turkey is ever present. All four children, but particularly the younger three – Newroz and Medya, both girls, and the youngest, Dilovan, a boy – are showing serious mental symptoms.

Yurdagul, their mother, mentioned to reporters that in Dungavel, Medya used to have screaming nightmares. Now all of the children do. Dilovan stated baldly that going to school was pointless because they will all be deported. The family live under a cloud of intense pessimism. Eventually they were granted the right to live indefinitely in Germany, but it is the UK that they long for. How are they – even the adults – to understand that their human rights as refugees from political oppression are of less concern to the British government than is furtherance of the arms trade?

However, as indicated above, the Ay family's plight is not at all unique to the UK's authorities. Thousands of children, often already traumatized by civil war in their own countries, are trafficked here for profit and are then dumped on the streets at or near their point of illegal entry. Most of them do not have the language skills to even attempt an 'explanation' (as though a child *could* explain such things). For such victims, asylum is routinely refused. They frequently therefore face being sent back to their home countries, often to be exploited or tortured. The *Sunday Times Magazine* of 4 February 2007 contained a report on two Angolan girls, aged 7 and 15 years, who were dumped illegally in the UK, and it described what befell them at the hands of Her Majesty's Government.[18]

Without dealing with the article in the depth that it merits, suffice it to say that it not only deals with the criminal exploitation of children by the traffickers, but also describes their totally insensitive treatment – in violation of the UN Declaration of the Rights of the Child – by government authorities in the UK. Moreover, it is not as if these events are 'accidental' or due to temporary breakdowns in the system. Nor are they outside the public eye. The treatment of these children is widely publicized, and one suspects that this is because the government is more anxious to counter accusations from the more right-wing media that they are 'too soft' on illegal migrants, bogus asylum seekers, etc. Indeed, such media presentations, and government acquiescence to them, are such that the very words 'migrant', 'refugee' and 'asylum seeker', rather than evoking feelings of sympathy from ordinary people, have been used as pejorative adjectives intended to generate suspicion and hostility, very much at variance with Britain's once international reputation for fairness and humanity. For instance, and perfectly reasonably, the British Home Office differentiates between adults (18 years or over) and children (under 18 years), but in testimony after testimony accounts are given of children being accused by immigration officials of lying about their age, and being treated as adults whatever they say. As adults they can be repatriated, even to countries where they will almost certainly suffer punishment, torture and exploitation, if not worse.

One of the cases reported in the above-cited *Sunday Times* article makes this point clear. Maria, aged 15 years, and her niece, Madalea, arrived in the UK from Angola. Maria, whatever her chronological age, had had her 'childhood' arbitrarily terminated, as her father had been humiliated and then slaughtered in her presence by Angolan government soldiers. In addition, she said that she was raped and otherwise tortured before she made her escape. On reaching the UK, neither her story of her rape nor her age were believed by the authorities. This is explicitly stated in the letter which she eventually received from the Home Office, and quoted in the *Sunday Times*, denying her asylum. Unlike the Ay family discussed above, she had been taken directly from her own country to the UK, without making a prior landfall anywhere else. Therefore she could not even be exported to another fairly safe European country, but faced being sent back to Angola itself. Even more extraordinarily, although it was well known that in that country civil society had been overwhelmed by violence, Angola was deemed by the Home Office to be 'safe.'

Neither of the girls was believed when they gave their account, without the aid of translators, to immigration officials. Indeed, the letter from the Home Office is a most extraordinary document in its insensitivity and blatant denial of human rights for anyone (let alone its flagrant violation of the Rights of the Child Declaration). Selectively quoting from that letter, we read that the girl's account of being helped to escape by various people was declared 'implausible.' One quote from it is as follows: 'Maria wanted me to believe that a complete stranger helped them. . . . It beggars belief that, once in the UK, neither Maria nor her legal representative nor a medical professional had sought to elicit information from Madalea about their treatment before they left Angola.' The letter took no account of the fact that for two months the girls had tried repeatedly to seek help from the local Social Services offices in London where they were staying, but were refused!

It is even worse when the letter deals with Maria's account of her 'alleged rape.' The letter states:

> There was no evidence that she suffered untoward consequences like HIV or sexually transmitted diseases. Even assuming she was raped, I do not find that it was for Refugee Convention reasons but for reasons of sexual gratification . . .

What this means is that her rape, even if it had occurred, did not contravene the Geneva Convention, for that document defines a refugee as a person persecuted because of their race, religion, nationality, social group or political opinion. The fact that Maria's father had been regarded as hostile to the Angolan government apparently made no difference! The letter concludes that the immigration official concerned 'does not accept' that returning them to Angola 'to live in conditions, wretched as they are' would breach their human rights.

In this particular case, luck was with the children because just over a year later, their accounts were shown to be true and they were granted refugee status. Such a happy outcome is exceedingly uncommon. In fact, of the 2,500 to 3,500 children who have arrived alone every year and seeking asylum since 1999, 5% or fewer per year are granted permanent refuge. Most are brought in on planes by adults whom they barely know, and abandoned at airports before being processed by immigration control or later at the roadside, in restaurants or close to Home Office buildings. Others are smuggled in via ports and caught by immigration authorities or dumped by the road. They are usually brought in by agents paid by relatives or others, or by traffickers trying to sell them for domestic servitude or sexual exploitation.

Until now, most such children have been given leave to remain in the UK until they are 18 years of age, after which, like unsuccessful adult asylum seekers, they have been liable to 'removal.' However, this temporary safety net now looks set to be taken away from thousands of children from some of the world's poorest and most dangerous countries, such as Angola and Congo, and from Vietnam, where children are particularly vulnerable to being trafficked abroad. Plans are being drawn up to repatriate children from these countries once their asylum claims are rejected and their appeals denied. This is part of the government drive to step up removals amid mounting pressure over immigration controls, which culminated in the Home Secretary John Reid's admission that the Immigration and Nationality Directorate was 'not fit for purpose' in the wake of the foreign-prisoners scandal. If such a 'pilot project' is deemed a success, child-protection experts fear it will mean that children from many more countries will be swiftly dispatched back home.

The reporter who wrote the *Sunday Times* article goes on to state that she spoke to 10 youngsters:

> which is the average number arriving 'unauthorized' in the UK every day. Finding those willing to speak is no easy matter. Many are afraid. Since news of the government plan leaked out several months ago, some have gone on the run out of fear they will be returned.

Of those she met in different parts of the country – four boys, four girls and two young women, including Maria, who arrived here as children – only Maria and Madalea have been granted asylum. Half have already received the standard letter sent out to failed asylum seekers offering them financial incentives worth around £3,000 to go home voluntarily before risking arrest.

The article goes on to say that when the children tell their stories it becomes clear – as the UK charities that work with them say – that the government views them as foreigners first, and children second (that is if they are seen as children at all). Because their passports are frequently kept by those who bring them into this country, many cannot prove their age. In recent years, growing numbers are not even believed when they say how old they are. Many are wrongly deemed to be already adult, often after little more than a swift visual assessment by immigration officials.

Such age disputes have serious implications for the level of support that the children receive. Those who are believed when they say they are 16 years or under are placed in the care of social services, many of them with foster families. Those aged 16 to 18 years receive more limited support in bed-and-breakfast accommodation or shared housing, and can gain some access to further education, while those who are deemed to be adults receive the most basic support and face being sent to immigration detention centres, where the holding of children is prohibited.

Maria, for instance, was initially considered to be lying about her age and told that she must be 'at least 18' on the basis, she says, 'that they didn't believe a 16-year-old would be able to look after my niece the way I did.' Even when social services did finally help, she was treated as an adult, left to care for her young niece alone in a hostel, and then put in a shared house with adult asylum seekers. 'It was terrible', she says. 'As a child you know your age, but they don't even believe that.'

'The culture of disbelief is so widespread that these children are thought of just as people who have been sent by their parents to get a job or an education', says Nadine

Finch, a barrister and co-author of the recent report *Seeking Asylum Alone*, partly sponsored by Harvard University.

'All too often the children are not held to be credible because what they have gone through is beyond the experience of the person assessing them', says Sheila Melzak, principal child and adolescent psychotherapist at the Medical Foundation for the Care of Victims of Torture, which counsels hundreds of such children every year. 'There is this dance that goes on between adults who don't want to hear and don't want to think about a child experiencing grotesque violence, and the children themselves, who don't want to or are unable to speak about what they have gone through.' The halting steps that children take in such a dance begin to fall into a familiar pattern, marked by long silences during painful recollections.

One could quote from hundreds of such accounts, but the human rights issue is clear. The UK, along with several other developed countries, is just as guilty of violating the Universal Declaration of Human Rights as less developed countries. Indeed, Human Rights Watch commented in this vein as far back as 2001, when the UK adopted anti-terrorism legislation to bring it into closer alignment with the US War on terrorism. The Human Rights report stated that ' . . . the legislation adopted in the UK marks another step in the UK's retreat from human rights and refugee protection obligations.'[19]

In that report, Elizabeth Andersen observes that 'The September 11 attacks in the US raised serious security concerns. But the UK legislation is unfortunately a frontal assault on fundamental rights.'

In a critique issued on 16 November 2001, in advance of the bill's parliamentary readings, Human Rights Watch urged parliamentarians to reject provisions that would define terrorism so broadly that individuals could be found 'guilty by association.' Human Rights Watch was also critical of provisions that would permit prolonged indefinite detention of terrorist suspects without charge, would allow the UK to derogate from certain obligations under the European Convention on Human Rights, and would severely undermine the right to seek asylum in the UK.

Although the definition of a terrorist in the new law has been refined to include those who 'support or assist' terrorists, these terms remain vague and undefined. The status of the Special Immigration Appeals Commission (SIAC) is also enhanced, but suspects' access to judicial review before a court remains restricted to questions of law. Moreover, the provision for secret proceedings before the SIAC remains intact. None of the amendments to the bill effectively responded to Human Rights Watch's concerns.

The group also expressed a broader concern that the UK's derogation from certain provisions of the European Convention sends a signal to other Council of Europe member states that obligations under the convention can be disregarded with ease.

'The passage of the Human Rights Act in 2000 was a milestone', said Andersen. 'But now the UK is departing from the European Convention and adopting a law that permits indefinite detention without trial, and a denial in some cases of the right to seek asylum.'

Human Rights Watch criticized the UK's then Home Secretary, David Blunkett, for equating critics of the bill with supporters of terrorism. Among those critics were a number of members of the House of Lords, who complained in debate that certain provisions could lead to human rights abuses without significantly improving UK security. Many human rights and civil liberties organizations with large UK-based memberships also opposed the bill.

'By impugning opponents to this bill, the UK is trying to silence anyone with a genuine concern for the effect these new measures will have on their rights', said Andersen. 'Immigrant and refugee communities in particular will feel the full force of a new law that implicitly makes them suspect.'

'Human Rights Watch expressed concern for the law's impact on the right to seek asylum in the UK and the obligation not to return a refugee to a country where his or her life or freedom could be threatened. This week the UK stated at a high-level ministerial meeting on the Refugee Convention that the anti-terrorism law "will in no way undermine the UK's obligations under the Convention. Indeed, it is not designed to do so."'

'In fact, the new law explicitly undermines the Refugee Convention at the expense of those the convention was designed to help', said Andersen. 'The long rights tradition in Britain is not well served by this law.'

Human Rights Watch has been erratic in providing positive criticisms of the UK's policies with regard to the asylum process, and has put forward various suggestions for ameliorating it. So far, none of these have made much difference. For instance, in September 2003 they made a direct submission to the House of Lords Select Committee on the European Union on the issue.[20] Paragraphs 8, 9 and 10 of that submission are worth quoting in full:

> 8. The proposals also threaten the right to seek asylum, enshrined in the Universal Declaration of Human Rights. They also risk undermining the fundamental right of refugees not to be returned to a country where their lives or freedom are threatened because of persecution (nonrefoulement), guaranteed in Article 33 of the Refugee Convention, Article 3 of the ECHR, and Article 3 of the Convention against Torture. As outlined in paragraphs 13 and 22–28 below, Human Rights Watch believes that abuses encountered by refugees either inside or outside of the proposed centres may cause their transfer to the centres to result in refoulement.

> 9. The transfer of asylum seekers arriving illegally in the UK to centres abroad, where they will be detained pending the outcome of the asylum process, also constitutes a penalty in violation of Article 31 of the Refugee Convention. Asylum seekers should be detained only in exceptional circumstances, not routinely, and on a case-by-case basis in accordance with the UNHCR Guidelines on Applicable Criteria and Standards Relating to the Detention of Asylum Seekers. Moreover, the UK proposals make no mention of safeguards for undocumented migrants transferred to such centres for processing. Article 5 of the ECHR permits the detention of undocumented migrants pending an active process undertaken 'with a view to deportation.' Our research in several West European countries has revealed the systematic abuse of migrants who are detained without any prospect of being returned to their home countries, due to armed conflict, political obstacles or administrative policies.

> 10. Targeting asylum applicants by nationality or geographic region of origin and transferring them to processing centres in regions where they will enjoy

fewer Refugee Convention rights than refugees located on British soil could violate Article 3 of the Refugee Convention, which stipulates that the provisions of the Convention must be applied to refugees without discrimination as to race, religion, or country of origin. In August 2003, the UN Committee on the Elimination of Racial Discrimination expressed concern about discrimination in the UK against asylum seekers, and recommended that the UK adopt 'measures making the asylum procedures more equitable, efficient and unbiased.' The current proposals do not appear designed to make the asylum process either more equitable or more unbiased, and may make it worse.

What must a solution involve?

Everything that has been said so far in this chapter raises questions about the rôle of the UN in promoting its own Universal Declaration of Human Rights. Those issues will be considered in detail in the final chapter. However, from what has been said so far, it is clear that the incidence of asylum seekers coming to the UK is often considered by the authorities in the light of 'refugee status', as opposed to what is often referred to as 'economic migration.' In terms of human rights, especially health rights, it is difficult to make this distinction meaningfully.

The official attitude is that people who enter the UK illegally, 'merely' to enhance their economic prospects, should apply for entry at a British consular office in their own country. Otherwise they can be sent back on landing in the UK. Genuine asylum seekers, on the other hand, can apply for refugee status – provided that they do so as quickly as possible on arrival, and provided that the UK was the first EU country in which they landed. However, there are all kinds of problems with these categories and provisions.

First of all, people trying to enter the UK 'merely to improve their economic status' may, under the Universal Declaration of Human Rights, have every justification for doing so. For instance, a Zimbabwean man who is unable to provide for his family's needs, even basic healthcare and schooling, because his employment doesn't pay enough, especially under astronomically high inflation, has every right to wander the world in search of more propitious conditions. The UK is a preferred target – something about which UK citizens should feel pride – because it has an international reputation for tolerance, and also because English is the most widely spoken foreign language in Europe, Africa and Asia.

However, it is obvious that a totally laissez-faire approach would have serious consequences for British civil life. In the author's view, this has to be regarded as a transnational problem, solved by a transnational organization like the UN being able to intervene in sovereign states whose domestic administrations create conditions that are not in accord with the Universal Declaration of Human Rights. As presently constituted – and for the reasons already discussed – the UN cannot meet this demand. Clearly, however, if there were an agreed transnational mechanism for enforcing human rights, the need for people to 'wander the world' in search of economic security and basic human rights would not exist. Anyone who really believes that people are easily persuaded to forsake their culture, language, family and established social habits for the chance of economic gain alone knows little about human psychology. The author has dealt with this issue in a previous publication.[21]

Again, it is obvious from what we have already said about the asylum issue that trafficking in people has played a huge role, and continues to do so. Such trafficking is, of course, an unspeakable crime, but one that is very profitable. Indeed, it is reckoned that it is now more profitable than the trade in illegal narcotics.[22] However, as with the violations of human rights already dealt with in this chapter, the UK is heavily involved in the crime of trafficking people and all of the human rights violations that stem from it.

The UK's involvement in people trafficking and slavery

Most readers will recall the incident in 2004 in which 23 Chinese cockle-pickers were drowned by rising water levels in Morecambe Bay. As illegal migrants they had been working under a gangmaster and were outside any kind of legal control or requirement for health and safety. The incident so horrified people that the British government made trafficking for forced labour a criminal offence. But what is 'forced labour' if not slavery? And slavery has been illegal in the UK since the late nineteenth century. In 2004 a licensing system came into force in support of which the government set up a Human Trafficking Centre with a mandate to prevent human trafficking.

However, despite this long overdue measure, not a single successful prosecution for the offence has occurred as of 2007. Even worse, no assistance has been made available to people who have been so trafficked, nor has any guarantee been given that such victims themselves will not be punished for violations of immigration regulations. Indeed, the British government has not even signed the Council of Europe Convention on Action Against Trafficking in Human Beings. Such a move would, at the stroke of a pen, guarantee that such trafficked people would be offered protection and support. Over 30 other European countries have already signed. One can be excused for being puzzled at the delay, but the reasons for it are not difficult to adduce. Independent News and Media Limited[23] published an article in December 2007 commenting on this issue and pointing out that government officials are under pressure to reflect a tough line on illegal migrants to the UK.

For the police to have any prospect of catching those who run international networks, they must have the co-operation of the victims. However, when the victims have irregular status in the country, there is limited incentive for them to co-operate with the police. The police cannot guarantee them protection, access to services or an opportunity to regularize their status. They can only try to negotiate protection for them with the Immigration Service, which often attempts to deport victims who the police would regard as witnesses and expect to be treated as victims of crime.

This is because the Immigration Service works on a quota system of deportations. So for immigrations officials, there is limited incentive to stop the deportation of victims of trafficking, even if it assists police enquiries. This situation is likely to get worse, not better. The government seems much more interested in placating its right-wing critics than in human rights. They are anxious to show that they are taking a hard line on migrants. Under the Government's latest proposals, the number of deportations will increase. This will further hamper the pursuit of criminals, for the victims of trafficking are even less likely to co-operate with the police if they are immediately to be deported back to the very countries where those criminal gangs still hold sway.

The result is a system whose priorities are upside down. Instead of protecting the rights of victims, the system punishes them. Trafficked people can be detained, charged or prosecuted for immigration offences such as illegal entry or destroying their documents, although this is most likely to have occurred as a result of coercion from the traffickers. What all this means is that trafficking people to the UK remains a high-profit, low-risk business for those criminal gangs who organize it. In countries like Germany and Italy, which have signed the European Convention Against Trafficking – and where minimum standards of protection for the victims of human trafficking now exist – prosecutions have increased. In the UK there has still not been a single prosecution. As the *Independent* article further points out, this situation has always been unacceptable from a human rights perspective. What is clear now is that it is unjustifiable from a law enforcement perspective as well.

McQuade claims that 'Britain has created a legal framework which makes it virtually impossible to take action against trafficking. The result is that despite what British history teaches us about Bishop Wilberforce and the outlawing of slavery back in the nineteenth century, there are still slaves in Britain today. Of course, nowadays the practice is carried on discreetly, but both the Police and the Home Office acknowledge that it is happening. However, it is not in the government's interest to draw the situation to wide popular attention because the government is so badly compromised because of the contradiction between its public statements about 'control of immigration' and its legal commitment to prevent people trafficking.'

The International Labour Organization (ILO) estimates that there are as many as 360,000 slaves living in the world's developed countries. About 70% of these people were pushed into slavery, at considerable profit, by people trafficking, thereby creating an industry valued at a minimum of US$ 32 billion annually. No one knows for sure how many of these people are in the UK, mainly because the individuals themselves – knowing that they are virtually unprotected – are afraid to reveal themselves to the authorities. The victims are to be found working in agriculture, construction sites, cleaning crews for agencies with contracts to clean office buildings, academic institutions, etc. Ordinary domestic work accounts for more than a few, as does food processing, restaurant work and even agency nursing. These 'slaves' are even sold from one owner to another.

Occasionally criminals involved in the trade are caught and prosecuted, but not with the frequency or in the numbers that would represent a serious obstacle to its continuation as a profitable enterprise.

One case that attracted widespread horror was exposed in Dover on 18 June 2000. On that day, port officials, while checking a lorry from the Netherlands, found in it the bodies of 58 Chinese people (54 men and 4 women). The lorry was driven by a Dutch citizen, Perry Wacher. He was, of course, arrested and was eventually sentenced to 14 years for trafficking and manslaughter. Before the rough channel crossing from Belgium – a journey that took 5 hours – Wacher had sealed the only air vent in the container so that outsiders would not hear the people inside crying out. As it was, two other people in the crate survived.[24]

According to that bulletin, senior British police officers were quoted as warning that UK-based criminal gangs trading in people and fake documents are now out of control. The BBC broadcast gave details of four cases – including that of Wacher.

Another was that of an Indian gangster, Sarwan Deo, from Punjab. He was working with four British confederates who for 13 years had successfully been trafficking people into the UK from India. The gang charged each 'customer' up to £8,000, supposedly to secure their safe passage and employment in the UK. They were each provided with a fake passport and flown to Heathrow. At its height, 10 people a week were being brought into the UK – more than 500 a year. Over the 13-year period they thus accounted for thousands of people who, instead of finding 'security' and 'employment', were exploited. When he was tried, it emerged that Sarwan Dao had made about £50 million from his activities.

The other two cases were similar, although run by different gangs. In June 2003, immigration officers, while searching for only one illegal immigrant in a house in Croydon, uncovered a complete travel document factory. They discovered £5 million worth of forged documents, including 1,335 fake passports and 2,000 credit cards. The police also seized forgery equipment, even card-scanners and government stamps from a number of EU countries. The result was the arrest and jailing of a Romanian husband-and-wife team. It also emerged that not only had the pair cleared a huge profit from those activities, but they were also involved in then tricking their 'clients', selling some of them into various forms of slavery, confident that they were too intimidated to speak out. In this belief they were correct, and these serious breaches of human rights would have gone undetected but for that one lucky breakthrough during a routine immigration investigation.

The fourth case mentioned on the BBC Radio broadcast exemplifies the most common form of slavery in the UK. A gang of Albanian pimps, six of whom had resident status in the UK, tricked teenage girls into London brothels. They successfully carried on their trade for 7 years until they were caught and convicted in December 2005, because one of the girls plucked up enough courage to go to the police. On arrival in the UK, the girls' passports and travel documents were taken from them and they were threatened with being revealed to the authorities as illegal migrants if they spoke out.

At the trial in Southwark Crown Court, one young Lithuanian student testified that at 16 years of age she was still a virgin, but on arrival in London she was sold to a British confederate, and within the hour was forced by him to lose her virginity. She earned tens of thousands of pounds for him before she escaped.

In view of all of this, what has been the British government's reaction? As indicated above, there are some who argue that the UK's stand on human rights, and their effectiveness in promoting it, have been particularly compromised by the UK's present Prime Minister, Tony Blair, and his administration.

Attitudes to human rights in the UK today

A number of serious lapses, especially in the Home Office and also with regard to 'dangerous people' of various categories slipping out of the frame of official super-vision, have recently occupied a high profile in the UK media. The general tenor of this commentary is that the government has been too concerned about the human rights of various antisocial elements, and correspondingly inadequately concerned about their victims. In recent years this has encouraged a whole spate of highly florid public comment to the effect that Britain's agreement to respect the EU's human rights legislation has tilted the balance of justice too much in favour of the wrong-doer, while leaving potential victims more vulnerable. On the *Guardian* website this phenomenon was made the subject of an article by Ned Tanko and Janice Doward[25] in the *Observer* of 14 May 2006.

The article claims that, in mid-2006, Tony Blair was actively planning an attack on human rights law in the UK. In particular, the Prime Minister was said to want the government to have the power to override court rulings based on consideration of human rights. Only a few days earlier, Blair had caused controversy by criticising a senior judge for blocking the repatriation of nine Afghan refugees who had hijacked a plane to the UK. It was further reported that Blair had declared that the ruling was 'barmy.' The article goes on to explain the processes invoked by the Prime Minister to make his point clear, even though a variety of responsible sources had maintained that the refugees had been driven by terror to flee their country by any means possible to escape torture and/or death for their opposition to the Afghan government. However, before citing details of the report, let us be clear as to what is meant by 'human rights' in the context of EU law and incorporated, in 2000, into British law.

The Human Rights Act, originally framed in the EU in 1998, came into force in the UK 2 years later. It integrated into British law the entire 1950 European Convention on Human Rights. Its effect is to render inalienable a number of civil and political rights enforceable under UK law. Indeed, in 2000, Prime Minister Blair had welcomed it as a flagship piece of legislation that highlighted the Labour Party's commitment to justice! It was only called into question when it was seen as potentially interfering with actions that the Blair government was anxious to promote, both to placate critical media comment in the UK and to avoid disrupting the close acquiescence with US military and political objectives.

The above paragraph serves to account for the series of events catalogued in the cited *Observer* article. Blair unveiled his plans in a letter to the new Home Secretary, John Reid, in which he set out his 'most urgent policy tasks.' Legal experts and civil liberties groups accused Blair of playing politics with fundamental rights. The *Observer* has obtained a copy of the letter, which says that it is essential to 'ensure the law-abiding majority can live without fear.'

It adds: 'We will need to look again at whether primary legislation is needed to address the issue of court rulings which overrule the government in a way that is inconsistent with other EU countries' interpretation of the European Convention on Human Rights.' A Downing Street source said that a range of existing laws could be reviewed and new legislation was also possible. One option under consideration was to amend the 1998 Human Rights Act, which wrote the European Convention into British law, to require a 'balance between the rights of the individual and the rights of the community to basic security.' He said that 'although British judges should already take that balance into consideration, it's clear that sometimes they don't.'

He said that the act could be further amended if British courts blocked moves to deport terror suspects on the basis of 'memorandums of understanding' that they would not be tortured. A further possibility would be for the UK to consider withdrawing from specific clauses of the European rights convention if they led to court rulings which put 'community safety' at risk.

Such cavalier attitudes towards human rights on the part of the British government do not bode well for hope that the government will, or even can, become proactive in co-operating with the UN in mediating the Universal Declaration of Human Rights.

Indeed, there is every indication that even greater pressure is building up in the 'anti-migrant' lobby to use the 'war on terrorism' as a justification for urging former Prime Minister Blair to intervene more actively in the courts. The *Observer* article, for instance, went on to say that it had learned that the Police Federation (representing 130,000 officers in England and Wales) would use its imminent national conference to pass a motion calling for the government to intervene directly in the administration of justice. It would urge the government to completely overhaul current sentencing protocols under which some offenders can qualify for early release.

Considerations of space alone prevent this author from presenting further detail about the UK's current equivocation with regard to human rights. As with any of the other countries mentioned in previous chapters, as well as a number of other countries not dealt with specifically in this book, the question must be raised as to what the UN can do to effectively compel adherence to the Universal Declaration of Human Rights. We are accustomed to calling on the UN to intervene in less developed countries, but how can that body be effective in this respect in developed countries? Unless we can solve that problem, we will soon come face to face again with international inequity. These matters will be considered in Chapter 10.

References

1 Bosely S. British children: poorer, at greater risk and more insecure.
   The Guardian, 14 February 2007.

2 Raphael D. Politics and health outcomes; http://tinyurl.com/gpn34 (accessed 20 February 2007).

3 Control Arms. *G8 Arms Exports Fuelling Poverty and Human Rights Abuses.* Report issued through Amnesty International, 22 June 2005; www.controlarms.org/latest_news/g8report.htm (accessed 20 February 2007).

4 *Hansard*, 9 November 2006. Column 554W; www.ucl.ac.uk/Library/accso5o7.shtml (accessed 28 July 2007).

5 House of Commons, Defence Committee. *Second Report: the appointment of the new Head of Defence Export Services. HC 147.* London: House of Commons; 1999.

6 Campaign Against Arms Trade (CAAT). *Call the Shots: DESO campaign briefing;* www.caat.org.uk/publications/government/desobriefing0106.plp (accessed 20 February 2007).

7 Campaign Against Arms Trade (CAAT), op. cit., p. 3.

8 'UK sells arms to both sides.' *Private Eye*, 27 December 2002.

9 Foreign and Commonwealth Office. *Human Rights Annual Report;* www.fco.gov.uk/servlet/Front/pagename=OpenMarket (accessed 20 February 2007).

10 Campaign Against Arms Trade (CAAT), op. cit., pp. 8–9.

11 Amnesty International. *Annual Report: the state of the world's human rights;* www.web.amnesty.org/ailib/aireport/index.html (accessed 4 March 2007).

12 *Defence Director Magazine.* Key Milestones for Future Rapid Effect Systems (FRES); www.govnet.co.uk/heading.php?magazine=2-29k (accessed 4 March 2007).

13 Defence Secretary in Riyadh to lobby for deal on fighter aircraft. *The Guardian*, 27 September 2005, p. 2.

14 BBC (Radio) News. Broadcast 10am, 21 December 2005.

15 Leigh D, Evans R. Blair forced Goldsmith to drop BAE charges; www.guardian.co.uk/armstrade/0,,2003233,00.html (accessed 5 March 2007).

16 Ibid., p. 2.

17 Taylor D, Hattenstone S. A life on the run. *The Guardian*, 20 January 2007, pp. 33–5.

18 Toomey C. Dumped on our doorstep. *Sunday Times Magazine*, 4 February 2007, pp. 53–8.

19 Human Rights Watch. *UK's New Anti-Terror Law Rolls Back Rights*; http://hrw.org/English/docs/2001/12/14/uk3427.htm (accessed 1 March 2007).

20 Human Rights Watch. *New Approaches to the Asylum Process. Submission to the House of Lords Select Committee on the European Union, Sub-Committee F (Social Affairs, Education and Home Affairs)*; http://hrw.org/backgrounder/eca/asylum-process.htm (accessed 17 February 2007).

21 MacDonald T. *Third World Health: hostage to First World wealth.* Oxford: Radcliffe Publishing; 2005. pp. 53–5.

22 MacDonald T. *The Global Human Right to Health: dream or possibility?* Oxford: Radcliffe Publishing; 2007. pp. 107–8.

23 McQuade A. 'Why do we punish the victims of slavery?'; http://comment.independent.co.uk/commentators/articcle2105971.ece (accessed 17 February 2007).

24 BBC News. News item broadcast on 14 February 2002; http://news.bbc.co.uk/1/hi/uk/4942764.stm (accessed 1 February 2007).

25 Tanko N, Doward J. Revealed: Blair attack on human rights law. *Observer*, 14 May 2006; http://observer.guardian.co.uk/polotics/story/o,1774399.html (accessed 2 February 2007).

Chapter 8

WHO mediates the global right to health?

The UN, the WHO and the Universal Declaration of Human Rights

The World Health Organization (WHO) was one of the first agencies established, in 1948, by the UN to mediate the UN Charter and the Universal Declaration of Human Rights. However, as was explained in Chapter 2, the UN finds itself in some important respects compromised – not only by the conflict created by having to 'respect the integrity of nations' and 'prevent international conflict', but also by virtue of the fact that not all of its several agencies are co-operative in promoting the aims of the UN Universal Declaration of Human Rights. For instance, the author has already shown how the UN 'adopted' some agencies (such as the International Monetary Fund (IMF), the World Bank (WB) and the World Trade Organization (WTO)) whose actions conflict with such UN agencies as the WHO, the United Nations Children's Fund (UNICEF) and the United Nations Educational, Scientific and Cultural Organization (UNESCO). The reasons for this are basically ideological and political. The last-mentioned agencies were created in order to further and strengthen key clauses in the Universal Declaration of Human Rights. The first-mentioned agencies, on the other hand, were established to protect the rights of the banks and corporations in 'developing' countries in keeping with financial policies that were advantageous to the stockholders in those banks and corporations. The pivotal policy in promoting and sustaining such 'development' is global 'free trade' (as opposed to various forms of 'fair trade'). However, as this author has shown,[1] such globalization of free trade under neoliberal fiscal policies actually undermines such human rights as primary healthcare (PHC).

As has already been indicated in Chapter 2, the WHO – operating in the spirit of commitment to ensure global equity in access to PHC – made slow but systematic progress towards this goal up until Dr Halfdan Mahler from Denmark became the Director-General of the WHO in 1973. At that point this progress accelerated greatly. He set the year 2000 as the target date for his campaign of 'Health For All' (HFA 2000), and identified 38 specific targets by which this could be achieved.[2] However, during the 1980s the grip of the IMF (through its Structural Adjustment Policies) and of financial and banking interests in the highly developed countries made itself increasingly felt in constraining health and educational programmes, and other human rights, in many less developed nations. This gradually slowed down efforts to elaborate and implement HFA policies. Dr Mahler's term as Director-General of the WHO came to an end in 1988, and by the early 1990s it had become abundantly clear that the goals of HFA 2000 would not be met, even though some of the goals had been set back to 2015 or even 2020. To add insult to injury, the WHO was gradually made to play second fiddle to the fiscal development interests of the WTO. A WHO delegate was allowed to attend the WTO annual meetings, but only as an observer, being unable to vote or to take part in the debates!

Indeed, the years 1990 to 2006 could in many ways be regarded as years of eclipse for the influence of the WHO – but not entirely, because they did accomplish much in the control and elimination of various diseases. As described by the author,[3] Kofi Annan (the General Secretary of the UN) was concerned about the undermining of the WHO, and in 2000 put forward a package of proposals designed to put the UN back on track. These were called the Millennium Development Goals (MDGs). There were eight of them, and this author pointed out in the book cited above that even if these had been achieved, this would only have represented a minimum starting point for really effective UN reform. The MDGs are listed in Chapter 10.

In July 2006, the then Director-General of the WHO, Dr Lee Jong-wook, died suddenly. During his period in office, he had mediated the most consistently successful attack on HIV/AIDS. His death, of course, meant that another Director-General had to be appointed, and in the mean time Dr Anders Nordström served as Acting Director-General. It was well known that a new Director-General would be appointed towards the end of 2006. President Bush and several of his advisers were promoting Dr Julio Frenk for the post. This filled with dread those who were anxious to get the WHO 'back on track' in the quest for HFA. Julio Frenk was a strong advocate of poor countries solving their healthcare problems in a manner consistent with the demands of the WTO, and of global neoliberalism generally. In particular, he was an exponent of various private health insurance initiatives, and played a decisive rôle in preventing a left-leaning government from coming to power in Mexico in 2006.

However, the power and influence of US corporate interests were so strong, especially with the Bush protégé John Bolton, Acting US Ambassador to the UN and awaiting his endorsement as Ambassador in January 2007, that many felt that Julio Frenk was sure to become the WHO's next Director-General.

As most readers are aware, things did not turn out that way, because of democracy in the USA itself. On 7 November 2006, the USA held its mid-term elections. At the time, President Bush's party – the Republicans – had majorities in both Congress and the Senate. This power seemed untouchable, but the opposition party, the Democrats, made staggering gains in both houses, ending up controlling both on 8 November 2006. Not only did this mean that John Bolton's nomination as US Ambassador to the UN would not now be endorsed, but it also meant that Julio Frenk would not become Director-General of the WHO because neither house would allow such a Bush favourite to be endorsed. To cut a long story short, this allowed Dr Margaret Chan to be appointed as Director-General.

Her appointment has generated great optimism among progressive thinkers who are committed to the realization of global human rights. There is real hope that she may take up where Dr Mahler left off, and commit the WHO afresh to the goals of HFA. Whether this will or will not occur will be discussed later in this chapter. However, buried in the foundation documents of the WHO itself lie the causes of many of the weaknesses in that agency, which only began to make themselves obvious as financial considerations, under neoliberal globalization, gradually overtook the WHO's basic orientation in the 1990s. In order to understand this thoroughly, we need to consider more carefully the origin and development of the WHO.

Origins, policies and development of the WHO

When the UN brought the WHO into being in 1948, its broad mandate was to ensure access to PHC for all, to strive to eradicate disease and to promote public health. However, the WHO itself states that it was established in 1948 to:[4]

1 direct and coordinate international health and promote technical cooperation in this field
2 assist governments, upon request, in strengthening health services
3 provide appropriate technical assistance and, in emergencies, necessary aid at the government's request
4 stimulate and advance work on the prevention and control of epidemic, endemic and other diseases
5 promote and coordinate biomedical and health services research.

I would invite the reader to carefully scrutinize the second and third of these aims. The second aim suggests that the WHO could only work to 'strengthen health services' in any given nation if that nation requested this. One can think of nations which have not made such a request – for example, Burma and Sudan. Yet the Universal Declaration of Human Rights states that all people have the right to PHC. In cases in which PHC is not being provided to, say, certain minority groups to the same extent that it is to the rest of the population in a given nation, that information can – according to that second clause – be withheld from the WHO, which would have no automatic right to investigate by sending in field officers. The third clause can, in the same way, also be used to effectively deny PHC to many people.

Despite the many wonderful positive achievements of the WHO, the very ambiguity of the UN is putting a brake on its capacity to act wholeheartedly to fulfil the objectives of the Universal Declaration. We have seen how this has made it easy for the WTO, for instance, to use its legislation under TRIPS and such instrumentalities as GATT and GATS to force many nations into situations that are deleterious to their health. The extent to which, at this early stage in her tenure of the office of Director-General, even Dr Chan might be deflected from her goals has been well expressed in an open letter to Dr Chan from Dr Alison Katz. This author was given permission to quote extensively from the letter by Dr Katz on 3 February 2007. Alison Katz is a social scientist and clinical psychologist who has worked in the field of health and development for 20 years, and in several UN agencies, including the World Health Organization for 17 years, as well as for various NGOs. She is a member of the People's Health Movement.[5]

> Dear Dr Chan, You have taken office as Director-General of the World Health Organization after two discouraging decades in which the international health authority has been progressively subjected to pressure from powerful minorities, separated from the people it serves and diverted from its public health mission. In short, WHO has fallen victim to neoliberal globalization – as have most social and economic institutions serving the public interest. A number of WHO staff, in senior and less senior positions, have struggled against the worst excesses of this process, but the damage has been extensive. In addition to the tragedy (and scandal) of continuing, avoidable disease and death, WHO has lost friends among the people it serves and has gained rich and powerful 'partners' in search of new areas of influence.

Almost certainly, the world's people will force a return to the goal of social and economic justice, and in the area of health, to the promise of Alma Ata – which was itself explicitly predicated upon a new international economic order. 'Health for All' became WHO's slogan at the end of 'Les Trentes Glorieuses' (1945–1975) – thirty years of genuine progress towards a fairer – and therefore a healthier – world. This was the era of decolonization, when the need for redistribution of power and resources, including the rights of peoples to self-determination and control over national resources, was widely recognized and there was strong commitment to universal, comprehensive public services to meet basic needs for health. A time of optimism, moral vision and genuine progress.

Optimism was fully justified because the world had (and still has) ample resources to ensure peace, security and the wellbeing of all. Health for All is no utopia. It was and is achievable even if it is far more ambitious than the Millennium Development Goals which are – quite literally – a set of half measures defined and delimited by the G8. If thirty years is the length of cycles of progress and backlash, with social progress for people always overtaking, if only by a small margin, the backlash of powerful minorities to maintain their privileges, we are embarking now on the new 30-year cycle of progress. And your five years as Director-General (DG) of WHO coincides with that new cycle of progress. I would like to comment on some of the excellent points you have made in various speeches[6] since your election, confident that your vision – if you can realize even part of it unimpeded, will reinforce and accelerate that progress. You identify poverty and insecurity as two of the greatest threats to harmony which as you rightly state is 'a word at the core of the WHO constitution.' You state that 'health is intrinsically related to both development and security, and hence to harmony.' The social justice perspective would go further by stating that peace and security cannot be achieved without justice, and health cannot be achieved without equitable and emancipatory development.

Our focus today should be on inequality rather than poverty, not because of a preference for the relative over the absolute, but because unequal power relations are themselves the root cause of both poverty and insecurity, and because inequality, over and above any level of material wealth or deprivation, is bad for health and for cohesive, safe, healthy societies. Current inequalities – in which the richest 1% of adults alone owned 40% of global assets in the year 2000 and the richest 10% of adults accounted for 85% of the world total – are not only grotesque in their divisiveness, they are lethal. It has become fashionable to focus attention on the poor but to meet – and establish partnerships with – the rich. In order to address the fundamental problem of inequality, this pattern must be reversed. It is time to focus attention on the rich and powerful because they are the experts in the mechanisms of unequal power relations, and the architects of policies and strategies which produce, reinforce and accelerate inequalities. Those systems must be closely examined and opened up to public scrutiny and democratic control. To clarify, this is not a discourse on good and evil; the issue is one of profoundly antisocial and violent systems, not of the use made of those systems by a handful of rapacious individuals.

Poor people do not attend G8 summits, board meetings of the latest 'Global Fund' or 'philanthropic' foundation, let alone the World Economic Forum – where Chief Executive Officers of transnational corporations are offered even more privileged access to political leaders than they already enjoy. Poor people also hold meetings and they are represented – if imperfectly – at the World Social Forum (and in national and regional social fora) and in trade unions, social and political movements and elsewhere of course. As Director-General of WHO, you are committed to 'the people of Africa who bear an enormous and disproportionate burden of ill health and premature death' and you have made this 'the key indicator of the performance of WHO.' Your presence at the next World Social Forum on Health (Nairobi, 21–23 January 2007) which unfortunately coincides with your first Executive Board, and many other such events in the future, would represent real hope and inspiration for the world's people and an essential counterbalance to high-level meetings with government leaders and their corporate backers/advisers – who are increasingly one and the same.

You note that 'the landscape of public health has become a complex and crowded arena for action, with a growing number of health initiatives' and you remind us that WHO is 'constitutionally mandated to act as the directing and coordinating authority on health.' As you know, public–private partnerships have become the policy paradigm for global health work, despite the evident conflict of interest which would have outlawed such arrangements thirty years ago. Agencies and organizations with public responsibilities are 'partnering' with the private sector for one reason. It [appears to have] become the only source of funds. This situation has arisen because under neoliberal economic regimes, public sector budgets have been slashed and tax bases destroyed. Those developments are themselves the result of the influence of transnational corporations on governments and the international financial institutions. The solution to this problem is not for public bodies to go begging to the private sector, nor to the foundations of celebrity 'philanthropists' with diverse agendas, from industry. The solution is economic justice, including an adequate tax base, both nationally and internationally, to cover all public services, as well as proper funding of public institutions such as WHO through regular budgets so that they may fulfil their international responsibilities unimpeded by corporate interests.

You report that 'the amount of money being made available by foundations, funding agencies and donor governments is unprecedented.' This will be entirely positive if you are able to use these funds to pursue your vision and priorities, as is your right and your duty. It can be argued that if WHO had operated exclusively on regular budgets, even with a significantly smaller workforce but one that was dedicated to WHO's constitutional mandate, far more progress towards Health for All would have been achieved. As you say, 'Primary health care (PHC) is the cornerstone of building the capacity of health systems. It is also central to health development and to community health security.' PHC will remain health rhetoric if it is not supported by a solid, equitable tax base and other forms of redistributive justice (debt cancellation and reparation, fair trade, abolition of tax havens, democratic control of TNC activities, etc.). WHO itself needs to set targets for the level of core funding, starting perhaps at 70% of total expenditure, and increasing annually until undue influence is removed. The private sector has no place in public health policy-making at global or national level. This does not of course exclude responsibly designed interactions as in the past, but it does exclude partnerships, because partners must share the same goal.

You cite technical authority as one of WHO's four unique assets, and you state that 'we can be absolutely authoritative in our guidance' and that 'WHO must influence the research and development agenda.' WHO's rôle as the technical health authority is indeed the jewel in its crown. All the more important then to address the current crisis in science and reclaim knowledge systems for the public good. The commercialization of science and the close relationship between industry and academic institutions should be at the centre of WHO's concerns.[7] In this regard, the public has every right to insist that assurances be provided that WHO's recent reports on the health effects of Chernobyl and on the safety of genetically modified foods were researched, developed and produced in full consultation with independent scientists, unimpeded by other interests.

In relation to the corruption of traditional ideals of science, an editorial in the *Lancet* reported that 'Academic institutions . . . have become businesses in their own right, seeking to commercialize for themselves research discoveries rather than preserve their independent scholarly status.' Equally worrying is the new trade-related intellectual property regime which represents an unprecedented privatization of knowledge. Knowledge should be in the public domain, accessible to all. It must above all be truthful and reliable – a reminder which is not superfluous today. Given continuing high levels of avoidable disease and death, alarming resurgence and emergence of old and new infectious disease, respectively, and the devastating effects of environmental degradation and resource depletion on population health, the world cannot afford corporate 'science.' As the world's technical health authority, WHO must take the lead in transforming the way scientific research is conducted and funded and the way knowledge is acquired and applied.

You state that 'We share the ethical foundations of the health profession. This is a caring, healing and science-based profession dedicated to the prevention and relief of human suffering. This gives us our moral authority and a most noble system of ethical values.' It has not always been easy for staff to stay close to WHO's mandate or to maintain respect for ethical values either as public servants or as colleagues during the neoliberal decades. The pressure often proved overwhelming while the independence of international civil servants was increasingly undermined. As you know, staff–management relations reached a low point and resulted in the first industrial action in WHO's history in November 2005, a massive work stoppage involving 700 staff. This was despite threats of disciplinary action including dismissal from the Director-General's Office, which reflected not only deep dissatisfaction on the part of staff but astonishing disregard for international labour standards on the part of a UN agency.

The work stoppage was not an event to be deplored or lamented, let alone sanctioned.[8] It was a needed signal to Member States and WHO's wider constituency that radical change was needed.

Staff who struggled against the tide during these past two decades were often 'guilty' of their attachment to the Declaration of Alma Ata, which clearly identified social and economic root causes of avoidable disease and death, placed the debate squarely within international power structures, and insisted on a broad public health perspective which addressed non-health-sector determinants of health. They were part of the broad movement led by civil society organizations promoting a return to the values and principles of Health for All, which was instrumental in the creation of WHO's Commission on the Social Determinants of Health. Some, through the Staff Association, were also guilty of revealing to member states, as is their duty,[9] corruption, nepotism, abuse of rules and procedures and an ineffective internal justice system. In an exemplary response, member states called for a progress report on staff–management relations at the next EB (January 2007) and an audit of all direct appointments at and under the D1 level.

The response, however, of the last administration was dismal. WHO staff are now represented by a 'Staff Committee' which, apparently in collusion with administration, opposed discussion of the application of international labour standards (human rights in the workplace) in WHO, at the Annual General Meeting of the HQ Staff Association. This is an absurd situation, unworthy of a UN agency. Today, there is an opportunity for civilized and dignified staff–management relations in which staff concerns and perspectives are welcomed with interest and respect. The first step will be to declare that WHO supports not only a rights-based approach to health but a rights-based organization which fully respects the ILO Covenants. Staff morale and motivation will soar, as will confidence in their leadership.

In discussion with colleagues about all the above concerns, I have often heard that with my views, I should rather work for an NGO, that my perspective is 'political' and that WHO is not an implementing agency. My response to the first comment is that WHO staff should surely be more committed to the values and principles of Health for All than staff of any other organization, just as all UN staff should be at the frontline of the defense of the UN Charter. My response to the second comment is that health is political and that the PHC approach and Health for All was and is an explicitly political project – as is the neoliberal project for health and health care. Today's international health establishment denies any political values, intentions or interests, and presents itself as neutral, objective and armed with scientific facts. But scientific objectivity requires awareness and acknowledgement of underlying values and principles. The States Parties to the Constitution, in line with the Charter of the United Nations, accepted a set of nine ethical principles when they established the World Health Organization. This is the source of our 'moral authority', and it is a value-laden and highly political document – if one accepts that politics is about the organization of societal structures and functions, in particular in relation to the distribution of power and resources, for the benefit of its members.

My response to the third comment is that although WHO is not an implementing agency, it has a clear advocacy rôle in terms of identifying and promoting policies and strategies – on the basis of serious science and sound evidence – that will ensure the meeting of basic needs for health, among other things. In the neoliberal decades, WHO staff, and other international civil servants, have found themselves in an uneasy position with conflicting duties of loyalty on the one hand to WHO's constitutional mandate and the UN Charter, and on the other hand, as WHO is an intergovernmental agency, to member states and current office holders and their interpretation of these mandates. The most obvious examples are UN sanctions and the invasion of Iraq, which have caused public health catastrophes. These actions have been qualified as war crimes and genocide, respectively.

Less spectacular examples of conflicting loyalties relate to certain policies and strategies which do not make the headlines, but which cause illness and death on a daily basis and an even larger scale. WHO has failed to denounce, in the strongest possible terms, unfair rules of trade and commerce, odious debt, ruthless liberalization of economies and privatization of public services, and continued exploitation of people's national resources. This is despite ample evidence that these create poverty and inequality, interfere with people's capacity to provide themselves with adequate supplies of food and water, and maintain more than half the world's people in unspeakably miserable living conditions. At least 10 million children die every year, and the vast majority of those deaths are avoidable. Life-threatening, structural violence requires principled, unambiguous resistance, not cautious admonitions, let alone timid acquiescence.

We live in exceptional times when leaders of powerful nations, who scarcely represent their own people let alone all member states, embark on illegal actions leading to death and destruction, and when transnational corporations, in collusion with international financial institutions – with no democratic legitimacy or accountability – are allowed to impose policies which have been shown to have devastating effects on population health. Should staff choose loyalty to current office holders and selected member states rather than loyalty to the mandate of their organization and the world's people, who are often very poorly represented by their governments? Should respect for human rights and confidence in our own moral judgment tip the balance in these conflicting loyalties? 'The way in which citizens of the rich countries currently live their lives is, on the whole, morally acceptable.'[10] Recognition that 'everyone's favourite prejudice' is profoundly wrong is fundamental to the struggle for social justice and Health for All.

WHO (and other UN) staff may be misinformed (by failing to consult alternative sources of information) and disinformed (by accepting la pensée unique of mainstream and conventional sources of information). However, none of us can claim lack of access to full information. It is time to consider whether the way in which UN and WHO staff serve the UN Charter and WHO's constitutional mandate, respectively, is, on the whole, morally acceptable or whether this belief is 'our favourite prejudice.'

Dr Chan, the vision you have articulated is exemplary and an inspiration to staff. But you will need them to summon up the courage of their convictions, stand strong in the face of powerful opposition, and keep close to WHO's constitutional mandate, if they are to assist you in its realization.

Sincerely,

Alison Katz

The author has quoted this letter in full for two reasons. First, it draws together so many of this author's concerns about human health rights being hostage to the financial 'rights' of the powerful nations, their corporate interests, banks and stock-holders. Any transnational mediator of human rights must be able to distance itself from the influence of, and certainly control by, interests that are essentially inimical to the human rights it is there to protect.[11] The UN, as presently constituted, is unable to do this. If we are serious about the indivisibility of human rights, we are left with two choices – either we set about reforming the UN or we replace it. Chapter 10 deals with this issue. However, secondly, we have the testimony in the letter quoted of someone with 17 years of faithful service to the WHO behind her, whose services were so easily dispensed with when it became evident that she did not agree with the WHO being a docile handmaiden of neoliberal needs. This, as much as anything stated above, makes the point rather well.

To gain insight into many of the points made by Alison Katz, and to understand better the precise relationship between the UN and the WHO, we need to consider how the WHO's mandate was defined by, and then changed by, the background to 'Health for All.' It did not start with Halfdan Mahler, although he had done more than any other Director-General of the WHO up until 2006 to organize and promote it.

Origins of the 'Health for All' enterprise

At the 59th World Health Assembly held in Geneva in May 2006, the WHO was challenged by one of the delegates to 'return to the principles of the Alma Ata Declaration.'[12] The challenge was thrown down to the WHO by Dr Hani Serag at a special meeting convened by the World Health Assembly's Commission on Social Determinants of Health, and was attended by Dr Halfdan Mahler. The reader will recall that Dr Mahler was the energetic promoter of the HFA 2000 project during the 1970s and 1980s, while he was Director-General of the WHO. The major emphasis in the Alma-Ata Declaration (1978) was to make PHC available globally, without distinction as to race or wealth. By 2006, as this author argues,[13] the HFA campaign had been knocked well down the list of priorities as the WHO became increasingly pressured by the globalization of finance under neoliberal ideologies.

The briefing seminar at which Dr Serag made his comments focused on the necessity for major health stakeholders worldwide to act more decisively in addressing the social (rather than purely clinical) causes of ill health. Referring to the work of Halfdan Mahler, one of the delegates, Dr Giovanni Berlinguer stated: 'He gave us the dream. He launched new ideas and made us realize that it was possible to achieve health for everyone on the planet.'[14] He went on to show how, since 1990, global health politics had evolved under financial pressures that were inimical to the values of HFA. He lamented the impact of changes in global political economy which saw the interests of public health recoil because of the actions of major financial institutions. It was of crucial importance, he asserted, for the Commission of Social Determinants of Health to act energetically to renew the Alma-Ata spirit and add momentum to a global movement to see health inequities addressed. Many delegates, especially those from the less developed countries, made similar exhortations. For instance, Bolivia's Health Minister, Dr Nila Heredia, pointed out her country's challenges to address inequalities in health, citing the low health budget and historical factors as some of the major obstacles. She mentioned poverty, poor housing and low levels of education, particularly among women, as some of the key social determinants of health in Bolivia. The government was exploring several programmes to address health inequalities, which included a 'zero malnutrition' programme and the promotion of a social security system that would allow segments of society to gain free access to health.

Civil society representative Dr Hani Serag challenged the WHO and the Commission to address the 'profound determinants such as violence, wars, and neoliberal policies', and to allow the different components of the Commission to work independently. Dr Serag further challenged the WHO to return to the principles of the Alma-Ata Declaration. Commissioner Dr Ndioro Ndiaye stressed the importance of including sectors outside the health domain to be part of the developing healthy societies: 'If we do not look at the intersectoral angle, that health is not just a medical problem . . . we will not succeed.' The Commission already engages different ministries and sectors outside health to work collaboratively on social determinants of health and equity.

Given that Alma-Ata has occupied such a high profile in health promotion for nearly three decades now, it behoves us to consider the Declaration that bears its name in closer detail. The International Conference on Primary Health Care was convened by the WHO at Alma-Ata in the former Soviet Union from 6 to 12 September 1978. It was called specifically to express the need for urgent action by all governments, all health and development workers and the entire world community to promote and protect the health of all the people of the world. The conference was the brainchild of Dr Halfdan Mahler, the then Director-General of the WHO. Of course, it was not as if the WHO had accomplished nothing between 1948 and 1978. As we shall see below, it had achieved a great deal, but overwhelmingly in addressing clinical/biomedical aspects of health.

However, during those 30 years many physicians had begun to realize just how much social and economic factors could affect health and – especially in socialist societies – how much could be done to improve public health by political decisions alone. It was with these realizations in mind that Dr Mahler assumed the leadership of the WHO in 1973. He convened committees to look into the findings of the then infant science of epidemiology, and specifically addressed the relationship between poverty and ill health. By the time he had organized the 'Health for All 2000' programme, a great deal of optimism about the possibility of creating global equity had come to the fore in the social sciences and among progressive thinkers in general.

The Alma-Ata Conference ended with the release of its Declaration. This document is now regarded as a keystone of most considerations of public health and epidemiology. It is divided into 10 clauses, the most crucial of which is the seventh one, devoted to primary healthcare.[15] Briefly, these clauses can be summarized as follows:

I Defines 'health' as 'a state of complete physical, mental and social well-being, and not merely the absence of disease or infirmity. It goes on to assert that the attainment of health is 'a fundamental human right', and is a worldwide social goal whose realization requires the action of many other social and economic sectors in addition to the health sector.

II Existing conditions of great inequality in health, both between and within nations, are unacceptable. They therefore need to be the concern of all countries.

III Economic and social development, based on a New International Economic

Order (NIEO), is basic to the reduction of these inequities. The promotion and protection of health are essential to economic and social development and to world peace.

IV The people have the right and duty to participate individually and collectively in the planning and implementation of their healthcare.

V Each government is responsible for the health of all its people. By 2000, all people should have attained a level of health that will allow them to lead socially and economically productive lives. Primary healthcare (PHC) is the key to social justice.

VI PHC has to be based on practical, scientifically valid methods, and available through careful and participative education at the community level. It should be an integral part both of each nation's health system and of overall social and economic development at the community level.

VII Primary healthcare has to fulfil seven criteria:

1 It must be derived from the social and economic realities of the nation/ community itself.

2 It must address the major health problems of the nation, and citizens must participate in identifying these.

3 It must involve education, through all available media and institutions, about these problems.

4 It must involve the broadest possible sources – political, economic and social, as well as clinical – of insight into the problems.

5 It must require and promote maximum community impact.

6 It must be sustained by mutually supportive referral systems, calling on all other social agencies (police, education, businesses, etc.).

7 It must rely on a congress of health workers specifically trained to involve everyone in the public health enterprises.

VIII All governments should formulate national policies and plans of action to sustain programmes of PHC. This requires political decisions – both domestic and expatriate.

IX All countries need to cooperate in promoting and sustaining PHC. The UNICEF/WHO reports on PHC constitute an ideal basis for such development.

X An acceptable level of health for all people by the year 2000 can be attained through better use of the world's resources. At present, many of these are wasted on arms and warfare.

As can be seen, most of the clauses of this Declaration emphasize the paramountcy of health rights, implying that where expense is required to sustain them, this must be regarded as a priority item. This, of course, is not only humane and ethical, but also socially logical, for health both underlies and presupposes all other human rights. It is the overarching theme which renders the human rights enterprise coherent. A world community guided by PHC as its basic sustaining right would be one characterized by the kind of sentiments expressed in the following short poem, which was written in homage to the HFA by the Danish poet Halfdan Rasmussen.[16]

> I fear not execution
> Not torture and not hate
> Not death from rifle barrels or
> The shadows on the gate

> I fear not restless nights with
> Shooting stars of streaking pain
> I fear but blindness from a world,
> Indifferent and insane.

Although health rights are perceived by many in health promotion or global health as being particularly relevant to the welfare of the less developed countries, this is not the case. As Chapter 7 made clear, basic human rights to health are violated on a large scale in the UK. As Tony Pugh[17] demonstrated in an article he wrote in February 2007, economic conditions in the USA – the world's richest nation – are such as to promote serious inequities in health within the USA itself. Excerpts taken from that article report the following.

The percentage of poor Americans who are living in severe poverty has reached a 32-year high. Millions of working Americans are falling closer to the poverty line, and the gulf between the nation's 'haves' and 'have nots' continues to widen.

The latest analysis of the 2005 census figures (the most recent available) found that nearly 16 million Americans are living in deep or severe poverty. A family of four, with two children and an annual income of less than $9,903 (half the federal poverty line) was considered severely poor in 2005. So were individuals who earned less than $5,080 a year.

It is interesting to note how widespread poverty actually is in the USA. People, even those in the USA itself, often imagine that certain states are rich (e.g. California) and others are poor (e.g. Mississippi), but this is not entirely true. What American political practice has produced is great inequality within the same areas of the country, even down to municipal level. The article referred to above, for instance, cites the states with most people in deep poverty as follows:

> California – 1.9 million
> Texas – 1.6 million
> New York – 1.2 million
> Florida – 943,670
> Illinois – 681,786
> Ohio – 657,415
> Pennsylvania – 618,229
> Michigan – 576,428
> Georgia – 562,014
> North Carolina – 523,511

Pugh reports that the number of severely poor Americans increased by 26% between 2000 and 2005. That's 56% faster than the overall population in poverty increased over the same period. The report also found statistically significant increases in the percentage of the population in severe poverty in 65 of 215 large US counties, and similar increases in 28 states. The review also suggested that the rise in severely poor residents was not confined to large urban counties, but extended to suburban and rural areas.

The plight of the severely poor is a distressing sideshow to an unusual economic expansion. Worker productivity has increased dramatically since the brief recession of 2001, but wages and job growth have lagged behind. At the same time, the share of national income going to corporate profits has dwarfed the amount going to wages and salaries. This helps to explain why the median household income of working-age families, adjusted for inflation, has fallen for 5 consecutive years.

These and other factors have helped to push 43% of the nation's 37 million poor people into 'deep poverty' – the highest rate since at least 1975. The proportion of poor Americans in deep poverty has climbed slowly but steadily over the last three decades. However, since 2000, the number of severely poor has increased more than any other segment of the population.

This was the precise opposite of what was expected when the analysis was undertaken. The researchers expected to see decreasing levels of deep poverty and increasing levels of moderate poverty as those formerly in deep poverty gradually moved up. This, of course, is a variant of the well-established myth of the 'trickle-down effect' so beloved by advocates of the 'inevitability' of neoliberalism. Instead what they found was that the growth spurt, which levelled off in 2005, in part reflects how hard it is for low-skilled workers to earn their way out of poverty in an unstable job market that favours skilled and educated workers. It also suggests that social programmes are not as effective as they once were at catching those who fall into economic despair.

About one in three severely poor people is under the age of 17 years, and nearly two out of three are female. Female-headed families with children account for a large share of the severely poor.

Nearly two out of three people (10.3 million) in severe poverty are white, but blacks (4.3 million) and Hispanics of any race (3.7 million) account for disproportionate shares. Black people are nearly three times more likely than non-Hispanic white people to be in deep poverty, while Hispanic people are roughly twice as likely to be.

Washington, DC, the nation's capital, has a higher concentration of severely poor people – 10.8% in 2005 – than any of the 50 states, topping even hurricane-ravaged Mississippi and Louisiana, with 9.3% and 8.3%, respectively. Nearly 6 out of 10 poor District residents are in extreme poverty.

The study found that, with the exception of Mexico and Russia, the USA devotes the smallest portion of its gross domestic product to federal anti-poverty programmes, and those programmes are among the least effective in reducing poverty (again, only Russia and Mexico do worse).

We can summarize much of the above by pointing out that the HFA (2000) movement, followed by its demise, may suggest that the WHO is not up to the task for which it was created. However, this is not true, as we shall now show. But what it *does* show is that, for HFA to be given a chance to work, we must make radical changes to the way in which the UN as a whole discharges its responsibilities with regard to promoting the Universal Declaration of Human Rights (*see* Chapter 9). We shall now briefly consider the achievements of the WHO in implementing programmes for the eradication of specific illnesses, and the bases for Dr Margaret Chan's optimism in undertaking her rôle as the WHO's Director-General.

The WHO's achievements

Since its establishment in 1948, the World Health Organization has collected many feathers in its cap. For instance, it has allowed the world to save up to US$ 1 billion every year in vaccination expenses since smallpox was eradicated in 1977. In the early

1950s – 150 years after the introduction of vaccinations – an estimated 50 million cases a year occurred worldwide! The WHO had been running vaccination campaigns since 1948, and by 1967 the figure had fallen to 10–15 million cases annually. Then, in 1967, the WHO launched an intensified offensive against the disease. The 'ancient scourge' threatened 60% of the world's population, killed one in four of its victims, scarred and/or blinded most survivors, and eluded any form of treatment. However, through the success of the global eradication campaign, smallpox was finally pushed back to the horn of Africa and then to a single last natural case, which occurred in Somalia in 1977. A fatal laboratory-acquired case occurred in the UK in 1978. The global eradication of smallpox was certified, based on intense verification activities in all countries surveyed, by a commission of eminent scientists in December 1979, and subsequently endorsed by the World Health Assembly in 1980.

They expected to consign polio similarly to the dustbin of history by 2005, but – as we shall see later – were prevented from doing so by a combination of reactionary religious forces and military conflict. Even at the level of only eradicating disease, the WHO still has much to do, for each year 17 million people, equivalent to the combined populations of Switzerland and Belgium, still die of infectious diseases, most of which could comparatively easily and cheaply be prevented in the context of appropriate social values and political will. Compared with the money wasted on war, the financial outlay required for the WHO to be optimally effective in the field is just a drop in the bucket. For instance, it only costs US$ 15 to immunize a child against the six deadliest diseases. Of special significance to people in the developed world is the fact that 24 million people worldwide die of various cancers, diabetes or cardiovascular diseases. Medical research is also continually discovering new diseases – 30 more diseases have come to light in the last two decades, largely through the coordination by the WHO of armies of research scientists, epidemiologists and medical workers.

Cholera, for instance, is another disease against which the WHO's field workers are racking up impressive victories. Consider the following extract, covering 3 days in 1997, based on the diary of a WHO doctor, Dr Maria Neira. Her account is reported by the WHO.[18]

> 5:00 a.m., Northern Uganda. A small aircraft takes off from a rural airport near Entebbe carrying Dr. Maria Neira, a WHO epidemiologist in charge of the WHO Task Force on Cholera, to a refugee camp in Adjumani. In the past, cholera vaccines provided little but a false sense of security. After years of extensive field trials, the WHO eventually found two new oral vaccines that show promise.
>
> 'We are still in the very early days with the new cholera vaccine, which potentially could be used in similar settings. But we seem to be moving in the right direction', says Dr. Neira. 'Cholera is not only a feared killer disease. It wreaks havoc on economies of developing countries, seriously hurting trade and tourism. Cholera vaccine is a welcome development, but fighting the disease with medications only is an uphill battle. The root causes of the virtually global cholera outreach go much deeper, and poverty is by far the most important one.'
>
> After three days of efforts by Dr. Neira and her colleagues, 38,000 Sudanese refugees have made history: they were part of the first large-scale trial involving a new cholera oral vaccine, which so far is proving effective.

The hunt for Ebola

An example of a disease that had not even been heard of 20 years ago is Ebola. In 1994, a team of WHO researchers investigated what appeared to be a highly contagious disease among chimpanzees, and therefore a potential threat to humans, in the Tai Forest of Côte d'Ivoire. One of the scientists indeed became infected – presumably as a result of dissecting one of the chimpanzees that had died. The disease turned out to be Ebola, a disease that has only occurred comparatively recently among native people of the area. It was the first time that the Ebola virus had been isolated in the wild.

Realizing the possibility of identifying the natural host or 'reservoir' of this horrifying condition, WHO scientists – in collaboration with staff from the Paris-based Pasteur Institute and the government of Côte d'Ivoire – have established a laboratory and camp in the Tai Forest, including the construction of platforms at the edge of the forest canopy, some at heights of 35 metres, to enable scientists to capture animals and undertake sampling of vertebrates and arthropods in the various strata of the tropical forest.

'I have seen with my own eyes the impact of the disease, and the wide swath of death that it leaves behind, scarring families and entire communities', said Dr Pierre Formenty, the man in charge of the project. 'Finding the reservoir requires a substantial investment in time and money, because the source could be any of the millions of plants or animals in the jungle. So, the mystery remains.'[19] If and when the scientists find the natural reservoir of Ebola, they hope that it will help to predict when and where outbreaks of Ebola infection are most likely to occur.

One could give many other uplifting examples, and the reader is encouraged to check the WHO website as cited above for further details. However, with regard to the eradication of disease, the WHO has run up against a particularly obstinate viral infection – polio. As stated earlier, the WHO had hoped to have completely eradicated the disease (as they did with smallpox) by 2005. They were making great progress towards this goal at the turn of the millennium, when the condition appeared to make a comeback in Pakistan, Afghanistan, India and Nigeria. From such widely separated sites it could easily spread internationally again. However, their efforts to mount intensive immunization programmes in the affected areas were stymied. For instance, in Pakistan and Afghanistan, the highest prevalence of polio has (even today) is in the border regions between those countries. However, the WHO cannot safely send immunization teams there because it is a war zone. In particular, Taliban forces regularly cross back and forth between Pakistan and Afghanistan, and any 'official' agents with other projects in mind are regarded with high suspicion and are frequently killed.

The situation in Nigeria is different again.[20] Many Muslims in the north believe that polio vaccination is being used as a ploy by Western countries to inject people with certain chemicals to reduce their fertility, or to infect them with HIV/AIDS, in order to reduce the population of Muslims.

'We put together a team that incorporates all the stakeholders so that they will see for themselves and be convinced whether or not the polio vaccine is safe', Nigeria's Minister of Health, Eyitayo Lambo, told reporters in Abuja in late 2004 as the team departed.

He predicted that the team would return with good news in time for the next round of nationwide polio immunization, due between 23 and 26 February 2005. In October 2004 the governors of three states in northern Nigeria – Kano, Kaduna and Zamfara – decided to suspend polio immunization until the vaccines were investigated and proven safe. They gave in to rumours and suspicions going back several years which had culminated in the widespread rejection of polio vaccination by people in the north. The rumour that polio vaccines were contaminated was first spread by some Islamic preachers. These claims were given greater credibility locally when they were endorsed by the Supreme Council of Shari'ah in Nigeria.

Following the suspension of polio vaccination by the three northern states, President Olusegun Obasanjo's federal government ordered that tests be conducted on the vaccines to determine their safety. Kano, Kaduna and Zamfara states also ordered their own separate investigations. However, tests conducted at the National Hospital in Abuja and at a laboratory in South Africa at the behest of the federal government showed the vaccines to be uncontaminated by any of the suspected chemical and biological agents.

Despite this, Kano state government said that its own tests showed the vaccines contained levels of the hormone oestrogen capable of lowering fertility in men. Neither Zamfara nor Kaduna states have made known the results of their own probes, nor have they lifted their suspension of polio vaccination. In the mean time, polio, which had been eradicated in almost all of Nigeria with the exception of Kano state (the last known reservoir), has made a comeback – not only in Nigeria, but also in several neighbouring countries where it had previously been wiped out. By 2005, it had crippled thousands of children in Thailand.

According to the WHO, strains of the virus traceable to Kano state have recently been traced to other parts of Nigeria, including the nation's commercial capital, Lagos. The WHO reported that more than 40% of the 677 new cases of polio recorded worldwide last year were in Nigeria. Recently, Nigerian strains of the polio virus have appeared in several west and central African countries, including Benin, Togo, Ghana, Burkina Faso, Cameroon and Central African Republic. This raised concern among international health experts that the world might be slipping in its efforts to wipe out polio by 2005, and indeed they were right!

The attempt to eradicate polio has already cost in excess of US$ 1 billion. It is estimated by WHO epidemiologists with whom this author has communicated that complete eradication will now take at least 4 more years and cost another US$ 1 billion. Success in the enterprise would require the UN to actively intervene as required in order to ensure that immunizations are carried out. In the mean time, Dr Margaret Chan is both confident and committed to the goals of HFA. I close this chapter with statements from her address to the WHO Executive Board, which met on 22 January 2007.[21]

In that very long and involved statement Dr Chan made it clear that on the whole she was optimistic, but that her basis for being so was her conviction that international co-operation at all levels could be challenged to address the imperative of HFA and thus fulfil a major aim of the UN's Universal Declaration of Human Rights. A typical source of her essential optimism is reflected in her comments on what she calls the 'spectacular success story of measles control.' She stated that on 15 January 2007, the WHO announced that ambitious targets for the reduction of measles mortality had been exceeded. The WHO had aimed for a 50% reduction in measles deaths by 1999, but by that date such mortalities were down by 60%.

Dr Chan went on to say that the news gets better by the day. WHO interventions are saving large numbers of lives among the very poorest people. These interventions include widespread provision of bed-nets to reduce the incidence of malaria, and vitamin A supplements that boost the natural immune system, which are bringing about a reduction in infectious diseases among African children. Dr Chan recounted many of the WHO's achievements before she became Director-General, and in all of her comments emphasized how the WHO could work effectively for human rights, even in co-operation with other agencies, but only if it set its own goals based solely on health needs and medical evidence. If she is successful in this, the WHO will soon be rescued from the subservient rôle that it has been compelled to play since 1990 to the goals of free trade and SAPs – monitored infrastructural projects that compromise the health rights of the poorest people in many of the less developed countries.

What all of this suggests is that the WHO *is* best situated to mediate the world's health needs, provided that it can control and promote its own programmes. However, the question remains as to whether or not the UN is best placed as a transnational mediator to allow the WHO the latitude that it needs to fulfil its HFA mandate. This issue will be considered in Chapter 9.

References

1 MacDonald T. *Health, Trade and Human Rights.* Oxford: Radcliffe Publishing; 2006. pp. 3–5.
2 MacDonald T. *Third World Health: hostage to First World wealth.* Oxford: Radcliffe Publishing; 2005. pp. 277–85.
3 MacDonald T. *The Global Human Right to Health: dream or possibility?* Oxford: Radcliffe Publishing; 2007. pp. 2–9.
4 World Health Organization. *The World Health Organization;* www.un.org/pubs/ourlives/who.htm (accessed 5 February 2007).
5 Katz A. Open letter to Dr Chan; www.lists.kabissa.org (accessed 19 February 2007).
6 Chan M. Speech to the World Health Assembly as D-G elect on 4 January 2007; www.who.int/dg/speeches/2006/wha/en/index.html (accessed 26 January 2007).
7 This section of Alison Katz's letter is drawn from the Convention on Knowledge, Institute of Science in Society; www.i-sis.org.uk/conventionknowledge.php (accessed 26 January 2007).
8 Alison Katz's post was abolished 3 weeks after the work stoppage, after 17 years' service with the WHO. This was obviously in retaliation for her involvement in promoting the human rights of UN staff.
9 According to WHO Executive Board Resolution BB91/1993/REC/1.
10 For example, the Initial Complaint prepared for the First Hearing by staff at the International War Crimes Tribunal; http://deoxy.org/wc/warcrim2.htm (accessed 31 January 2007).
11 Pogge T. *World Poverty and Human Rights.* Cambridge: Polity Press; 2002.
12 World Health Organization. *Managing the Politics of Equity and the Social Determinants of Health;* www.who.int/social_determinants/links/events/wha2006/en/in (accessed 10 March 2007).
13 Ibid., p. 1.
14 Ibid., p. 2.
15 World Health Organization. *The Alma Ata Declaration;* www.euro.who.int//aboutWHO/policy/20010827_1-333k (accessed 2 March 2007).
16 Rasmussen H. 'Poem in Praise of Health For All', sent as a gift to Alison Katz by H Mahler. Permission to include it was granted on 31 January 2006.
17 Pugh T. *US Economy Leaving Record Numbers in Severe Poverty;* www.commondreams.org/headlines07/0223-09.htm-27k (accessed 27 July 2007).

18 World Health Organization. *The World Health Organization;* www.un.org/pubs/ourlives/who.htm (accessed 5 February 2007).

19 Ibid., p. 3.

20 Science in Africa. *Nigeria: Muslim suspicion of polio vaccine lingers on;* www.scienceinafrica.co.za/2004.march/polio.htm (accessed 15 February 2007).

21 Chan M. Dr Margaret Chan on her appointment of D-G of WHO in an address to the Evaluation Board of WHO on 22 January 2007 in Geneva; www.archives.health.dev.net/af-aids/ms902848.htm (accessed 2 March 2007).

Chapter 9

Can the UN promote the WHO's objectives?

Health, human rights and the UN Charter

As has been suggested throughout this book, the UN has evolved in such a way that the goals of global human rights unambiguously enunciated in the UN's foundational Universal Declaration of Human Rights sometimes conflict with the goals of some of the UN's co-opted agencies, such as the International Monetary Fund (IMF) and the World Trade Organization (WTO). In addition, the fact that the UN is committed to the prevention of conflict between nations makes one of its rôles the protector of the integrity of nations, and this renders it difficult for it also to defend individual human rights as expressed in its UDHR. However, bacteria and viruses, to say nothing of industrial, environmental and even psychological causes of disease, are no respecters of national boundaries. There is increasing awareness, probably initially because of HIV/AIDS and TB, that health is a global issue of pressing importance. The politicians in different countries can no longer ignore the issue, largely because lay people are becoming broadly aware of it.

Although the World Health Organization is constituted to mediate such matters internationally, and has already made impressive gains in meeting that obligation, it has often been thwarted in the task by what can only be described as ambiguity, inconsistency and equivocation in the way that the UN Security Council addresses its mandate as the single authoritative transnational arbiter.

Of course health has been a global issue for most of recorded history,[1] but it has throughout most of that time been regarded as a low-priority issue. This has remained the case ever since the WHO came into existence, despite the fact that its major guiding principle is that 'the health of all people is fundamental to the attainment of peace and security and is dependent upon the fullest cooperation of individuals and states.'[2] Indeed, as has been shown in the preceding chapter, the 'Health For All' objective has not yet been recognized as a major foreign policy objective by most nations. In this respect, Cuba is an inspiring exception. Of course, the groundwork for making it a foreign policy issue has already been well prepared by the WHO in its immunization programmes, public health education campaigns and provision for global epidemiological research. However, in a sense this has all been seen by political figures working at government policy level as an excuse for not becoming involved themselves!

Only in the last two or three decades has foreign policy of major players on the international scene begun to recognize the cruciality of global health, and even then only because of wars and competition for economic advantages. For example, consider such events as the Soviet invasion of Afghanistan, the 1972 oil price crisis, the rise of militant Islam in Iran and elsewhere, and wars in Iraq, Somalia and elsewhere. Factors like this, combined with a looming global environmental catastrophe, have at last focused the political mindset on health as a pivotal issue. Some thinkers are far more optimistic than is this author about this growing awareness, as evidenced by the following recent comment by David Fidler in the *Bulletin of the World Health Organization*:[3]

> The current attention to the relationship between health and foreign policy indicates that the gulf between these two policy endeavours has disappeared, and that this process has changed both in ways that remain enigmatic. Perhaps most significantly for the relationship, health now prominently features in the permanent foreign policy dialogue between Rousseau and Kant. Foreign policy-makers regularly confront issues of population health that relate to national security, economic power, the protection of human dignity and the development of strategically important regions and countries. They must make decisions on these matters by setting priorities that protect national interests without losing sight of the universal aspirations of health policy. For the foreign policy community, the rise of health as an issue did not fundamentally change the permanent dialogue, but it did force foreign policy-makers to rethink, sometimes radically, how they view national interests.

Nowhere is this reality more apparent than in the relationship between national security and public health. Whether discussing biological terrorism, HIV/AIDS or pandemic influenza, foreign policy makers and public health experts have increasingly framed certain health threats as security challenges. Without question, the major powers of the international system have driven this process with their national interests in mind, which worries many of those involved in protecting and promoting global health. However, participating in the permanent dialogue of foreign policy does not allow health experts and advocates to avoid the pressures that leaders face to make decisions with scarce resources in volatile contexts of uncertainty, competition and vastly differing national capacities.

Noble words indeed, but for the gulf to 'disappear', the international community would have to do a great deal of reprioritising. For example, it would have to explicitly establish policies for promoting equity in PHC, adopt alternatives to neoliberalism in mediating international trade, etc. However, certainly there are indications that our political leaders are becoming aware that even narrow concerns with national financial interests require a more active engagement with global health issues. Research into the disease threats consequent upon global warming have acted as a wake-up call to many in this respect. Other factors have included such phenomena as the reappearance of TB in epidemic proportions in parts of the developed world only recently thought to be free from it and, of course, HIV/AIDS. Ease and speed of travel by air have created a situation in which millions of people are now travelling all over the world, sharing not only the wealth of cosmopolitan values but also once fairly isolated diseases.

The WHO's success in eradicating smallpox and its near victory over polio provide examples of what can happen when health issues assume a high profile in government thinking internationally. The polio issue, for example, has been rendered more involved by both warfare and religious obstruction, as dealt with in Chapter 8. However, the efforts made so far in the campaign have already involved levels of international finance and political co-operation that would have been unthinkable 30 years ago. In mediating such commitments, the G8 – not often regarded as being concerned with public health – has been pivotal. It would be difficult to attribute all of this solely to concerns for national security. Historically, especially since the nineteenth century, the promotion of economic advantage of one nation over others, and the prevention of political instability in allied governments, have been every nation's aims in security policy. Epidemics, be they HIV/AIDS, SARS or avian flu, impact badly on national security because they cause political instability.[4] In a similar way, HIV/AIDS was designated an issue of national security.[5] The same is true for all of the pandemic influenzas.

In many ways, such focusing on an international threat that cannot be addressed by armed conflict is beneficial over and above the obvious clinical implications. It tends to increase a readiness to co-operate, to become familiar with the problems of other nations, and to thereby broaden participation in each other's goals and build up diplomatic relationships.

The need for a politics of global health

The Alma-Ata Declaration of 1978 was firmly based on the knowledge that the success of its 'Health For All' objectives depended not only on international goodwill (which could hardly be said to be the case previously), but also on governments prioritising the UDHR claim that primary healthcare (PHC) was a human right. Nearly 30 years later, when this desideratum is finally being recognized as something more than a pious dream, the world community – led by the UN or some other transnational mediating body – has to urgently develop strategies for making global health a reality. In the last decade in particular, environmental and – of necessity – health issues have moved much further up the priority list of international affairs.

In the face of sudden outbreaks and the sudden spread of rogue diseases, such as various types of killer influenzas, there is a need to develop agreed international strategic approaches. The WHO has already led the way in this with regard to less spectacular, but crucial, health issues. One could cite the International Baby Food Action Network (IBFAN) and the Framework Convention on Tobacco Control. Indeed, it would take pages to list the number of organizations dealing with such specific health issues that have recently emerged. Some of these are not entirely controlled by the WHO, but are hybrid public–private initiatives. These will all need to be coordinated to prevent waste of resources by duplication or distortion through the need to meet the self-interest needs of private funders. Two national examples of how such enterprises might be organized are discussed in a recent paper in the *Bulletin of the World Health Organization*.[6] This is instructive, because Switzerland represents an advanced industrialized nation, widely recognized for its excellent public health initiatives, whereas Brazil is a less developed country whose major contribution to global health has been the manufacture of generic copies of antiretroviral drugs at a fraction of the cost demanded by transnational pharmaceutical corporations.

The Swiss approach

The Swiss government operates a joint strategic approach to global health developed by the Swiss Federal Office of Public Health and the Department of Foreign Affairs working together. They produced a document entitled 'Agreement on foreign health policy objectives', which was presented to the Swiss cabinet in October 2006.[7] This document incorporates three major strands of global health action. These are not specifically coordinated, but there is competition between them. They can be summarized as follows:

1 (a) addressing normative health issues
   (b) international agreement and avenues for co-operation
   (c) global outbreaks of disease and pandemics
2 commitment to health in the context of development assistance
3 policy initiatives in such other sectors as foreign policy with regard to trade.

The document emphasizes Switzerland's commitment to human rights through-out, and sets out three priorities in foreign health policy, as follows:

1 maintaining the health of the Swiss population
2 coherence between national and international health policy
3 strengthening international health co-operation in the furtherance of global health.

In furthering these aims, the Swiss government works eclectically with the WHO itself, various NGOs in the countries concerned, and private agencies.

The Brazilian model

Although Brazil is a less developed country in global terms, it is much better developed than, say, many of the poorest countries in Africa. In some statistics it is in fact classified as a 'middle-income country', but there is a huge inequality in the distribution of wealth there, and nearly 80% of Brazilians live at or below the poverty line. Since the election of Luiz Inacio Lula da Silva's reform government in 2002, the country's educational system has undergone a number of improvements, and this has included the institution of a vigorous public health programme. Also, and due to the same factors, Brazil has contributed significantly to global public health. The 2003 constitution lists health as a right of the people and an obligation of the state. However, it was a close call, because if Lulu had not been elected, Brazil would have completed the Free Trade Agreement with the USA and would not have been able to finance its health reforms. Brazil's global health diplomacy is now based on the premise that the first priority is the health of its people.[8]

Its paramount rôle in providing generic copies of antiretroviral drugs produced under trade names by the major pharmaceutical giants has already been mentioned. ARVs produced by the pharmaceutical firms are sufficiently expensive to be quite beyond the reach of HIV/AIDS victims in the less developed countries. The generic copies cost about 5% of what the pharmaceutical ones would cost, and have been shown to be just as effective. Recently the WTO has been active in trying to prevent Brazil from continuing with this practice, and in all likelihood will succeed, by bringing TRIPS to bear on the case. It has already stopped India from doing the same thing.

On another front, the participation of Brazil in the fight against tobacco has been strongly reinforced by its leading rôle in other international health forums. However, Brazil's international impact, through energetic health diplomacy in its foreign office diplomatic activities, has not been confined to smoking and HIV/AIDS. A spokesman from Brazil's Ministry of External Relations was quoted as saying that 'The visibility of our Ministry of Health, both at technical and political levels, has been crucial to the credibility of our health philosophy.'[9]

And it was exactly this philosophy that led to Brazil, in the person of Celso Amarim, being elected President of the Intergovernmental Negotiating Body. According to Kickbush and colleagues,[6] Celso reaffirmed the need to bring health into foreign policy, but also to bring foreign policy into health. Brazilian global health diplomacy was grounded on the country's solid preparation 'back home' with the National Commission for Tobacco Control, headed by the Ministry of Health and gathering representatives from different ministries (health, agriculture, international relations, treasury, education, environment, trade and industry, and communications). Again this illustrates the point that good global health governance begins at the national level, and this intensive multi-sector preparation allowed the Brazilian delegation to intervene in almost all working groups of the negotiation process. The final document therefore had major contributions from the Brazilian delegation, which highlighted the crucial link between the national and the global, and further manifested itself in the success of the Tobacco and Other Cancer Risk Factors National Control Program in Brazil.

Both of these examples clearly show that, before a viable foreign policy on global health can be mounted, two other factors need to be addressed.

1   There is a need to develop domestic public health programmes that are consistent with the Alma-Ata spirit. That is, they must be community based, accessible to all, and vigorous in soliciting lay input.
2   Foreign office diplomats working in other countries must be thoroughly aware of the health problems of the countries in which they serve, and be prepared to liaise with government health officials in both countries.

As Kickbush and colleagues[6] make clear, these examples highlight the need to build capacity for global health diplomacy by training public health professionals and diplomats, respectively. Two types of imbalance need to be addressed as a priority, namely imbalances that can emerge between foreign policy and public health experts, and imbalances that exist in the negotiating power and capacity between developed and developing countries.

Both Brazil and Switzerland have taken initiatives to address these imbalances through networking, experience exchange and capacity building. Switzerland has initiated an experience exchange between heads of department of international health from OECD countries to track their changing rôle in global health diplomacy. Brazil has made its experiences available through co-operation with most Latin American countries, and with the Portuguese-speaking African countries. The Ministry of Health has also embarked on a dialogue with the Brazilian School of Diplomacy to explore a two-way capacity-building exercise together with the National School of Public Health and the Oswaldo Cruz Foundation. The Swiss Federal Office for Public

Health is supporting an initiative to introduce global health into graduate studies in foreign relations at the Graduate Institute of International Studies in Geneva. A new programme entitled 'Global health diplomacy' will analyse the interface between the theory of international relations on the one hand, and the practice of international relations in health. It is in this kind of context that nations with different health perspectives and different cultural approaches to the contextual social issues can teach one another.

But the Empire strikes back

It must not be imagined that it is only carelessness or apathy that always prevents governments in the First World from doing the right thing. Neoliberalism is not an accident or some kind of economic phenomenon that has arisen organically without deliberate human intent. Indeed, it is often wrong to speak of 'laws of economics.' A people and their government can decide what they want their economy to do *and* go about creating the necessary legislative framework. Since neoliberalism, by its very nature, is quintessentially based on competition, it will itself take active steps to eradicate other forms of government operating on alternative models. A few pages back the author mentioned the 'inspiring example of Cuba.' However, its inspirational significance is due not only to its achievements in realising the politics of Health For All in its own country, and elsewhere, but also to its resistance to the attempts by neoliberal interests to destroy it. Various writers opposing neoliberalism have referred to it ironically as 'the Empire', after a famous Hollywood blockbuster film.

The author has had in-depth experience of the Cuba situation and has written extensively about it – for example, on its educational[10] and health[11] programmes. These ideas were long scorned by the neoliberal-controlled media, but recently new insistent voices have made themselves heard. For instance, Philip Agee was for many years a CIA operative involved in clandestine attempts to obliterate the forces opposing neoliberalism. However, he has come to see the error of his ways, and on 10 March 2007 he wrote an article[12] describing the persistent attempts made by neoliberal agencies to discredit Cuba's achievements. He describes what he calls 'Cuba's 50-year defiance of US attempts to isolate it as an inspiration to Latin American people.'

As the reader is no doubt aware, there has recently been a pronounced resurgence in Latin America of formal political opposition to neoliberal globalized finance and its negative impact on health (and other human rights) in Third World countries. Cuba, once isolated by the fact that most other Latin American countries belong to the Organization of American States (OAS), is now encountering a growing appreciation that its politics are the way forward in decreasing the global equity gap. Throughout all of that time Cuba held the torch high with its system of free universal healthcare and free and universal education at all levels, and world-class cultural, sporting and scientific achievements. As Agee comments, 'You won't find a Cuban today who says things are perfect, but they would also argue that there has been a world of improvement since the revolution.'

Throughout Cuba's revolutionary independence of US control since 1959, the US authorities have used every trick possible, including sabotage, terrorism, and economic and biological warfare, to overthrow the revolution. They have been both assiduous and resourceful in trying to foment internal conflict so that, if it should ultimately succeed, the USA can then put it down to an oppressed people rising up against the 'tyranny of totalitarianism'!

Philip Agee, of course, knows of what he writes, for he was a CIA officer in Latin America in the 1960s and was complicit in these attempts. In total, around 3,500 Cubans have been killed by US-sponsored terrorism and more than 2,000 permanently disabled. No other country has suffered terrorism for as long (nearly 50 years) or as consistently.

Since September 11, 2001, the USA has led in what it has called a 'War on Terrorism', but most people do not realize to what extent it has itself contributed to it! And what is also to be deplored is that many of those who do realize this fail to distinguish between 'US capitalism' (its government, bureaucracies and banks, etc.) and the ordinary US citizens. For the latter are also victims of neoliberalism, as any dispassionate analysis of their healthcare system, for example, would make clear. The 'empire' continues to strike back, even to the extent of ruining the lives of many of its own people.

Can we learn anything from this? We can, because the Cubans have not been slow in evolving strategies for defending the impressive gain they have made in globally promoting such basic human rights as health and education. They realize that to keep it to themselves would further isolate them and make it easier for the 'empire' to wipe them out. They have also taken steps to infiltrate the US government-sponsored 'anti-Latin' groups in Florida. Indeed, five Cubans who succeeded in infiltrating such groups, in the hope of warning Cuba of further terrorist initiatives, have been incarcerated in widely scattered prisons in the USA since 1998. The 'Miami Five', as they are called, were convicted by the US courts for 'espionage', and their trial was held in Miami, where of course there was little chance of them securing a fair hearing. So Cuba's persistent efforts to promote an alternative approach to neoliberalism continue to produce martyrs.

In our search for global equity in human rights, the Cuban alternative to neoliberalism may yet inform our efforts.

Education in global public health

In the UK, a number of health studies departments in colleges and universities already offer programmes dealing with global health issues. Despite this, and the fact that similar programmes exist in other countries, most of these courses do not specifically train people for work in desperately poor countries. In fact, the World Health Report (2006)[6] describes the lack of training of sufficient numbers of people in global public health as representing a serious and worsening problem.[13] Thus in a number of countries, public health programmes (run by clinicians with good biomedical training) fall foul of poor management, scarce resources inappropriately assigned and cultural misunderstandings due to the unintentional insensitivities of the practitioners to the contextual cultural subtleties. Adequate programmes of vigorous pre-service training must be developed and, as far as possible, run in conjunction with personnel from the target countries.

The students need to be sufficiently acquainted with world affairs and international relations to lend coherence to the particular situations into which they may be sent.

They must be thoroughly au courant with complex – but often highly localized – health problems and issues of inequities in health. They must be kept up to date about newly emerging diseases, and have a solid grasp of health as a socially determined phenomenon. In addition, of course, they need to be familiarized with other actors in the field, namely the relevant NGOs and local government agencies.

Also crucially important are newly emerging agencies and institutions which have arisen specifically in response to the crisis. The People's Health Movement, discussed earlier in the book, is one such agency, but there are many others. Another is the World Federation of Health Associations and various regional public health bodies. A further demand which must be made on these people is that they be encouraged to keep abreast of the relevant literature. When running such courses in developed countries, the author used to run a 2-hour per week programme in which students briefly reported on their journal reading, and would be expected to answer questions about the material raised by their classmates and/or the tutor.

One critical area in which appropriately trained workers in global health can be employed to good effect is the critical examination of government policies on large-scale developmental projects, which are likely to disrupt the lives of large numbers of people. Often these undertakings do not represent policy decisions by the local government, but are undertaken as part of 'development' programmes by overseas interests. Their primary aim, of course, is to render the target country more amenable to the dictates of free trade. As this author has amply shown,[14] such activities often have a huge adverse effect on local health and greatly widen the wealth gap within the target country.

Mary Robinson, former President of the Irish Republic, and named in 2004 as the UN High Commissioner for Human Rights, had a great deal to say about the intimate relationship between health and human rights,[15] and commented:

> The increasing links between domestic and foreign policy, and the growing prominence of health in both, raises new questions about national interest and national security in an interconnected world. Notions of human security and global public good have been enormously helpful in shifting debate away from narrow and short-term thinking. No one is suggesting that greater attention to human rights as part of health and foreign policy discussions will move issues of marginal strategic importance for the richest countries to the centre of the global agenda. Clearly, human rights cannot provide all the answers or make easier difficult public health choices concerning priorities and distribution of goods and services. But what other framework offers any detailed ethical, moral or legal guidance to policy-makers?
>
> Human rights are the closest thing we have to a shared values system for the world. We should take every opportunity to see them not simply as abstractions, but as guides to real action.

Examples of what she meant by 'real action' are highly instructive, and could act as a guide to the formulation of government policy generally. She pointed out that the global response to something like SARS, or even Ebola, is informed by irrational levels of fear, and thus powerful governments can – in order to please their electorates – respond well to this danger. However, this does nothing to address the levels of poverty and deprivation which are often the real reasons for the destructiveness of such diseases. Even the response to HIV/AIDS was slow because the wealthier nations regarded it as only affecting the poor countries. And even now the response is still hopelessly inadequate. Mary Robinson was quick to recognize that much of the reason for this was that the large pharmaceutical corporations could see little financial gain in developing drugs for people most of whom could not pay well enough for such firms to keep their shareholders happy. As Mary Robinson herself argues, this gives some indication of the mind-set changes which have to occur before the UN can hope to mediate health programmes of global benefit.

More than a billion people do not (at the time of writing, in 2007) have access to safe drinking water. As global warming increases, this situation will become much worse. More than 2.6 billion people lack access to sanitation. Every year 10 million children die of preventable diseases and one out of every 16 African women (not merely pregnant African women, which would be horrific enough, but all African women) dies as a consequence of pregnancy. Can anyone deny that these are political issues, not clinical ones, and that they can therefore be remedied without recourse to involved scientific/medical research? Generally speaking, lack of access to basic determinants of health only affects the poor – and the poor (under present systems) rarely have any political voice.

How then, Mary Robinson asks, can human rights be moved from philosophical/ ethical/sociological theory to action? She answers this crucial question along the following lines. First, human rights can help decision makers to assess risk. The human rights framework – by focusing attention on vulnerable populations, minorities, the rural poor and especially women, who are most often neglected and marginalized – forces those in authority to ask hard questions about whose needs are not being met, and whose voices are not being heard. Equally important, human rights provide standards against which government performance can be measured over time. Today the right to health or, in some cases, the more limited right to healthcare, first affirmed at the international level by the WHO in 1946, is constitutionally recognized and protected in nearly 100 countries. This means that governments have not voluntarily committed to progressively realizing the right to health, and can be criticized for not achieving sustained progress.[16]

Secondly, human rights principles and legal obligations can be used by advocates and authorities to help to diagnose the effectiveness of current health policies and to develop new approaches. Human rights organizations have become skilful (at both national and international levels) in using documentation and other evidence to highlight the impact of policies on vulnerable or marginalized groups and to demand changes which can promote health. For example, the efforts to frame HIV/AIDS as a human rights issue, by emphasizing how the spread of the disease has been affected by rights violations such as discrimination and gender inequities, have played a key rôle in strengthening public health responses. By focusing on principles like participation, transparency, accountability and non-discrimination, human rights provide an overarching framework in which detailed decisions can be made in the light of national and local priorities. Robinson goes on to say that two projects that she and her colleagues at Realizing Rights – the Ethical Globalization Initiative, are developing, in co-operation with the WHO and other partners, seek to take these lessons forward. These efforts aim to raise awareness of how a rights-based approach can work in practice and to help to forge common interests and solutions to major health challenges.

The first project, the Ministerial Leadership Initiative for Global Women's Health, is a new network of female health ministers from around the world who represent an untapped, powerful force for highlighting the right to health and the importance of prioritising health for women and girls worldwide. One of the group's aims is to build support for using the human rights framework to address a broader development of questions between donor and recipient countries.

A recent study by the Organization for Economic Co-operation and Development (OECD) showed that donor-country policies are increasingly integrating human rights both as guiding principles and as operational priorities for development programmes. However, more must be done, particularly in the area of health. They hope to convene a group of health and finance ministers from developing countries with senior development officials from key donor countries that have prioritized health funding. By examining development assistance trends, such as the move to greater general budget support, through a human rights lens, they see the need for intensified support to parliamentarians and civil society groups. These actors can hold their governments accountable for policies that progressively implement without discrimination rights to health, education and food security, among others. It is hoped that this type of analysis will raise awareness and test the degree to which policy priorities in donor and recipient countries are changed by attention to the rights of the most vulnerable.

The second project addresses the issue of health worker migration from developing to developed nations. Growing public concern about the movement of health professionals from poor to rich countries has not been matched by effective joint government action. Some steps have been taken, such as the Commonwealth code of conduct which is aimed at curtailing unethical recruitment, but leadership on this issue is still lacking. In co-operation with the Global Health Workforce Alliance and the WHO, they are seeking to encourage policy dialogue and joint action between sending and receiving countries on the health worker crisis. Their aim is to forge a greater sense of shared responsibility for addressing this growing problem, and to promote agreements that take into account the human rights implications for sending and receiving countries, as well as the right of individual health workers to migrate. The challenge is to advance realization of the right to health while protecting health workers' rights to seek employment in fair conditions.

The need to legislate for international health impact assessment

A particular piece of international legislation that needs to be passed, as mentioned above, is one that would give the UN the right to insist that an international Health Impact Assessment (HIA) be made as a precondition to any large-scale infrastructural project anywhere in the world. However, mandatory HIAs would be of greatest benefit to countries already living on the edge of economic ruin. A brilliant exposition of the link between HIAs. human rights and global public health was published in 2007.[17] As the author has already argued in a previous publication,[18] health rights equity cannot even be entertained as a long-term aim as long as health in less developed countries is routinely sacrificed to development. This raises fundamental issues about inter-national politics and economics generally, the kind of issues about which people would prefer not to think. However, unless we do face them at the radical level – as discussed in Chapter 10 – we can forget about prospects for global equity.

These points are well made in the paper by Scott-Samuel and O'Keefe.[17] Those authors point out that, over and above the need for HIAs to deflect health abuses that would otherwise accompany the infrastructural projects that are often associated with 'development' for the benefit of international free trade, HIAs have to be much more formally enshrined in UN law. This would entail three broad and salient contextual issues. First, we cannot simply acquiesce to the widely promoted view that neoliberalism is here to stay and is the only way forward. Instead, we have to ensure that wherever it is being applied – commonly in an IMF-funded and SAP-constrained 'development' project in some poorly developed country – the entire enterprise is guided by HIA funding. Secondly, HIAs must be explicitly wedded to the foreign policy of both participating nations to such an extent that ignoring their recommendations would itself constitute a violation of UN human rights law, including such specific conventions as Rights of the Child and the UDHR itself. Thirdly, and perhaps most importantly, the rôle of HIAs must be explicitly framed in the context of rights legislation and even added as extra clauses to the UDHR.

Of course, HIAs are already sometimes used in public policy decision making in industrialized wealthy countries by local green groups or health advocacy councils, but firm and internationally accepted legislation is now called for. At present, the WHO already requires accountability based on HIAs of national governments within their own borders. This sort of thing needs to be made global if its application is going to promote health equity. This author argues that if the UN is to be able to mediate such an undertaking, it needs to be extensively restructured, as discussed in Chapter 10.

For instance, it is often assumed that the existence of an international law (e.g. a prohibition against torture) would be sufficient for each nation to make it part of their national law. We have seen matters work this way in some cases with regard to the EU and individual states within it. However, with something involving heavy cost implications, such as HIA, an international law would be much less likely to be enforceable unless it was widely in force at the national level. Therefore, it would seem that while international HIA should ideally be part of the foreign policy of each nation in the UN, it will not be realized at the practical level until most member states have embraced HIA as domestic law.

Foreign policy with regard to trade and health

As this author has argued in a previous publication,[1] international trade and health have been deeply interconnected throughout recorded history, and no doubt earlier. Bubonic plague is a good example, going back at least to the sixth century BC. Nowadays, the speed and ease of travel and of importing and exporting trade products have greatly speeded up the process and have led to the wide-scale generation of the possibility of pandemics. At another level, the promotion of almost completely unregulated free trade, a requirement for sustaining neoliberal global finance, has vastly undermined the health of millions of people. Therefore, for the WHO to succeed in applying the Alma-Ata Declaration, international trade has to be governed by policies with regard to health. International and national HIAs are part of the solution, but the issue involves even wider consideration. This point has been argued by many researchers, and a good example is provided by a recent publication by Chantal Blouin.[19]

Using international pharmaceutical corporations as an example, she argues that the trading practices of such enterprises exemplify 'policy' incoherence at the interface between trade policy and global health. A more insidious reflection of such policy incoherence is provided by health tourism. For some years after the establishment of the NHS in Britain, people from other Commonwealth countries and/or from the USA 'visited' Britain in large numbers and, while there, underwent surgery or treatment for conditions that would have been ruinously expensive back in their home countries. The matter becomes much more serious when such an interface occurs between a highly industrialized First World country and a desperately poor Third World country, because such a situation redounds to the disadvantage of the former. However, as we shall see, it is much more likely to work the other way.

Organ transplants now represent big business in health tourism – from the EU and the USA to countries like India, Nepal and various South American republics. While in Ankara, Turkey, in the 1980s, this author met people who had raised much needed cash by selling one of their kidneys and, in one case, an eye. At a less desperate level, many drastic treatments are likely to be much less expensive in the Third World than in, say, the USA. However, the use of these facilities by health tourists effectively deprives local people of similar treatments.

As this author has shown in another publication,[20] the trade has for years gone in the opposite direction – to the great financial advantage of the already wealthy nations and to the manifest disadvantage of the poor. In this he refers to the degree to which First World countries exploit Third World countries by recruiting their medically trained personnel. Not only are these doctors and nurses often paid considerably less than a metropolitan country would have to pay its own graduates, but their medical training has cost the First World countries nothing, and the already acute shortage of such people in their own countries is exacerbated. Of course, the blandishment of higher pay and better working and living conditions would not cause the 'ideologically pure' to emigrate to the EU or the USA, but that is not really the point.

The above-mentioned paper by Blouin[19] suggests that five conditions are necessary – but not sufficient – to ensure that trade policies are coherent with national health policies. It goes without saying that this assumes that the national health policies are already informed by the global perspective of the Alma-Ata Declaration. These five conditions are:

1 dialogue between participating nations such as to establish the relevant health issues that stand to be affected
2 leadership by the respective ministries of health rather than by corporate interests or market forces alone
3 well-established institutional mechanisms in both countries, for coordinating the project
4 transparency in nominating and engaging financial stakeholders – because such a project will involve costs
5 an agreed commitment to abide by the dictates of a common set of evidence-based criteria.

As Blouin's paper shows, these five conditions involve a huge matrix of other considerations – political, financial and administrative. For instance, the dictates of the WHO and their readiness to apply TRIPS and the consequent plethora of patent-protection legislation has rendered it more difficult for really crucial drugs – such as antiretrovirals – to be made available on the basis of need. Blouin also observes that the benefits of a policy change are large and involve a small group of participants, who will have a strong incentive for supporting the policy change. However, it is usual that only minor advantages are anticipated by large numbers of people who, collectively, are likely to have less influence on policy because it is so much more difficult for diffuse groups to organize. The implication is that, where trade policy and health have the potential to interact, the policy preferences of actors with large benefits to gain would prevail. This invariably redounds to the disadvantage of the most needy, who already have little enough voice. The examples that Blouin cites are huge international pharmaceutical corporations or banker-backed firms selling health insurance under GATS provision. Because only small, tightly knit and highly articulate groups of people are involved, it is often politically expedient to accommodate them. However, to meet the objective of large-scale community-based health projects, such as those enjoined in the Alma-Ata approach, it will be necessary for national governments to facilitate trade policies that actually promote the achievement of wide-scale national and global health objectives. These are precisely the objectives of least interest to the small corps of special-interest advocates referred to above.

The question then arises as to how the necessary mechanisms for broad-based collaboration, based on popular need rather than on financial gain, are to be established. Already some countries (e.g. Sweden, Norway, and to some extent the UK) have inter-ministerial committees that are constituted to meet this need. They can concentrate their efforts on encouraging policy coherence across issues affected by international trade. For example, Blouin cites procurement, environmental policies and public services (of which schooling and healthcare are significant). In the best run of these, the rôle of public health is paramount. This author has observed that there is an increasing tendency to include the private sector – sometimes as dominant in decision making – along with the relevant government departments. He regards this as wholly undesirable on several grounds. Private involvement has to create profits (otherwise why do it?) and there is a consequent need to meet the expectations of shareholders. Such a situation tends to distort the incentive from meeting patients' needs to gaining kudos in the boardroom. Hence they cost more in the long run and often fail to fully address unprofitable pockets of health need in the community.

These objections are, in effect, highlighted in Blouin's paper by citing the example of Thailand. In Thailand, the Ministry of Health made estimates of the financial costs, taking TRIPS into account under the GATT and the fact that the US delegate to the WTO had requested a longer period of patent protection. The Thai Ministry had attempted to modify the negative impact of this by advocating a policy of intellectual property provision, but without the negative public health implications ordinarily consequent upon strict adherence to TRIPS. The minority put forward an alternative model to that piloted by TRIPS. They did this upon discovering that the prevailing Thai policy was attracting health tourists to the country. The Ministry of Health, reports Blouin, had been monitoring the impact of this health tourism and found that the increased demand for doctors and nurses to care for foreign patients had led to an internal brain-drain from the rural public sector to the urban private sector. Thanks to this monitoring capacity, the ministry could adopt a policy for scaling up the training of doctors and nurses under a special curriculum to facilitate rural distribution.[21]

Blouin argues that often a regional approach to obtaining the relevant data is a better way of sharing limited resources. Such data, of course, are required to create a trade policy that reflects community health needs as opposed to a national approach.[22] Other examples are cited, but it is obvious that not all countries would be able to mount the necessary legal and academic infrastructure to lay the required groundwork. In such cases, a process of regional collaboration would represent an optional approach to internal coherence. This could in fact be part and parcel of the author's recommendation[23] that 'Regional Trade Zones' be established to mediate GATS in that area initially, but possibly globally if applicable. Needless to say, such an approach would be quite contrary to the policies and objectives of the WTO.

What should be obvious is that the policies of the WTO, and the ways in which they are applied, are themselves 'national policies', but principally of the powerful nations in the developed world. As discussed earlier, although the WTO is democratic in that every nation – large or small, rich or poor – can have a seat in the WTO, there is no limit as to the number of lawyers and other advisers that can accompany any one national delegate. The practical effect of this is that the will of a few very powerful nations tends to prevail at the annual WTO ministerials.

It is in this regard that the WHO can occupy a pivotal position, consistent with its Alma-Ata mandate, in acting as a collaborator and in providing the technical assistance in assembling a strong evidence base for elaborating trade policies consistent with global health rights. Over and above these considerations, the problems imposed by large discrepancies in national wealth globally will continue to be reflected in grievous levels of health inequity unless we vigorously address the wealth divide. The WHO cannot do this. The UN, on the other hand, could – if it could only somehow reorganize itself to do so. That matter is the subject of the next chapter, but to close this chapter, what can the really wealthy nations, the G8, do in the field of elaborating health policies and also to finance the process more realistically than they are doing at the moment?

The G8, population health and foreign policy

In recent years a number of scholars have concerned themselves with determinants of health, other than the purely biomedical ones, in the world. People like David Raphael, Alex Scoot-Samuel and others have already been cited in this book, and the issue is increasing in urgency by the day. In March 2007, two well-known authorities on the social and political aspects of health promotion – Ron Labonte and Ted Schocher, both at the Institute of Population Health at the University of Ottawa in Canada – published a paper dealing specifically with the theme of the issues discussed above.[24]

If we care to discuss the rôle that the wealthy G8 nations seem to play, both in elaborating foreign policies that are conducive to global health justice and in financing much of the undertaking, it is reasonable to assess the potential of these G8 nations. All eight of these countries (Canada, France, Germany, Italy, Japan, Russia, the UK and the USA) occupy a high international profile in supporting the UN and in the global fiscal and political order generally. Some of them have also played a leading rôle in aggressively researching the social and political determinants of health. As Laboute and Schocher aver, the G8 nations are a 'logical starting point for any enquiry into the relations between foreign policy and health.' As well as being rich, these eight countries have enormous influence. They account for 48% of the global economy and 49% of global trade, they hold four of the five permanent Security Council seats in the UN, and they are majority shareholders in the IMF and the World Bank.[25]

The question arises as to whether there is any explicit commitment on the part of the G8 nations to play a significant rôle in trying to achieve global health equity. Unless they are going to achieve national advantage by such actions, what should be driving them to so involve themselves? They are not under any moral, religious or political 'contract.' However, as has been observed already, there are factors other than sheer goodwill that impel them to act for the global good. The G8 itself is expected to address itself to at least five altruistic commitments.

1 Their communiqué from Geneva[26] states that the G8 is committed to make globalization work for all their citizens, but especially for the world's poor. At the very least this means ensuring that their PHC needs are met.

2 The UN General Assembly, and hence all the nations in it, is committed to achieving the Millennium Development Goals (MDGs) by 2015. The MDGs can be found on the Internet,[27] but three of them relate directly to sustaining global health, while the others (extreme poverty, poor nourishment, inadequate housing, oppression of women, and lack of access to safe water and sanitation) impact directly on health. As this author has pointed out previously,[28] the MDGs (listed in Chapter 10) will not all be met. In fact most of them won't be met. Moreover, much of the reason for this failure is due to WTO requirements, IMF Structural Adjustment Policies, etc., in which the G8 nations are deeply complicit.

3 The huge disparities in wealth between the G8 countries and most of the others is unsustainable and will lead to a collapse of global social order unless the G8 addresses the issue as a priority. Even at the purely epidemiological level, the ability of the G8 to cheaply and easily counter such pandemics as HIV/AIDS, and even TB, while many in the rest of the world cannot afford to do so, means that – given the speed with which pandemics can now spread – we in the G8 nations will not remain safe for long.

4 Under neoliberalism, we in the G8 nations are regarded by much of the impoverished world as being actively involved in condemning them to degradation and death. Modern means of communication ensure that we know about them and they know about us. No one can plead ignorance. This is a recipe for upheaval, if not the end of civilization as we know it.

5 The Universal Declaration of Human Rights unambiguously commits the wealthy nations to policies for reducing the (at present) widening equity gap. Article 25 of the UDHR states that everyone has a right to an 'adequate standard of living', and Article 28 refers to 'a social and international order in which the rights and freedoms' set out in the rest of the UDHR 'can be fully realised.'

There is not a great deal of ambiguity here! Can the world meet the challenge? The answer is 'Yes, rather easily, if we change our national priorities.' For instance, in order to meet the goals set out in the MDGs, we need somewhere between US$ 25 billion and US$ 70 billion. However, the UK alone has already spent around US$ 3.6 billion during 2006 on the wars in Afghanistan and Iraq.[29] In 1999, the UN set a target of 0.7%

of gross national income as an appropriate *minimum* contribution from each of the G7 countries (this was before Canada was added) in order to ease the wealth discrepancy. Although Canada, Japan and the USA did offer increases in their foreign aid at the 2005 G8 meeting, they still did not reach 0.7%, and now all the G8 countries lag behind this minimum figure. Norway, Sweden and Denmark – none of which are in the G8 – currently exceed this level of support.

And cash-flow donations are not the only aspects of G8 failure. There are also the problems of debt relief and trade. As the author has made clear from previously cited sources,[8] despite promises that were made at the 2005 G8 meeting regarding debt relief, various bureaucratic delays have resulted in some clawing back of this money. Likewise, promises of trade liberalization – by which poor countries could gain access on an equal footing to First World markets for their goods – have not turned out as hoped, sometimes due to governments of the EU countries and the USA providing such generous subsidies to their farmers that Third World producers just couldn't compete. In fact, to make matters worse, WTO regulations required them to allow the EU and the USA access to the Third World markets, undermining even further the economic and health prospects of their own farmers.

As we have seen in this chapter, the UN has the research base necessary to further all of the Alma-Ata aims, but it is not doing so at several levels. It could be convincingly argued that it is prevented from doing so for various reasons internal to its own constitution – some of its agencies have aims that conflict with the original aims of the UN. It is also caught in the catch-22 situation of having to mediate between nations to prevent war or disruption of international affairs, and thus cannot intervene in the internal affairs of a nation that is causing no international disruption, while at the same time supposedly acting as both advocate and mediator in defence of individual human rights as defined in its own UDHR.

In the next chapter we shall closely analyse the UN's many rôles, first of all by considering the various types of breaches of human rights that have been outlined in Chapters 3 to 8, and then by examining ways in which the UN could be used to mediate these breaches more effectively. Of course, it might be that the UN, as presently constituted, is unfit for purpose. In this case, there remain two possibilities. The first is to redesign the UN so that it does not include some of its existing agencies, and another body is set up to mediate global finance. The alternative is to scrap the UN altogether and to create some other means of transnational mediation.

References

1 MacDonald T. *Health, Trade and Human Rights*. Oxford: Radcliffe Publishing; 2006.
2 World Health Organization. *Constitution of the World Health Organization: preamble*. Geneva: World Health Organization; 1949. p. 1.
3 Fidler D. *Reflections on the Revolution in Health and Foreign Policy*; www.who.int/bulletin/volumes/85/3/07-041087/en/index.htm (accessed 12 March 2007).
4 Price-Smith A. *The Health of Nations: infectious disease, environmental change and their effects on national security and development*. Cambridge, MA: Massachusetts Institute of Technology Press; 2002.
5 National Intelligence Council – United States. *The Global Infectious Disease Threat and its Implications for the US*; www.fas.org/irp/threat/nie99-17d.htm (accessed 12 March 2007).
6 Kickbush I, Silberschmidt G, Buss P. Global health diplomacy: the need for new perspectives, strategic approaches and skills in global health. *Bull WHO*. 2007; **85**: 230–32.

7 Agreement on Foreign Health Policy Objectives, adopted by the Swiss Federal Department of Foreign Affairs in Berne, Switzerland on 9 October 2006; www.bag.admin.ch/international (accessed 10 March 2007).

8 Kickbush I, Silberschmidt G, Buss P., op. cit., p. 232.

9 Kickbush I, Silberschmidt G, Buss P., op. cit., pp. 27–33.

10 MacDonald T. *Making a New People.* Vancouver: New Star Books; 1985.

11 MacDonald T. *Health Care in Cuba: an analysis of developments since 1959.* Lampeter: Edwin Mellen Press; 1999.

12 Agee P. A shameful injustice. *The Guardian (Section 1),* 10 March 2007, p. 27.

13 World Health Organization. *World Health Report: working together for health.* Geneva: World Health Organization; 2006. pp. 163–4.

14 MacDonald T. *Health, Trade and Human Rights.* Oxford: Radcliffe Publishing; 2006. pp. 4–15.

15 Robinson M. *Realizing Rights: the ethical globalization initiative;* www.realizingrights.org (accessed 4 March 2007).

16 Ibid., p. 12.

17 Scott-Samuel A, O'Keefe E. Health impact assessment, human rights and global public policy – a critical appraisal. *Bull WHO.* 2007; **85:** 212–17.

18 MacDonald T. *Health, Trade and Human Rights.* Oxford: Radcliffe Publishing; 2006. pp. 67–9.

19 Blouin C. Trade policy and health: from conflicting interests to policy coherence. *Bull WHO.* 2007; **85:** 169–73.

20 MacDonald T. *The Global Human Right to Health: dream or possibility?* Oxford: Radcliffe Publishing; 2007. pp. 160–62.

21 Blouin C, op. cit., p. 173.

22 Reichmann J. *Managing the Challenge of Globalised Intellectual Property Regime;* www.iprsonline.org/uncladisictsd/bellagio/docs/Reichmann_Bollagio2.pdf (accessed 9 March 2007).

23 MacDonald T. *Health, Trade and Human Rights.* Oxford: Radcliffe Publishing; 2006. pp. 121–3.

24 Labonte R, Schocher T. Foreign policy matters: a normative view of the G-8 and population health. *Bull WHO.* 2005; **106:** 185–191.

25 Corlazzoli V, Smith J, editors. *The G8 and African Final Reports: an overview of the G-8's ongoing relationship with African development from the 2001 Geneva Summit to the 2005 Gleneagles Summit;* www.g8.utoronto.co/evaluation/osed/g8africa_0506244.html (accessed 8 March 2007).

26 G-8. *G-8 Communiqué,* 22 July 2001; www.g8.utoronto.co/summit/2001genoafinalcommuniqu.html (accessed 8 March 2007).

27 The Eight Millennium Development Goals: www.un.org/milleniumgoals (accessed 2 February 2007).

28 MacDonald T. *The Global Human Right to Health.* Oxford: Radcliffe Publishing; 2007.

29 Griffiths R. War costs hit $1.8 billion. *Morning Star,* 27 April, 2007, p. 1.

Chapter 10

Transnational advocacy and mediation

Cops and lawyers for the global village

Probably it was the speed and frequency of air travel, combined with a growing awareness of our mutual interdependence, that gave the phrase 'the global village' its ring of authenticity for most of us. More recently, the imminent prospect of irrevocable global warming and the threat of a looming environmental disaster have acted to shrink the global village still further. More people then ever now see beyond narrow sectional or national interests. New potential pandemics such as SARS or avian flu have helped to imbue something even more inclusive than mere internationalizing, pushing beyond that to a longing for a productive, sane and co-operative cosmopolitanism. Perhaps as never before, the very idea of war strikes people as unimaginably stupid, a form of chauvinistic self-indulgence which we can no longer afford.

However, even a village needs a police presence to mediate neighbouring disputes and even to intervene to protect the safety of our daily coming and going. On top of this, even a village needs a lawyer or two to act as advocates when a case comes up for mediation.

At the end of World War Two, the world was a very different place. Most people did not travel much, and different countries seemed far away, remote and strange. In small clusters of religious or political faiths, of linguistic and cultural enclaves, we pretty well remained sequestered in our mutual suspicion and hatred. Indeed, such sequestration engendered its own sense of cosy warmth, security and – above all – moral certainty. Nationalities or blocs of nations could derive advantage by cultivating cordial bonds of mutual mistrust.

It was in such a context that the UN came into being. People looked to it as a kind of referee – not only to protect us from another international conflict, but also to protect the cultural certainties of the victorious powers. In its rôle as a defender of peace, it gradually became assumed that the UN was there to ensure and promote peace based on existing power relationships. The UN's second General Secretary, Dag Hammerskjold, who served two terms in that capacity from 4 April 1953 to 18 September 1961, made this quite clear both in his writings and his actions. He was very active in defending US foreign policy and in arguing that a neoliberal approach to international business was the way forward. Furthermore, in 1963 a book which he had written, entitle *Markings*, was published. It explicitly stated that he regarded Christianity as the ultimate faith, and he classified himself as a 'Christian Mysticist.' He died in a plane crash while on his fourth visit to Congo – where he had played such a prominent rôle in helping the USA to dispose of the newly emerged African nationalist, Pratice Lumunba, and the establishment of Moise Tshombe as Lumunba's (eventual) replacement.[1] As it turned out, even the plane crash was probably not accidental, as the media proclaimed it to be at the time. Desmond Tutu, not yet an Archbishop, saw

Dag Hammerskjold's body after the crash. He apparently survived for long enough to crawl some distance from the aircraft before dying and, according to Tutu, he had a bullet hole in his forehead which was subsequently airbrushed out of all newspaper photos of his corpse.

This author, who once had the privilege of interviewing Patrice Lumunba, has a clear recollection of Congo's independence from Belgium and its subsequent decline into the anarchy, corruption, warfare and despair that now characterize the region. He has included this account of the UN's Secretary General of the time to illustrate just how compromised it was possible for the UN to become, even that early in its existence.

However, if the UN is to be a successful 'village policeman' for the world, it has to find some way of separating its 'advocacy' and 'mediator' rôles.

Clearly, the UN of today, on top of and perhaps because of its internal constitutional problems (already discussed in previous chapters), still reflects a high degree of inconsistency. To make the point, compare its response to the situations in Iran and Sudan. Iran, whatever distaste one may feel for its leadership, has not as yet done anything illegal. No one denies its right to develop a capacity for the peaceful use of atomic energy, and surely suspicion that its real intention is to produce nuclear arms cannot be regarded as a reason for threatening to bomb it! In fact, even if Iran were – God forbid – set on developing bomb-grade uranium, nuclear powers which themselves are further enhancing their nuclear arsenals contrary to the Nuclear Non-Proliferation Treaty,[2] which they signed in 1968, are hardly in a position to condemn Iran for materially adding to the danger. In fact, in 1995 the 88 signatories (India, Pakistan and Israel did not sign, and North Korea withdrew after signing) further agreed to extend the treaty 'indefinitely and without condition.' This became a UN Declaration. It began to unravel in 2005, when India tested a nuclear bomb and the USA was supporting it by providing material and technical advice for peaceful uses of nuclear energy. Later that same year the USA argued that the treaty should be changed to ban proliferation only. This would effectively allow India to retain its nuclear material but prevent countries like Iran and North Korea from actually developing nuclear weapons.

The original three pillars of the treaty are as follows:

1   non-proliferation – existing nuclear powers are not allowed to supply other states with such material
2   disarmament – nuclear states must disarm their nuclear weapons as quickly as possible
3   the right to develop and use nuclear power for peaceful purposes (e.g. electricity generation) is protected.

With regard to (2), the UK, for instance, should not be embarking on updating its Trident missiles. In the light of (3), Iran is not in violation of any UN Declaration.

Despite all of this, the UN Security Council has acted with commendable speed in confronting the 'threat' posed by Iran. It passed a resolution on 3 March 2007, condemning Iran for breach of a UN requirement that it cease work altogether on developing its nuclear industry. US spokespersons have assured the world that they 'cannot rule out' invoking direct military attacks on Iran to enforce compliance with UN dictates. They also state that, while they might not 'attack' Iran, they might 'target its nuclear facilities' (which are scattered widely over Iran) with 'surgical strikes.' If this is not war, what is? However, as we well know from the first and second Iraq wars, 'surgical strikes' are not quite as target-focused as the military intend, and still end up killing and wounding significant numbers of innocent civilians.

Now let us turn to Sudan. As we saw in Chapter 3, the Khartoum government has been in breach of specific UN demands since 2003, and in obvious breach of human rights clauses of the UDHR for even longer. On 6 March 2007, a US-based group, Academics Against Genocide, explicitly referred to the Khartoum government's actions in Darfur as 'genocide.' They stated that the gross violation of human rights continued unabated, despite UN statements of disapproval.[3] Yet not even trade sanctions have been declared by the UN as pressure to keep the Khartoum government in line. UN field officers and NGOs linked to the UN have frequently brought the most appalling and persistent violations of human rights of the people of Darfur to the attention of the Security Council. In fact, a lack of action on the UN's part can now no longer be predicated on the fact that it has not involved other nations – the reason used to prevent the government of Burma from being censured (*see* Chapter 4) – for the Darfur crisis has now also involved at least two other countries, namely Chad and the Central African Republic.

The Government of Sudan has already broken commitments it made to the UN to permit human rights agents into Darfur, while such people apparently move in and around and out of Iran virtually at will. Sudan won't even allow the UN to send in more peacekeeping forces, despite the fact that the present contingent of African Union forces is too small to be adequate for the task. It seems as though the President of Sudan can act autonomously and even set conditions as to how and when the UN can intervene. This apparent immunity of Sudan from direct UN-sponsored invasion on 'humanitarian grounds' (as discussed later in this chapter, a bad idea in any case!), or even from such sanctions as trade embargoes, when contrasted with the UN response to the situation in Iran, may have something to do with 'balance of power' politics. Such considerations almost certainly influenced UN action in the former Belgian Congo in 1961.

In the present situation, action against Iran is in the interests of the USA and its corporate oil and banking hunger for economic control over global oil supplies. It is also very much in the interests of Israel. The matter of 'inconsistency' with regard to UN behaviour is even further complicated by the fact that certain key nations – Russia (replacing the former Soviet Union), the USA, China (People's Republic of China), France and the UK – have the power of the veto. Even if every nation except one of these 'Big Five' (as they are known) vetoes a motion, that motion will not be carried, for that sole Big Five member's veto would be enough to scupper it.

Therefore it is important that we examine the issue of the veto, because it may well be a major factor in rendering the UN less effective as a transnational mediator. As will be discussed later, for the UN to be optimally effective, each representative of a member state – on entering the General Assembly Chamber or meetings of the Security Council – must somehow be able to think over and beyond the immediate advantages of the nation that they represent, and vote in accordance with the global good alone! Any changes that are made to the UN need to address this psychological hurdle. Information on any of the material that follows can be found in any quality encyclopaedia. This author has drawn on Wikipedia.[4]

The veto in the UN

The veto cannot be used to prevent discussion of an issue. Thus any resolution – even if it is known ahead of time that it will be vetoed – can be debated. For instance, the US embargo against Cuba, which even extends under certain circumstances to preventing other countries from trading with Cuba, is regularly debated by the Security Council, even though it is appreciated that it will be vetoed by the USA and also voted down by Israel. Likewise, debates about the national rights of the Palestinians routinely share the same fate. As stated above, the UN veto power is wielded solely by the five permanent members of the Security Council, enabling them to void any Security Council substantive resolution, regardless of the level of general support. This power is exercised when any permanent member enters a 'nay' vote. An abstention vote or absence is taken as allowing the measure to pass.

However, as implied earlier, the very establishment of the UN embodies a distinct bias towards US values and interests. This has become noticeably less so since Russia assumed the former Soviet Union seat on the Security Council and Communist China likewise assumed the seat of the former Kuomingtan regime in that country. However, the bias persists, as clearly stated in the founding Charter of the UN. The veto system was established to protect the interests of the founding members of the United Nations, which were the countries that won World War Two. At the UN founding conference in 1944, it was decided that the representatives of Britain, China, the Soviet Union, the USA and, 'in due course,' France, should be permanent members. France had been defeated and occupied by Nazi Germany, but its rôle as a permanent member of the League of Nations, its status as a colonial power and the activities of the Free French forces on the allied side allowed it a place at the table with the Big Four.

In other words, the victorious countries of World War Two assumed the mantle of responsibility for determining how human rights were to be interpreted globally! This built-in imbalance has had predictable consequences, which become evident if we consult the UN Charter of 1944.

Article 27 of the United Nations Charter states:

> Each member of the Security Council shall have one vote. Decisions of the Security Council on procedural matters shall be made by an affirmative vote of nine members. Decisions of the Security Council on all other matters shall be made by an affirmative vote of nine members, including the concurring votes of the permanent members; provided that, in decisions under Chapter VI, and under paragraph 3 of Article 52, a party to a dispute shall abstain from voting.

During the Korean War the Soviet Union left an 'empty chair' with the aim of preventing any Security Council resolutions on the matter. Despite the apparently clear wording of the Charter, this was treated as a non-blocking abstention, and since then all abstentions and absences have not been treated as being a veto. This has the unexpected advantage of allowing a permanent member to express its opposition to a measure without blocking it by abstaining. The majority – more than half – of all vetoes in the history of the Security Council were exercised by the Soviet Union. Since shortly before the fall of the Soviet Union, the USA has been the most frequent user of the veto.[5]

Between the fall of the Berlin Wall in 1989, and the end of 2004, vetoes were exercised on 19 occasions. For that period, usage can be broken down as follows.

- The USA used the veto on 13 occasions (11 regarding Israel, one regarding Bosnia and one regarding Panama).
- Russia/the Soviet Union used the veto on three occasions (two regarding Cyprus and one regarding Bosnia).

In the early days of the UN, the Soviet Union commissar and later minister for foreign affairs, Vyacheslav Molotov, said 'no' so many times that he was known as 'Mr Veto.' In fact, the Soviet Union was responsible for nearly half of all vetoes ever cast – 79 vetoes were used in the first 10 years. Molotov regularly rejected bids for new membership because of the USA's refusal to admit the Soviet republics as separate members. Since the collapse of the Soviet Union, the Russians have used their veto power sparingly.

Of course, this is mainly because Russia is now much more ideologically aligned with the values of neoliberal globalization. However, it doesn't hesitate to use its veto, even against the USA, if its own national interests are at stake, with complete indifference to the justice or otherwise of the human interests issues involved. A good example of this emerged at a Security Council meeting on 12 January 2007, when Russia and China vetoed a USA-supported proposal to censure Burma (Myanmar) for its human rights record. The USA, needless to say, is equally partisan in its use of the veto. It first used its veto power in 1970, for until then it had always secured its own way, and it first issued a lone veto in 1972 to prevent a proposal criticising Israel.

In fact, in the early years of the UN's history – up until 1955, say – the USA was one of the only countries that was able to pay its dues. Such financial clout was good for business, because it gave it – and capitalism – immense leverage. While the 'Russian' veto was used so prodigiously by the Soviet Union, that all changed and now the USA is the most frequent user of the veto – often to further Israel's initiatives in the Middle East. Its reflex support of Zionist interests has generated immense friction between the General Assembly and the Security Council. This was evident, for instance, in the mass opposition within the General Assembly to the 2003 Iraqi war, which was not endorsed by the UN. The members of the General Assembly include the less powerful nations, and their political orientation is, for obvious reasons, often opposed to the interests of US and EU corporate power, the banks linked to the IMF and the WB, and to the WTO. However, their votes routinely count for nothing because of the veto. The question then has to be raised as to how the UN can effectively mediate the needs of the many economically disadvantaged countries. How can it realistically mediate equally between competing interests in our ever-shrinking global village?

This question becomes more pertinent when we analyse the extent to which the veto is used as a strategy for supporting national interests, not unlike those employed in a chess tournament. For example, consider the change in China's rôle in the Security Council once the Kuomingtan regime in China had given way to the modern People's Republic of China in 1971 and after the death of Mao. The reader will probably remember that, from 1949 until 1971, the Chinese UN Security Council seat was occupied by the island of Taiwan! This ridiculous state of affairs was again the result of US veto power in the UN, and the Taiwan regime really represented, in a most blatant manner, the international banking and industrial needs of US capitalism. During that entire time, Taiwan (representing all of China!) only used its veto once, and that was to prevent the People's Republic of Mongolia from becoming a UN member in 1955. Why was this? Simply because the Taiwan regime regarded Mongolia as really part of China. If the Republic of Mongolia *had* been admitted to the UN as a separate member, it would always have vetoed proposals put forward by China (which at that time was really only Taiwan) in the General Assembly. The upshot was that Mongolia was only admitted to its own seat in the UN in 1960, and this happened only because the Soviet Union made it clear that, unless Mongolia was admitted, it would block the admission of all of the newly independent African states. This forced Taiwan to back down.

After 1971, the Chinese seat was occupied by representatives of mainland China, the People's Republic of China (PRC). They exercised their veto for the first time on 25 August 1972 over Bangladesh's admission to the UN. They have only exercised their veto five times since, the last occasion being their infamous vote against the USA's proposed censure of Burma in 2007. And so the mad chess game will continue unless and until we drastically alter the system. And until that is done, the human rights of at least two-thirds of the world's people cannot effectively be protected or promoted.

Reform of the veto system

All that has been said above provides reason enough for trying to change the present veto system. However, other reasons also have to be taken into account, because the seats of the Big Five no longer represent the agencies that they did just after World War Two, and the members who have replaced them are not themselves necessarily stable forces on the international scene. Furthermore, veto power slows down attempts at reform and impedes the speed and/or efficacy with which the UN can use its authority when a crisis arises. Because of all the changes that have taken place in the Security Council since 1945, widespread dissatisfaction with the UN has arisen. We have to consider the possibility that the current permanent members of the Security Council are not the most appropriate states to hold the world community to ransom by the power of the veto.

Another argument against retaining the veto power is that it is detrimental to fast, balanced political decisions. The Rwandan genocide serves as an example of this, when the veto power proved detrimental to the genesis of a global relief effort that could have reduced the severity of the genocide.[6] There is also debate over the use of the veto power as a political aid to a permanent member's allies. The USA has used its veto power more than any other permanent member since 1972, particularly in blocking resolutions condemning Israel. This has spread concerns that the veto power serves as a medium for permanent members to benefit their allies with the power of the UN Security Council.

The veto power was originally intended as a preventative measure, to disallow brash resolutions that could have negative consequences. Advocates of the veto power believe that this is still necessary in the current geo-political landscape, and that without the veto power, the UN Security Council would be open to making 'majority rules' decisions that have implications on a global level.[7] Perhaps it should take two 'nay votes' from permanent members to be considered a veto.

This author would argue for a much more radical set of reforms. For instance, UN representatives are generally not elected, or if they are, they are not elected by a plebiscite of their nations' populations, but by a selection committee. The General Assembly members should be elected by balloting all of the adult suffrage that they will represent. If a smaller sub-group with veto powers is felt (by the General Assembly members) to be useful, then they should be elected regularly by the General Assembly. Permanent veto power is unacceptable. This would effectively guarantee that the economically powerful countries would not always wield all the power. There would have to be horse-trading, and this would lead to greater financial equity and might, at last, allow the Alma-Ata Declaration to be realized.

As far as the Security Council is concerned, even its present members recognize the need for reform, but are equally anxious not to lose all of their power and influence.

Along with discussions of expanding the permanent Council membership, there has been the issue of whether or not to extend the veto power to the new permanent members. The current members appear to be amenable to expanding the Council membership, but more ambivalent about (or firmly against) extending the veto power, arguing that doing so would paralyse the Security Council and make it ineffectual. On the other hand, members of the G4, consisting of India, Germany, Brazil and Japan, argue that the present Security Council composition represents the world of 1946 rather than that of 2006. According to these countries, the Security Council must represent a greater number of people, otherwise the importance of the Security Council might be lost and the UN would suffer the same fate as befell the League of Nations. All four countries have launched a massive diplomatic effort to create a general consensus in their favour.

Humanitarian intervention under the UDHR

Chapters 3 to 7 of this book have spelled out the details of just a tiny fraction of the day-to-day gross violations of rights to health – even of babes in arms and their mothers – and explicitly raises the following questions. Where was the UN? And what can the UN do? We only have to cast our minds back to the ghastly events that accompanied the dismantling of Yugoslavia to realize that even when the UN acts late in the day, it can still accomplish much and, in the same event, see the degree to which the UN is compromised in its efforts.

As we listened to newscasts from Sarajevo and read reports about it, many of us asked ourselves the following question. What can the international community do to bring justice to the victims? Or is there really such a thing as the international community? Can the UN Security Council meet its UDHR responsibility to defend the human rights of ordinary civilians? Or is the UDHR little more than a Trojan Horse designed to deflect popular attention away from the economic abuses practised by the 'haves' in exploiting the 'have nots'?

The appeal to higher moral purposes continues to infect the political discourse of the major influential powers. Today's 'humanitarian intervention' is only the latest in this long tradition of political mendacity. It is perfectly clear in such cases as the US-UK invasion and occupation of Iraq (which UK Prime Minister Tony Blair described as a 'humanitarian intervention'). But should intervention (even multilateral inter-vention, approved by the Security Council) be excluded in all circumstances?

No debate about these issues in the security of dining rooms in the First World is without the appeals to 'morality' alluded to above, and the desire to solve the problems by military means soon makes itself apparent but, as we have observed before, the nation state – whatever its pretences – generally acts so as to enhance itself. This author often gives the following definitions of a soldier and a diplomat:

> The soldier is willing to die for his country.
> The diplomat is willing to lie for his country.

However, as we know, the lying diplomat produces the dying soldier. The UN was founded in the ashes of horror and remorse of World War Two with the mandate to prevent that from ever occurring again. The degree to which it has so far failed to achieve this aim has nothing to do with some insane 'fixity' in what we call 'human nature.' Rather it is due to a calculated neglect of human rights. Concern with *that* as a priority issue would free both the soldier and the diplomat for much grander jobs. Therefore, how are we to regard the use of military force, even if endorsed by the UN? Very often the more thoughtful soldiers involved in such 'humanitarian interventions' are left wondering what the difference was between fighting for the UN and fighting for their country!

As Global Policy Forum (2006)[5] makes clear by implication, humanitarian interventions are rarely 'humanitarian' in their impact (the Iraq war was, after all, described as a humanitarian intervention). Nor are they usually guided by a dispassionate concern for human rights.

When nations send their military forces into other nations' territory, it is rarely (if ever) for 'humanitarian' purposes. They are typically pursuing their narrow national interest – grabbing territory, gaining geo-strategic advantage, or seizing control of precious natural resources. Leaders hope to win public support by describing such actions in terms of high moral purpose – bringing peace, justice, democracy and civilization to the affected area. In the era of colonialism, European governments all cynically insisted that they acted to promote such higher commitments – the 'white man's burden', 'la mission civilisatrice' and the like.

What all of this suggests is that, if human rights are the goal, then only very rarely would military intervention, even in the name of the UN, as in Korea from 1949 to 1951, be of any use in pursuit of that aim. In the next section we shall consider the already mentioned Millennium Development Goals that were put forward in 2000 by Kofi Annan (then Secretary General of the UN). These goals – to be achieved by 2015 (since extended to 2020) – are intended to establish a social and economic basis on which a programme of global human rights can be built.

However, we are at present governed to an astounding degree by people who hold that UN resolutions should be backed up by military forces. This is even stated in the Millennium+5 Document (MDGs to be completed by 2020 instead of 2015), released on 15 September 2005. The relevant passage states:[8]

> Heads of state who gathered at UN headquarters for the Millennium+5 Summit approved the final outcome document. Although the document insists on pursuing peaceful means to protect populations from crimes against humanity, it also accepts the need that the international community, through the United Nations, should 'take collective action, in a timely and decisive manner . . . on a case-by-case basis and in cooperation with relevant regional organizations as appropriate.'

Kofi Annan, while Secretary General of the UN, tended to put the idea of direct military intervention low down his list of sanctions to be applied to nations in breach of UN Security Council resolutions. He was aware, one suspects, of the growing dissatisfaction with the military option, and insisted that it is the responsibility of the international community to use diplomatic, humanitarian and other methods – to thoroughly exhaust these – before adopting a policy of armed intervention. And the UN's own history strongly suggests that trade sanctions and restrictions on the right of leading figures in the delinquent nations to travel freely have been most effective.

The Venezuelan President, Hugo Chavez, in a speech he made on 17 September 2005, criticized the UN's suggestion that invasion may sometimes be required.[9] His apparent scepticism about the good intentions of the governments aiding and abetting such policies was based on the belief that they only provided further opportunities for rich developed nations to elaborate yet more effective ways to exploit the mineral resources of less developed nations. To some readers this might seem far-fetched, but the important thing is that such conspiracies are widely believed in the poorer countries, and this informs their actions and their choice of political alliances. We neglect such feelings at our peril.

Having said that, however, it is important to remember that not all humanitarian interventions are beneficial. For instance, some authorities on humanitarianism have argued that attempts to promote and enforce, say, globalized democracy are much more likely to end up maintaining unfair globalized financial systems and to obscure these negative consequences.

Attempts to provide regime change in states whose leadership is regarded as hostile to international peace also tend to be counter-productive. A good example of this is provided by Canada's recent 'humanitarian' involvement in Haiti. A section of the Global Policy Watch article cited earlier considers this issue in detail,[10] and well illustrates the problems.

This two-part article discusses the extent of Canada's participation in the US-led 2004 coup that ousted Haiti's democratically elected President Jean-Bertrand Aristide. Publicly, Ottawa denies any involvement in the coup and maintains that Canada was seeking a peaceful settlement to the crisis. However, according to classified memos obtained by the various media, Canada was planning the removal of the Aristide government under the 'responsibility to protect' doctrine months before the coup. This principle justified the military intervention under the guise of 'humanitarian intervention for human protection.' However, rather than averting a crisis, the 'duty-to-protect' intervention in Haiti became the backdrop for a major escalation of atrocities, with thousands killed and hundreds jailed for their political views, all to serve Canadian, US and European political and economic interests in Haiti.

Many more examples could be cited, but it is becoming increasingly clear to many international observers that, if the UN is to promote the UDHR, its best means of doing so will need to rely upon international opprobrium backed up by properly enforced diplomatic sanctions, rather than military intervention. Along with this, as was so explicitly stated in 2000 by Kofi Annan,[11] an increase in direct funding from the G8 nations is required. His eight Millennium Development Goals,[12] which should ideally be achieved by 2015 (and by 2020 at the latest), would establish a minimum concrete basis for moving on to completion of the Alma-Ata Declaration's HFA campaign.

The eight MDGs are listed below.

1 Eradicate extreme poverty and hunger.
2 Achieve universal primary education.
3 Promote gender equality and empower women.
4 Reduce child mortality.
5 Improve maternal health.
6 Combat HIV/AIDS, malaria and other diseases.
7 Ensure environmental sustainability.
8 Develop a global partnership for development.

One can see that they all, directly or indirectly, involve the rights to health and require – as a minimum – universal access to primary healthcare (PHC).

If we examine them more closely, we can see that each 'goal' is predicated on the achievement of certain targets, and some of these suggest that achievement of the targets would often fall rather short of the relevant goal, as follows.

Goal 1: **Target 1:** Halve, between 1990 and 2015, the proportion of people whose income is less than one dollar a day.
Target 2: Halve, between 1990 and 2015, the proportion of people who suffer from hunger.

Goal 2: **Target 3:** Ensure that by 2015 children everywhere – boys and girls alike – will be able to complete a full course of primary schooling.

Goal 3: **Target 4:** Eliminate gender disparity in primary and secondary education, preferably by 2005, and at all levels of education no later than 2015.

Goal 4: **Target 5:** Reduce by two-thirds, between 1990 and 2015, the under-five mortality rate.

Goal 5: **Target 6:** Reduce by three-quarters, between 1990 and 2015, the maternal mortality rate.

Goal 6: **Target 7:** Have halted by 2015, and begun to reverse, the spread of HIV/AIDS.
Target 8: Have halted by 2015, and begun to reverse, the incidence of malaria and other major diseases.

Goal 7: **Target 9:** Integrate the principles of sustainable development into country policies and programmes, and reverse the loss of environmental resources.
Target 10: Halve by 2015 the proportion of people without sustainable access to safe drinking-water.
Target 11: Achieve by 2020 a significant improvement in the lives of at least 100 million slum dwellers.

Goal 8: **Target 12:** Develop an open, rule-based, non-discriminatory trading and financial system.
Target 13: Address the special needs of the least developed countries.
Target 14: Address the special needs of landlocked and small island developing states.
Target 15: Deal comprehensively with the debt problems of developing countries.
Target 16: Develop and implement strategies for decent and productive work for young people in developing countries.
Target 17: Provide access, in co-operation with pharmaceutical companies, to make affordable essential drugs in developing countries.
Target 18: Make available, in co-operation with the private sector, the benefits of new technologies, especially information and communications.

This is why this author has gone on record as claiming that the MDGs, if achieved, would only represent a minimal basis for possible achievement of HFA – and even then, at a later date.

Reform the UN or replace it?

We have so far in this book been made aware of many failings of the UN in its capacity to promote the articles of its seminal Universal Declaration of Human Rights. The UN has produced a number of agencies explicitly charged with rendering the UDHR operational, namely the WHO, UNICEF, UNESCO and several others. Since health is basic to all other human rights, we have devoted considerable space to an analysis of the WHO. Its pivotal rôle with regard to the UN's mandate in this respect was recognized by Kofi Annan, and his eight MDGs, listed above, clearly reflect his determination to get both the WHO and the UN itself back on track towards the aims of the 1978 Alma-Ata Declaration. That document, the HFA (2000) goals and the MDGs explicitly recognize that the social, economic and political determinants of health are every bit as pivotal in sustaining public health as are the medical sciences themselves. As far as the ordinary citizen is concerned, they are more pivotal, because citizens can – through thoughtful collective action – decide what they want their political, economic and social values to achieve. They can determine, through government, how to finance the medical sciences most effectively.

It is widely appreciated that this cannot, however, be a purely parochial concern. It must be global, and for that reason its transnational mediation is essential. That we need some kind of transnational 'world body' to accomplish this has been argued by this author in several of his previous books.[13]

Reform of the UN – so as to counter problems created by power disparities between members of the General Assembly and the Security Council, to prevent equivocation on the part of the UN as to how it reacts to human rights abuses in different countries, to overcome the strong tendency of member states to make decisions based on narrow national needs rather than global needs, and to somehow address issues of inter-agency conflict of aims (e.g. between the WHO and the WTO) – would not be a simple matter. Moreover, remediation of these problems lies less within the UN than with the political determination of each state in it. In this, the powerful states, including members of the G8, would have to lead the way. So far – for example, with regard to the Nuclear Proliferation Treaty and the percentage of gross national income allocated to the relief of desperately poor nations – the G8 nations have set an appalling example. Reforms at this level are best made by the determination of the citizens themselves to elect politicians who are committed to the project. In this regard the author remains optimistic, even though he entirely acquiesces with the view that the so far politically apathetic citizenry is becoming energized primarily by fear of environmental disaster. The global village must unite to preserve itself.

With regard to reform within the UN itself, the new Security General of the UN, Ban Ki-moon, promises to embark energetically on a reform programme. Kofi Annan was amazingly successful in generating and sustaining programmes aimed at global equity – the MDGs being an outstanding example – and in encouraging individual national leaders in their efforts. Now, however, to make such grand projects work effectively, we need a tough-minded organizer. So far, our new Secretary-General appears to be such a person.

On 5 February 2007, an official from the League of Arab States printed a statement strongly advocating Ban Ki-moon's approach. He stated that the nations of the Arab League strongly back plans to restructure the organization's peacekeeping and disarmament operations so that he can focus on tackling pressing international crises and global challenges.

The League's Permanent Observer to the UN, Yahya Mahmassani, who attended a private lunch on 5 February with Mr Ban and other key ambassadors, including members of the Security Council, said participants concurred that although they might have different views on some of the proposal details, they must come to an agreement quickly.

'We can't continue to just keep discussing it and putting forward our ideas without setting a consensus on this', he told the UN News Service and UN Radio. 'There was a general feeling at the luncheon that we must agree on this issue because the SG has too many other things to do. He has a big agenda to follow.'[14]

Under a proposal given to member states, Mr Ban wants to create a new Department of Field Support so that UN peace operations – whose numbers have reached an all-time high – can be supported more effectively and coherently. The Secretary-General has also suggested that the Department of Disarmament Affairs be constituted as an Office with a direct line of responsibility to him 'to ensure access and more frequent interaction,' his spokesperson Michele Montas said after the meeting.

Mr Ban and other senior UN officials have been holding talks with Member States about the proposals, and Mr Mahmassani said that this informal process would continue in the weeks ahead. He emphasized the importance of individual states prioritizing the issue.

Also speaking to the UN News Service and UN Radio, Under-Secretary-General for Political Affairs Ibrahim Gambari said Mr Ban stressed to participants at the luncheon that 'he wants to feel he has their support' for his vision for restructuring, so that he can implement it quickly and then concentrate on such issues as the Darfur crisis, the Middle East, Iraq and climate change.

Mr Gambari said Mr Ban wants Member States to at least support the framework of his changes, allowing any contentious details to be worked out in the second phase during meetings involving the General Assembly and its committees. This is crucial. The UN cannot change unless its members do.

He added that some participants voiced concerns about the process rather than the content of the planned reforms, given that they would have budgetary and resource implications.

The Non-Aligned Movement (NAM) and some other States also wanted assurances that the proposal for disarmament affairs did not represent a downgrading of its rôle, especially amid perceptions among some that non-proliferation was being paid more attention than was disarmament.

This observation is crucial because, as we have seen in previous chapters, in countries such as Sudan, Liberia, Burma, Israel and Palestine, and even in the EU and the USA, military spending detracts hugely from health and educational infrastructure. The same is true in almost every country. Nuclear disarmament – as promised by the Nuclear Non-Proliferation Treaty's three pillars – would alone create enormous savings and create many more jobs in such useful activities as health and education than would ever be lost by the cessation of a nuclear weapons commitment. However, over and above all of this, there is abundant evidence that any kind of military activity has a much more destructive effect on civilian life and health than it does on the military personnel on either side – even with modern non-nuclear weaponry.

At the Arab League meeting cited above we are also told that Mr Gambari said Mr Ban informed ambassadors that his plans were actually designed to upgrade the rôle of disarmament and ensure that it plays a more pro-active part in encouraging member states to reach agreement about issues on which they are divided. He added that representatives of the European Union and the USA, among others, indicated that they wanted to give Mr Ban plenty of room to organize the Secretariat in the ways he sought. Mr Gambari also noted that Mr Ban had already made some alterations to the initial draft of his plans to accommodate the views of member states.

It is encouraging to note that Ban Ki-moon's Secretary-Generalship has already gone much further than inspirational rhetoric. Only a week and a half after the Arab League meeting just discussed, he described precisely how he intended to strengthen and better coordinate the UN's peacekeeping programmes. As we have seen in Darfur and in the Occupied Palestinian Territories, the presence of UN peacekeepers in sufficient numbers would probably prevent continued wasteful military activity.

Ban Ki-moon proposes, as detailed in a letter he sent to the General Assembly on 15 February 2007, to split the current UN peacekeeping department in two in order to facilitate better planning and faster deployment. This, he states, can be done mainly by more effectively coordinating widely scattered missions and preventing duplication.[15]

The recommendations, detailed in a letter that Mr Ban sent to the General Assembly a week later as part of his ongoing consultations on his restructuring initiative, call for splitting the current Department of Peacekeeping Operations (DPKO) into a Department of Peace Operations and a Department of Field Support, both headed by an Under-Secretary-General, at the managerial level of the current DPKO chief.

'The number of peace operations is at an all-time high with almost 100,000 personnel in the field. It appears that the figure will rise still further in 2007', he said, noting that reforms in 2000 had aimed to equip the DPKO with sufficient capability to launch one new multidisciplinary mission per year.

'Yet the past 36 months alone have seen the start-up or expansion of nine field missions, with three additional missions currently in active start-up. Over the course of the next year, the number of personnel in UN peace operations could increase by as much as 40 per cent', he added. He stressed that the new arrangement would be resource-neutral because the two new departments would consolidate operations that are now spread among various offices and departments.

Perhaps his most encouraging proposal is to re-activate all three pillars of the Nuclear Non-Proliferation Treaty. He intends to do this by replacing the present Department for Disarmament Affairs, currently under the charge of an Under-Secretary-General, with a new department led by a High Representative for Disarmament Affairs. This proposal might at first appear to represent a downgrade, but in fact will give the portfolio greater impact, flexibility and a direct line to Mr Ban himself. In making this proposal, he expressed his dismay at the present disregard for the dangers of nuclear arms.

He referred to the failure of the 2005 review conference of Parties to the Treaty on the Non-Proliferation of Nuclear Weapons (NPT), the deadlock in the Conference on Disarmament, and the need for new impetus for the entry into force of the Comprehensive Nuclear Test Ban Treaty.

'This deeply alarming situation makes clear the need to revitalize the disarmament and non-proliferation agenda through a more focused effort', he wrote. 'I believe in the need for a greater rôle and personal involvement of the Secretary-General in this regard.'

The Secretary-General has briefed the General Assembly in closed session regarding the proposals, the second time he has done so within a month. All of these intentions augur well for the future but, as the reader will realize from Chapters 3 to 7, there needs to be both much more commitment on the part of national governments to address UDHR issues, and at the same time a much tighter mediation of these diverse activities at the centre. For instance, in both the Rwanda conflict between Hutus and Tutsis, and the Kosovo conflict between Serbs and Albanians, it was lack of clear and unambiguous lines of communication between various NGOs and UN peacekeeping forces and between the latter and the Secretary-General's office in New York that caused both conflicts to spin horribly out of control. An important aspect of reform so as to render the UN more effective in mediating human rights globally has to address this issue.

Guiding humanitarian initiatives worldwide

While working in various less developed countries, this author has frequently been struck by the frustrating lack of communication among NGOs in the field, and between those NGOs and such UN agencies as the WHO and UNICEF. Likewise, field officers in such UN agencies are frequently impeded by domestic governments striving to meet IMF or WTO requirements. All of this will have to be restructured. One way of doing this would be to separate the activities of financial agencies of the UN from those working at the health-related or other human rights interface.

This could be done by having an intermediary body in each nation or region, through which the relevant UN agencies and NGOs could coordinate their efforts with regard to both timing and efficiency. This would also simplify procedures for reporting and addressing clear breaches of the UDHR, both within and between nations. Many of Kofi Annan's recommendations started to address these issues, but especially during his second term of office, he often found his efforts blocked by the protection and advocacy provided by individual nations for their own financial advantage. As neoliberalism has gathered strength, these conflicts of goal became more and more obvious, and reached a crescendo during the last decade of the last millennium.

During that time, the world witnessed some of the worst violations of human rights on record. Worldwide, civilians became targets of unprecedented terror, as in Darfur and Burma, and often by and with support at government level. In some cases, the governments were unable to protect their own civilians. In others, the governments themselves took part in attacking civilians, especially minority ethnic groups. From Angola and Sierra Leone to Bosnia and Kosovo to East Timor, millions of people have been killed, over 30 million have been displaced, and countless men, women and children have been denied some of the most fundamental human rights.

Former Secretary-General Kofi Annan observed that the United Nations – and the international community – cannot accept a situation in which people are brutalized behind national boundaries: 'A United Nations that will not stand up for human rights is a United Nations that cannot stand up for itself. We know where our mission for human rights begins and ends: with the individual and his or her universal and inalienable rights – to speak, to act, to grow, to learn and to live according to his or her own conscience.' [16]

To address the new humanitarian challenges, in a report submitted to the Security Council in September 1999, he proposed specific recommendations for consideration by the member states, which can be summarized as follows.

- **Ratification and implementation of international instruments.** He urged member states to ratify the major instruments of international humanitarian law, human rights law and refugee law, and to adhere to them.
- **Accountability for war crimes.** When Governments or groups fail to comply with such international humanitarian law, enforcement measures should be considered. He asked the member states to ratify the Statute of the International Criminal Court.
- **Minimum age of recruitment by the armed forces.** He asked the member states to support raising the minimum age for recruitment in the armed forces to 18 years.
- **Intervention in cases of systematic violation of international law.** He asked the member states to consider appropriate enforcement action in the face of massive and ongoing abuses. This does not have to be military.

This alone would require that all states recognize the authority of the International Criminal Court – a desideratum so far not met by the USA, for instance. It should be obvious that for the UN to have effective transnational authority, all of its members should be constrained by the same laws.

One could say much more about these matters, but the critical issue is one of widespread involvement.

Should the UN be scrapped?

Because of the difficulties – both internal and external – besetting the UN, many of this author's colleagues who are deeply concerned about global equity argue that the UN has passed its 'sell-by' date and should be eliminated. The need for transnational mediation is obvious, but – as currently structured – the UN cannot meet its obligations.

However, whatever other transnational agency – let us call it the World Body (WB) to avoid the semantic difficulties of national integrity – is established would run into similar difficulties. Even if the concept of 'nation' were scrapped, and even if the fiscal and human rights mandates were coordinated so as to give priority to the latter, regional interests guided by trade would allow the WB to be manipulated as the UN is today by national corporate interests. The only way to avoid this would be to adequately represent a more socially responsive philosophy, essentially egalitarian and socialist in its world view.

In view of the fact that we really are a 'small global village' now, and one threatened by environmental catastrophe, this author has no doubt that we will ultimately have to meet the above demands. However, in the meantime we have no alternative but to reform the UN, both organizationally and philosophically. If we make even some headway in making global equity our top priority, we may yet end up with the kind of world mediation envisioned above.

Humans are far too wonderful a product of evolution to be regarded as a brief chapter in the history of our planet. As far as we know, we are the only animal so far evolved with the capacity to ask 'What if?' or to introspectively try to analyse our own motives and social values. We have much further to go and much more to do artistically, socially, materially and in every other way. Would it not be better to address the task head on, beginning with the proposition that, because our separate dignities presuppose 'human rights', we should start to work now towards the fairly short-term goal of ensuring 'health for all' – the absolute basis for all other human rights?

References

1 Spartacus. *Moise Tshombe, Katanga, the Congo Crisis and Dag Hammarskjold*; www.spartacus. schoolnet.co.uk/COLDtshombe.htm (accessed 13 March 2007).
2 Wikipedia. *Nuclear Non-Proliferation Treaty*; http://en.Wikipedia.org/wiki/Nuclear_Non-Proliferation_Treaty (accessed 13 March 2007).
3 Events. *Time to End the Genocide in Darfur*; www.timetoprotect.org/event/ (accessed 13 March 2007).
4 Wikipedia. *United Nations Security Council Veto Power*; http://en.Wikipedia.org/wiki/United_Nations_Security_Council_veto (accessed 9 March 2007).
5 Global Policy Forum. *Veto Database and Information*; www.globalpolicy.org/security/membership/veto.htm (accessed 9 March 2007).
6 www.zmag.org/content/showarticle.cmf?ItemID=5296 (accessed 9 March 2007).
7 www.mtholyoke.edu/acud/intrel/schles.htm (accessed 9 March 2007).
8 Global Policy Watch. *Humanitarian Intervention*; www.globalpolicy.org/empire/humaninf/index.htm (accessed 11 March 2007).
9 Ibid., p. 2.
10 Ibid., pp. 4–5.
11 UN Security Council. Excerpt from the Millennium +5 Outcome Document; www.global policy.org/empire/humaninf/2005/0915outcome.htm (accessed 11 March 2007).
12 Ibid., p. 2.
13 MacDonald T. *Third World Health: hostage to First World wealth*. Oxford: Radcliffe Publishing; 2005. pp. 222–3.
14 Mahmassani Y. *States Agree Ban Ki-Moon's Reform Plans*; www.un.org/apps/news/story.asp?NewsID=21458&Cr=UN (accessed 10 March 2007).
15 United Nations. *Ban Ki-Moon Details Plans for Restructuring UN Peacekeeping and Disarmament Work*; www.un.org/apps/news/story.asp?/NewsID=21601&Cr=restruct (accessed 10 March 2007).
16 Biodiversity. *Human Rights and Human Security*; www0.un.org/cyberschoolbus/briefing/rights/hrnesteps.htm (accessed 9 March 2007).

Index